John McDowell

John McDowell

Maximilian de Gaynesford

polity

First published in 2004 by Polity Press Ltd.

Polity Press
65 Bridge Street
Cambridge CB2 1UR, UK

Polity Press
350 Main Street
Malden, MA 02148, USA

ISBN: 0-7456 3036-7
ISBN: 0-7456 3037-5 (pb)

A catalogue record for this book is available from the British Library and has been applied for from the Library of Congress.

Typeset in 10.5 on 12 pt Palatino
by SNP Best-set Typesetter Ltd, Hong Kong
Printed and bound in Great Britain by MPG Books Ltd, Bodmin, Cornwall

For further information on Polity, visit our website: www.polity.co.uk

Key Contemporary Thinkers

Published

Michael Moriarty, *Roland Barthes*
Harold W. Noonan, *Frege: A Critical Introduction*
William Outhwaite, *Habermas: A Critical Introduction*
Kari Palonen, *Quentin Skinner: History, Politics, Rhetoric*
John Preston, *Feyerabend: Philosophy, Science and Society*
Chris Rojek, *Stuart Hall*
Susan Sellers, *Hélène Cixous: Authorship, Autobiography and Love*
Wes Sharrock and Rupert Read, *Kuhn: Philosopher of Scientific Revolution*
David Silverman, *Harvey Sacks: Social Science and Conversation Analysis*
Dennis Smith, *Zygmunt Bauman: Prophet of Postmodernity*
Nicholas H. Smith, *Charles Taylor: Meaning, Morals and Modernity*
Geoffrey Stokes, *Popper: Philosophy, Politics and Scientific Method*
Georgia Warnke, *Gadamer: Hermeneutics, Tradition and Reason*
James Williams, *Lyotard: Towards a Postmodern Philosophy*
Jonathan Wolff, *Robert Nozick: Property, Justice and the Minimal State*

Forthcoming

Maria Baghramian, *Hilary Putnam*
Sara Beardsworth, *Kristeva*
James Carey, *Innis and McLuhan*
George Crowder, *Isaiah Berlin*
Thomas D'Andrea, *Alasdair MacIntyre*
Reidar Andreas Due, *Deleuze*
Eric Dunning, *Norbert Elias*
Neil Gascoigne, *Richard Rorty*
Paul Kelly, *Ronald Dworkin*
Carl Levy, *Antonio Gramsci*
Moya Lloyd, *Judith Butler*
Nigel Mapp, *Paul de Man*
Dermot Moran, *Edmund Husserl*
Stephen Morton, *Gayatri Spivak*
James O'Shea, *Wilfrid Sellars*
Felix Stalder *Manuel Castells*
Nicholas Walker, *Heidegger*

Contents

Acknowledgements

The first drafts of this book were written for presentation at a week-long *Intensiv-Seminar* in the University of Bremen, two series of graduate classes in Oxford and an undergraduate course in the College of William and Mary, Virginia. In addition to the participants on these occasions, I am most grateful to David Bakhurst, Paul Davies, Simon Glendinning and two anonymous readers for encouragement and advice. I have made use of material from my 'Critical notice of *Mind and World*' (*Australasian Journal of Philosophy*, 74, 3, 1996, pp. 495–509) by permission of Oxford University Press; 'Object dependence in language and thought' (*Language and Communication*, 21, 2001, pp. 183–207) by permission of Elsevier; and 'Blue Book ways of telling: criteria, openness and other minds' (*Philosophical Investigations*, 25, 4, 2002, pp. 319–30) by permission of Blackwell Publishing. The book owes most to those who taught me critical evaluation, particularly Christopher Cherry, Edward Corbould, John Cottingham, James Howard-Johnston, Maurice Keen, Alexander Murray and Michael Rosen. However poorly I have learned from their example, I would not otherwise have seen how rigour grounded in the principle of charity makes criticism transcend disagreement. The book is dedicated to my mother and father, who have given me everything and more.

M. de G.
31 January 2003
Prenzlauer Berg, Berlin

Preface

This book is about the philosopher John McDowell and the main question posed by his work: what must be the case if things are as they seem and we are at home in the world?[1]

The issue is as old as philosophy and often identified with it. For Novalis, philosophy just is homesickness: 'the urge to be everywhere at home'. He meant that philosophers are driven to explain everything that is not philosophy by appeal to philosophy, and to make sense of philosophy itself in terms of a deep unified system. He thought the goal unattainable and the yearning to satisfy it pathological, a symptom of 'logical illness'.[2] But then one's view of philosophy would have to be pretty low to exchange it, as Novalis did, for work in the salt mines. Perhaps he considered it suitable preparation. Certainly it would not be much of a career change if the ideas presented in this book are correct. For in the light of McDowell's arguments, much modern philosophy seems simple drudgery; ineffectual labour to answer misguided questions in a doomed effort to disguise grotesque distortion at the core by spinning endless epicycles about the circumference. Even salt mines have a certain charm from that perspective.

How, then, should we regard our relationship to the world? What must be the case if we are at home in it? And why does philosophy tend systematically to falsify that view? McDowell has offered answers to these crucial questions that match his criticism of contemporary philosophy. Like Novalis, he thinks that what ultimately drives philosophical endeavour is the urge to be at home in the world. Like Novalis, he finds logical illness at the heart of the subject. But whereas Novalis thought the urge could not be satisfied and identified it with the illness, McDowell thinks it merely a symptom. We are already at home in the world; philosophy keeps us from being able to appreciate that; so we experience an urge to satisfy what is already satisfied. If we treat the logical illness in philosophy which prevents us appreciating what is the case, the urge itself will abate.

This book sets out to enlarge the group of those who know about McDowell's philosophical work, to extend the sphere in which his ideas are influential beyond the confines of professional philosophers, and to encourage those who wish to make our experience of the world their study to engage with his arguments. His deeply systematic writings are already exercising a profound influence on philosophy and the directions taken by research. Particularly well known are the papers 'On the sense and reference of a proper name' (1977), 'Are moral requirements hypothetical imperatives?' (1978a), 'Virtue and reason' (1979), 'Criteria, defeasibility and knowledge' (1982a), 'Values and secondary qualities' (1985b), 'Singular thought and the extent of inner space' (1986b), 'Might there be external reasons?' (1995b) and the collection of lectures *Mind and World* (1994a). Foremost writers who bear deep marks of his influence include Robert Brandom, Gareth Evans, Derek Parfit, Christopher Peacocke, Hilary Putnam, Richard Rorty and Crispin Wright.

McDowell's writing is not easy-going, which is one spur for an introduction of this sort. His work is characterized by formidable and elaborate chains of reasoning concisely and often metaphorically expressed. His arguments incorporate diagnoses, so that recognizing their steps is rarely simple. Seeing that some view is false, for example, is often made to depend on seeing what is nevertheless attractive about it. Engaging with any part of McDowell's work requires, amongst other things, some familiarity with the history of philosophy (particularly Kant, early Analytic Philosophy and Wittgenstein), some technical adeptness and acquaintance with many of his other philosophical interests. This last requirement is made more difficult by the bewildering range of those interests, from metaphysics through epistemology to ethics, aesthetics and moral psychology.

My main aim is to stimulate readers towards a thoughtful reading of McDowell; it is not to substitute for engagement of that kind. Engagement will not be possible unless the arguments contained in his work are made accessible. This requires description, elucidation, commentary. Hence there is a good deal of systematic exposition in what follows. But unless there is also a sense of involvement with these arguments, engagement will seem neither attractive nor important. So critical evaluation is basic to the book. Whenever questions of the form 'what does McDowell *say*?' are addressed, it is with the purpose of achieving that position from which the reader may judiciously ask whether he is *right*. There are four main aspects to the critical task undertaken here; I shall describe each in turn.

Some of the difficulties arising from McDowell's work are relatively superficial; the present book is an attempt to surmount them. But many of the demands placed on his readers are philosophically interesting and well motivated. If he is right, coming to our (common) senses about the way we are in the world requires strenuous and constant struggle with temptations to view things differently. So what is demanding about his work itself stands as a persuasive advocate for it. One would not expect this to be taken on trust; demonstrating it will play a considerable role in what is critical and not merely expository about what follows.

The second critical aim is to show that a unified response to a unified challenge lies at the heart of McDowell's writings. This is just as well, since a wide and diverse body of work can on closer scrutiny be made to reveal a network of deep and intricate relations. But defending this claim and making the underlying design salient present special problems, for the design itself is too dense to be appreciated from that distance at which alone it can be seen whole and entire. There is no clear solution to this problem, no way to avoid some form of trade-off between operations of analysis and synthesis. But the risk of distortion is very great if the various parts of McDowell's work are broken off in the traditional way for concentrated serial viewing – his views on the mind, for example, treated as separable from his views on language, on the world, on nature, on truth, on knowledge, on experience, and so on.

So I have chosen a different approach. The first part of the book describes the unified challenge McDowell takes himself to be facing. Knowing what his goals are, it is possible to judge how successful he is in achieving them. Understanding this challenge is also essential if we are to acquire a real sense for what McDowell thinks philosophy is and what its practitioners should be about, questions that are themselves quintessentially philosophical. The second part of the book takes a wide-angled focus, centring on the unified response that McDowell offers; naturalism is the key here. The third part narrows the focus on that same core, making repeated engagements with its main features: experience, the world, nature, knowledge, language. In the final part, the unified response is put to work and tested on a sample-group of specific problems: other minds, evaluative thought, colours, moral judgements. So the reader should be warned: the book is determinedly cumulative.

The third critical strand to the book is a set of comparisons and contrasts between McDowell's views and other well-known positions in contemporary debate. In order to keep the waters as clear as possible, I have chosen to make these discussions extended rather than frequent. So critical attention is restricted to discussion of McDowell's position in relation to various kinds of naturalism, Wittgenstein, neo-Kantianism, Quine, Davidson, Mackie, various forms of (non-)externalism, (non-)conceptualism and (non-)realism.

The possibilities for disagreement increase as the book proceeds and we have a better idea of what McDowell is saying. By part IV it is possible to discern reasons for concern about his project. In order to give due attention to what is salient here, I discuss a limited number of problems at length. Some arise over implications of the project: the epistemology associated with the notorious 'other minds' question, for example; the description of what it is to think evaluatively; the status of moral judgements. These concerns dominate the final part of the book. In the conclusion, I raise questions about the roots of McDowell's project: in particular, whether his attempts to put us 'at home' in the world rest on and require bias in favour of one particular element of the whole natural order, human beings; and whether his effort to 'give philosophy peace' does indeed leave us without the need to engage in further philosophizing. This is the fourth aspect of the book's critical dimension.

A final comment about the nature of this book. It is written to be intelligible and of interest to an audience without background in philosophy. So I explain technical concepts where they arise but keep them to a minimum. I quote from the most straightforward and readily available sources, confining to the notes the apparatus on which the analysis depends.[3] And, most important, I emphasize narrative line; there is a story in McDowell's philosophical work and I try to tell it. Pursuing what is at the core has meant being selective. This is not the place to chase up arguments as zealously as scholars need or chase down counter-arguments as tirelessly as adepts desire. McDowell's readings in the history of philosophy and his views on moral psychology, for example, depend on background that I have not the space to describe. Omissions are necessary, painful, but not I hope damaging to the overall enterprise. For there is a deep unity to McDowell's views, as I hope to show; hence none are neglected once their core is exposed.

Alice looked round her in great surprise. 'Why, I do believe we've been under this tree the whole time! Everything's just as it was!'

'Of course it is,' said the Queen. 'What would you have it?'

'Well, in *our* country,' said Alice, still panting a little, 'you'd generally get to somewhere else – if you ran very fast for a long time as we've been doing.'

'A slow sort of country!' said the Queen. 'Now, *here*, you see, it takes all the running *you* can do, to keep in the same place.'

Lewis Carroll, Through the Looking-Glass

Part I

Overview

1

Challenge

The fox knows many things; the hedgehog one big thing.
                                    Archilochus, *Fragment 201*[1]

Isaiah Berlin famously used this ancient saying to distinguish between those (he is primarily concerned with thinkers and artists) who are essentially characterized by the diversity of their projects, and those whom one would fail to depict correctly except in relation to some single overriding design.[2] What Berlin highlights in the original saying is a distinction in the defence strategies adopted by animals. For thinkers and artists, this becomes a distinction in the way they respond to how things are, or are taken to be.

But the original saying can be interpreted at another level. Animals distinguish themselves not just by how they act in response to danger, but also by what they perceive the danger to be. For some, the kind of hazards faced are essentially many; we cannot make sense of the 'fox's' behaviour unless we ascribe it a readiness to recognize and respond to variety. The 'hedgehog', on the other hand, perceives uniformity in danger; the one big thing it knows is that behind any particular manifestation, there is a single kind of opponent or challenge. The same distinction holds for thinkers and the problems they confront. Some take difference and diversity to lie at the heart of what challenges them, others unity and likeness.

The two levels are connected, of course; how one perceives things to be will help determine how one acts in response. But we cannot assume that what essentially characterizes the way in which thinkers perceive will be essential to characterizing the way in which they act, or vice versa. For it would be perfectly consistent for a thinker to deny that there is, at heart, any uniformity to the kinds of problem they face, and nevertheless to address the questions raised in a standardized way. Conversely, a thinker's response to problems might be fundamentally characterized by multiplicity, even though they think of such challenges as only superficially distinct, as mere forms of what is genuinely challenging, something they take to be basic, constant and single.

John McDowell is like the hedgehog, and in both respects: he perceives a uniformity to the problems confronted, and he responds in a unified way. That this is the essential characteristic of his contributions to philosophy has become steadily clearer since he began publishing at the beginning of the 1970s. Indeed, for a period, McDowell's published work seemed eminently fox-like. Entirely made up of separate articles on a bewildering variety of topics, his output ranged from inquiries into what there is (metaphysics) and how we know (epistemology), through problems set by our psychology and mental lives (the philosophy of mind) and by our linguistic skills and ability to communicate verbally (the philosophy of language), to questions about how we should live (ethics) and how we reason about how we should live (moral psychology), even touching in passing on certain puzzles raised by our appreciation of art (aesthetics).[3] What united this diverse body of work was more obviously a matter of style and tone than of theory or subject-matter.[4] But in the past two decades, it has become obvious that something far deeper connects up McDowell's output: the reflection of a systematic and integrated response to the perception of a specific and unified challenge.[5]

The Default

Aurelio Zen was dead to the world. Under the next umbrella, a few desirable metres closer to the sea, Massimo Rutelli was just dead.
Michael Dibdin, *And Then You Die*[6]

The unified challenge which McDowell faces can be expressed crudely as follows (we shall find various ways to refine it). Our experience of the world gives us reason to form beliefs about it which we express in language. I see this computer screen before me, for example, and I believe on the basis of this experience that there is a computer screen before me; this belief I might express by telling you 'there is a computer screen before me'. If this is so, then our experiences are *of* worldly things; moreover, we must have ways of thinking *about* such aspects of reality, of forming justified beliefs *concerning* them; and, finally, it must be the case that we use language to *refer* to things in the world, that what we say *has to do with* those things. We can say, for short, that our experience, thought and language are *directed on* the world. The world, in turn, has a *bearing on* our experience, thought and language. For how things are in the world (whether there is indeed a computer screen before me, for example) informs and helps determine what I experience, what reasons I have for my beliefs, whether what I say is true, and so on. This is the sense of being alive or dead to the world which is captured in Dibdin's description of Zen and Rutelli. If we are alive to it, it lies open before us; if it is closed to us in some way, we can be dead to it without being (quite) dead.

McDowell often uses the phrase 'openness', and it should be introduced with care.[7] 'Openness' is a metaphor whose home is in characterizations of contact (and the lack of it) between rational human beings; so the appropriate antonyms are caginess, reserve, restraint, constraint, confinement, isolation, (self-)containment, withdrawal, loss, and so on. Some uses of openness are not obviously appropriate guides to McDowell's use. So although we may describe someone as 'open to new experiences', it should not be thought that McDowell makes ambition or a sense of adventure essential to the way in which our experiences, thoughts and use of language are about the world. Again, we should not model that relationship of aboutness too closely on the description of someone as 'having an open mind'; openness, in the sense to which McDowell is alluding, is avowedly not inconsistent with judgement, resolution and endorsement. A use that is more apt to explaining McDowell's can be discerned in the phrase 'I am open to other suggestions or criticisms.' This carries the sense that judgement has been made but is revisable; that the subject is vulnerable to reasons, such as those provided by the way the world is, and can be changed by them; that the subject's relationship with the world is one in which he can be affected or altered in these and other ways; that the world can act as a cause, for example, in what the subject takes to be true.[8] The subject's openness to the world, then, is not a stark impressibility, a helpless exposure to the 'bright obvious',[9] but a relationship which makes possible, evokes and on occasion elicits a reflective, rational, critical response.

Now this basic background description of intimate relations between us and the world needs filling out; that is a major task for the body of this book. But it is important for the moment to note that it is not immediately problematic, and to see what follows from this. The description *should* seem straightforward, in McDowell's view. We enjoy a standing right to look at things in this way, one that we need not excuse, justify or validate. It is a starting point and stance that we would need to be argued out of, not one that we need to be argued into. Call what this description represents, then – our openness to the world in experience of it and thought and talk about it – *the Default*.[10]

And this is precisely where the challenge arises. For, so it turns out, there are all kinds of ways of conceiving the components of our openness to the world in experience, thought and talk – experience itself, the self having the experience, the world, having reasons, reference, and so on – which make holding on to that description seem not merely difficult, but quite impossible. And the effect is to make it seem that we are closed off from the world; that the world cannot have its bearing on us; that we are (or could be) dead to the world while yet being very much alive.

The challenge is not merely to show how we should keep hold of the Default in the face of these various temptations to let it go. The point is to acknowledge the full force of such enticements, and at the same time to retain our initial impression of the description as being precisely natural, an obvious and straightforward description of how things are – something which, it might be appropriate to say, any fool can see.

Given the demanding challenge McDowell sets himself, then, the kind of achievement which alone would constitute a satisfactory result in his regard would indeed be significant. To recognize, comprehend and appreciate the forces at work behind all apparent rivals to the original description, our Default; to advance no new position or theory; to secure the original description; and to show how what appears to be a contest between that description and its alleged rivals is no contest at all, for there are in fact no real forces behind them; even the notion that the Default faces competition turns out to be, in a straightforward sense, simply illusory.

What are the tempting thoughts which would cause us to find the original description problematic, if not false? That is very much the subject-matter of what follows, for tracking down and exposing the harmful patterns of thought which make problematic views seem attractive is subtle work. But it is possible to pick up the scent from grosser, more obvious lines of thought. It can seem, for example, that the differences between the constituents of our mental lives (our thoughts, desires, emotions, experiences, etc.) and the constituents of the world (ordinary objects, properties, states of affairs) are so very great that the Default must be false. The internally generated and appreciated freedoms we enjoy thanks to our having ('leading') mental lives, for example, contrast with the external forces determining the behaviour of objects. Moreover, the activity of the one is set against the passivity of the other. And the explanations of behaviour differ. With people, we allow for the possibility that they move for reasons which are goals for them: 'X runs because he wants to keep fit.' Since the Scientific Revolution, we have learned to give up such explanations for the behaviour of objects. Their movements are accounted for by reference to laws ('that glass fell because there was no equal and opposite force to support it against the effects of gravity', for example). Such thoughts might suggest that mind and world are hopelessly distinct and could not interact; or, at best, that there is a gulf between them which it is the purpose of experience to 'bridge'. On either view, of course, the Default must be rejected.

There are other reasons for drawing this conclusion. Thinking about one's present state of awareness is perhaps the most common way to generate the relevant kinds of worry.[11] Such thoughts need motivating, so consider this. It bothers you that you never seem to find the ideal situation for reading books of this sort. Your eyes are strained slightly; no matter how the lighting is arranged, the white page either glares or has shadows cast upon it. That background noise distracts you a little. Your legs feel uncomfortable positioned as they are, but if you move them your back tenses up. Was that someone at the door or were you imagining it? You could do with a hot drink; that whisky was a mistake. You rearrange things, and there is some improvement, but the situation is still not entirely conducive to concentrating on the words before you. In doing all of this, you are consciously aware of having certain kinds of sensory experience, of seeing this page, of hearing that background noise, of feeling your body positioned in a certain way. You are also conscious of having other kinds of thought; of understanding what you are reading, of wanting to be comfortable, of imagining someone at the door.

In such a case, it might be asked what sorts of thing there are of which you are conscious. Ordinary objects like books and chairs and glasses, certainly; and properties, like the weight of the book, the strength of the chair, the position of the glass; and events, like the sudden noise. These are items in the world; indeed, items of types whose totality makes up the world. But there are other sorts of thing of which you are conscious also. You are aware, for example, of the thoughts and beliefs you have about such worldly items. You are conscious not only of the background noise, but also of what you think about it (it disturbs you); you are aware not only of your body, but also of what you believe about it (it is uncomfortable). These thoughts and beliefs of which you are aware seem to be different kinds of item altogether from the worldly items you are also aware of. For one thing, your belief 'it is uncomfortable' is about your body; your thought 'it disturbs me' is about the background noise. But there is no sense in which that noise is about your thought, or your body is about your belief. Again, your thoughts and beliefs seem to represent worldly things to you in these various ways, but there is no obvious sense in which the worldly things represent your thoughts or beliefs to you.

So there seem to be at least two very different sorts of thing of which you are aware in even the most normal circumstances. There are worldly things like noises and bodies, on the one hand, and things like thoughts and beliefs, on the other. And one might mark the difference by saying that these latter items are not in the world at all but are distanced from it somehow; they exist, if anywhere, in your consciousness. Of course, these thoughts and beliefs must nevertheless be related to worldly things. For how else could your belief 'it is uncomfortable' be about your body, or your thought 'it disturbs me' represent that noise to you? But this might not seem to present much of a problem. For a picture of some particular dog is obviously a very different type of thing from a dog, and yet, by resembling the animal in various ways, it can be about or represent that dog.[12] If one regarded thoughts and beliefs as being like pictures, one could preserve the sense in which they are quite different from worldly things and yet nevertheless represent or be about them. So one might think of thoughts and beliefs as items in one's consciousness which represented other things: mental images, for short. And since it is useful to see how general a theory might be, one might propose viewing the totality of one's conscious awareness in this way, as composed of items that picture what they are about or represent.[13] When you are conscious of seeing this page, for example, your experience puts you in touch with the way that worldly thing is by presenting you with a mental image of it. So it might be plausible to say that what you are seeing directly is the mental image of a page, and via that, the page itself. Indeed, that since it is not the page itself that one sees directly but rather its image, it is not really the page one sees at all, strictly speaking, but its proxy. And since the properties of that image cannot be exactly the same as the properties of the page (the image must be two-dimensional, for example), we must then make an educated guess, given the properties of the one, what the properties of the other might be . . .[14]

At which point one might continue unabashed or panic at how very decisively one has departed already from the Default, and how tempting it is to continue. For suppose that what our experience and thought are really directed on are the mental images which represent the world to us.[15] This seems to place a definite borderline on our experience and thought, making it difficult to see how our minds could then be said to reach beyond those images, out into the world.[16] In which case, of course, we have to ask what right we have to say that our experience and thought are about the world at all. It would seem more accurate to say that they are about that proxy world in our consciousness, composed of mental images, to which alone our minds can stretch. The problems ramify. If words would be mere sounds unless they represented thoughts, language inherits the problem.[17] By saying 'this book', I have said not anything about the worldly item, but about the mental image which represents it. If knowing something depends on having beliefs about it, then knowledge is also affected. Since we have no beliefs about the world but only of mental images, we have no knowledge of the world, but only the possibility of knowing about its mental proxy.

This is a crude theory arrived at through crude means. It is meant to illustrate with a gross example how certain forces might tempt one to depart from the Default; it is not meant to set out the pattern which any thought-process would have to follow to constitute such a departure. But we may go on using the example for the moment to gain a further sense of the challenge McDowell sets himself. There are several points to be made about that challenge which follow directly from what has already been said.

Intentionality vs epistemology

The Default and temptations to depart from it are primarily concerned not with our knowledge of the world, but with our ability to experience it and think about it. So the challenge McDowell confronts does not primarily concern whether we know there is a world beyond our minds, or whether we know what it is like. That is a knowledge-based problem, termed 'epistemological'. Rather, it is about whether our experience is even of the world, whether our thoughts are even directed on the world, whether we even speak about the world. And since 'intentionality' is the technical term used for the relation of directedness or 'aboutness' that obtains between our experiences, thoughts, language and the world, it is appropriate to describe McDowell's challenge as fundamentally concerned with intentionality.

True, there are major implications for epistemology, and problems relating to knowledge will often crop up in what follows. For if none of your experiences, or beliefs, or uses of language were really about the world, but were about something else entirely (mental images, for example), then it might be difficult to say what, if anything, you know about that world. Some form of scepticism about the world would then be in order. 'For all you know', it might be said, 'the world outside your mind does not exist at all; or if it exists, it does so in a way that is quite different from anything you suppose or ever will suppose.'

But the door to scepticism is opened here because your knowing some fact about the world (that this book is before you, for example) depends on your having thoughts which are about, or are directed on, aspects of the world (in this case, the book and your body). And it is precisely this deeper claim which certain tempting thoughts (like those strung together in the crude theory) either qualify dangerously or deny. The claim is deeper because although one cannot know about some particular thing without having beliefs that are about it, the converse is not the case. If you were to think 'this book is a light comedy', for example, what you think might very well be about this book. But if it is indeed about this book, then it is certainly not something you know, for your belief is patently false.

So the intentionality-based challenge McDowell faces runs deeper than any epistemological problem such as scepticism. To put it bluntly: you do not get to claim that you know anything at all about some worldly item unless you at least have thoughts about it. So worrying over theories of intentionality at the point where they challenge knowledge is to worry too late. That damage has already been done which would be irreparable if we were constrained to use epistemological resources alone.

Deconstructive vs constructive philosophy

If the Default merits that title, it is not to be regarded as a 'position' or 'theory', a set of claims which can be promoted as the successful outcome once its rivals, like the crude theory, have been defeated. Indeed, any such relation of 'rivalry' between the Default and the crude theory can only be apparent. For the phrase misleadingly suggests that there is some arena and some common set of rules and assumptions within whose context the one is sufficiently like the other to submit to being tested against it. And since that cannot be the case, McDowell must find another way to resist the crude theory and promote the Default. Instead of constructing a rival theory, he must deconstruct positions like the crude theory.

The meaning of these remarks will not be immediately obvious, so consider them in the light of a pair of analogies. You see two small children come to blows over which animal would defeat the other: a shark with wings or a wasp with sabre teeth. Or you hear two theists accuse each other of heresy for promoting erroneous doctrine about the divine nature: they agree that there is only one God, but disagree about whether God is two or three. There are various options available to you. You might simply ignore these debates, or insist that nothing you can say would impinge upon them. Alternatively, you might wade in on one side of the argument and support the shark's advantage or the trinitarian's belief. Or you might expand the argument by rejecting the present constraint on alternatives: a rhinoceros with a machine gun would beat both shark and wasp; God is many.

But suppose that you are an adult responsible for the children, or a hard-headed logician. You might then try hard to convince all parties not simply that their own positions are false, but that their disputes are misguided. The very physical and biological laws which alone would permit brutish contest between animals rule out the possibility of winged sharks or toothy wasps; the selfsame logical laws which govern the claim that 'there is only one God' rule out the possibility of there being three.

In maintaining this, you have not taken sides in the dispute, nor have you advanced an alternative. Instead, you have undermined assumptions common to all actual and even possible parties to the dispute, assumptions that are necessary if it is even to take place. So it is not quite correct to say that you have 'overcome' the disputants; you have simply dissolved the dispute. Nor have you, in conciliatory fashion, 'bridged the gulf' between the different actual or possible participants. To describe matters in that way is to assume that the dispute was in good order; that the positions taken were defensible; that the assumptions leading to debate were sound; and that, in order to defuse the situation, it only remained to point out some further information or reasoning. There is nothing conciliatory about your strategy.

No rival position or theory has been offered, nor has the attempt been made to convert anyone to a new point of view. You have merely offered reminders to the disputants of what they must already know if their talk was even intelligible. To talk intelligibly of sharks' behaviour is itself to announce conformity with those physical laws which rule out the possibility of their being winged; to talk intelligibly of some thing's being one is itself to recognize application of those logical laws which rule out the possibility of its being three. You have returned the disputants to phenomena with which they are perfectly familiar – with which they would have to have been for their dispute to have got under way; phenomena which they had forgotten, or not kept sufficiently in focus. And you have shown how these vital elements in the structure of the disputants' positions not only count against those positions themselves, but annul any possibility of conflict on the grounds chosen with any other position. So this strategy may be termed 'deconstructive', as opposed to 'constructive'. Instead of destroying a position from without by constructing an alternative, this method destroys the position from within by pointing out sufficiently deep inconsistencies in its own construction to make it untenable. The strategy reveals how the position was constructed as an alternative to other positions, using grounds for contrast with those alternatives that turned out to be no grounds at all; hence the position itself turned out to be no position at all.

So there is a clear sense in which the deconstructive method has simply left things as they are; the sense in which 'things' stands for the overall situation (including physical and logical laws, for example) which recognizes some debates as well founded and others not. This is the sense of 'things' in which we may say that you and the disputants share the same general conception of what you are doing. In another sense of 'things', of course, the deconstructive method has produced a dramatic alteration. This is the sense of 'things' in which we may say that you and the disputants differ, at least prior to your interruption. For you have tackled the positions taken, dealt with the mistakes which led to misguided alternatives, and corrected the notion that the debate itself was something to become heated about. Your point has been absolutely conclusive, and a genuine contribution has been made, one that leads to intellectual tranquillity about the issues raised.

If the Default is to count as such, then it must be used by McDowell in precisely the same way. For it would not count as such if there were a real contest between that description and its alleged rivals, or if there were real force behind those problematic positions. This is part of the challenge he sets up for himself then.[18] The point is to remind those who advocate positions like the crude theory of those very things (familiar but, with varying degrees of subtlety, out of focus) which would annul any possible conflictual relation with apparent rivals. And, since the construction of these positions depends on the actual or possible existence of such conflictual relations, this reminder should be sufficient to dissolve those positions. To accomplish the task set, then, McDowell must destroy theories without proposing new, alternative ones. So his method must be deconstructive, not constructive.

And this makes McDowell both like and unlike Socrates' self-description when he drew the famous analogy between his philosophical role and that of a midwife.[19] As with babies, so with philosophical theses, both Socrates and McDowell produce none themselves but draw them out of others and test them for their 'health' (correctness). But what Socrates thought was a risk, McDowell takes as a certainty: that these tests will reveal the pregnancy to have been false, no matter how convincing the signs or how painful the process. There are no offspring; to think otherwise is to be seriously misled. And what Socrates largely ignores, McDowell goes on to make central to his study: the circumstances which made the sham possible and the situations in which it seemed convincing; all with a view to extirpating those conditions.

McDowell himself uses the phrase 'deconstruction' to describe the enterprise in which he is engaged, styling in this way, for example, his alignment with Davidson in response to the dualism of Scheme and Content,[20] and his interpretation of Wittgenstein in response to constructive philosophical accounts of how meaning and understanding are possible.[21] McDowell is often labelled a (Wittgensteinian) quietist, with his own apparent acquiescence, on the basis of the kinds of evidence just noted.[22] But since this label often misleads people into thinking that neither he nor Wittgenstein tries to offer conclusive arguments, attack positions, correct mistakes, dissolve theories or, more generally 'have effects' on philosophical debates, 'deconstructive' is preferable.[23]

An alternative label for McDowell's general approach, with some claim to accuracy, is 'genealogy' in its Nietzschean usage.[24] Roughly, this means a descriptive evaluation of some cultural feature or trend in terms of its history; a narrative detailing how it came about, or at least how it might have come about. McDowell certainly accepts the necessary assumption of this approach: that the cultural features to be dealt with (in this case, those conceptions of mind–world relations which resist or obstruct the Default) are deeply contingent.[25] The problems which he wants to dissolve arise perennially in philosophy; but that is not to say that they are timeless. The form in which they occur changes, renews itself; hence they require *re*-solution in a manner that is as timely as their form. Moreover, McDowell evidently recognizes the usefulness of narrative evaluation as a strategy.[26] It can provide a usefully exculpatory explanation of how one came to a false conception for plausible reasons (precisely what one needs in order to be convinced to change one's views for the better, incidentally, if those views are at all deeply held).

But there are two good reasons to avoid characterizing McDowell's whole approach in this way. First, genealogy requires a strong measure of patiently documented historical evidence and interpretation which McDowell does not provide or seek to provide. This is not surprising given the second reason. Genealogy alone would not suffice to undermine our false conceptions unless we were unconscious of the route by which we acquired them. For genealogy just provides a narrative linking our current conceptions to their roots. On occasion, we might renounce a view knowing no more than how we acquired it. But there may be conceptions whose origins we are aware of that turn out to be false. McDowell is concerned to press this point. Hence he might use genealogical methods, but genealogy itself could not characterize or determine his enterprise.

Knot-unravelling vs therapy

McDowell is a difficult philosopher to read.[27] This is largely because the demands placed on him by the challenge he confronts are also placed on the reader. There are two, rather different, ways to explain why McDowell's texts are demanding. Either would justify engaging in the complex process of reading him. But I believe only one is truly accurate and philosophically satisfying.

The first explanation has to do with producing conviction in others.[28] You would probably believe me if I simply told you the time without producing my credentials. But it is usually not enough simply to state the truth about some complex matter to convince anyone else of it. If I were a Flat-earther, for example, convinced that this is the only way to interpret a wealth of evidence, merely hearing you say that the earth is round will not correct me. In some way or other, you must find out how and why I hold the views I do and, by distinguishing for me what should convince from what is false or confused, lead me out of error. There is an apt analogy with psychotherapy here. In both cases, bewildered people caught in the clutches of confusion are freed by being made aware of what they believe and do and of the various forms of deception and tension lying therein. This work is necessarily as complex as the illusion it works on. So if McDowell wants to convince others of the falseness of various problematic theories, he is justified in going by circuitous routes which demand the kind of persistence and inner searching expected of psychoanalytic patients. His philosophizing is a form of therapy, guiding the confused from error to truth. And if ordinary philosophy of the constructive type turns out to be the cause of our bewilderment, then therapy will prove exceedingly convoluted and hence demanding. For it will be philosophy itself which is both the disease in search of a remedy and the cure for that disease.

But this explanation/justification of the difficulty in reading McDowell does not go as deep as it could. It is the nature of the challenge McDowell sets himself, quite apart from the desire to convince others, which necessitates the demanding route he follows. To dissolve problematic positions without advancing any alternative requires that we work from those positions, transforming what is mistaken about them into what is true. And work of that sort is very much more complicated than what is more common in philosophical debate: simple rejection of a position by pointing out the absurdity of its consequences. To pursue the course set by the challenge he faces, McDowell cannot afford to look for errors in the consequences of problematic theories. That would be to confront the problem too late. Anything that might be said at that point would be as useful as offering the notorious advice to someone who asks for directions to another town: 'I wouldn't start from here.'

Many of the problems with which McDowell has to deal are, at root, forms of (more or less wilful) self-deception. Part of the mind knows very well that the Default is true; but the temptation to indulge trains of thought which undermine it is so strong that this knowledge remains somehow isolated, inaccessible to reason, powerless to influence one's thoughts. So, to confront what is truly problematic, McDowell must uncover the sources of the errors which make it seem that there are rival positions; become intimate with the metaphors, descriptions and pictures which explain why the notion that real conflictual relations exist between them are so tempting; search for what makes those same patterns of thought compelling; expose the fissures and subtle flaws within those patterns; and thus loose their hold on us, a resolution that allows us to give up supposing that there exists what would be necessary to sustain sufficient contrast between rival positions to make them possible.

To prefer this deeper explanation/justification of McDowell's demanding writing is to prefer one Wittgensteinian metaphor to another. Instead of a likeness between philosophizing and (psycho)therapy, compare the former with straightening a complex knot.[29] You can look for the ends and pull, in which case you will very likely make the knot smaller and harder. Or you can try to unravel the knot, in which case you will have to look sufficiently carefully into it to make precisely the same complex moves which led to its creation, and all in reverse. The main point is this: with McDowell's challenge, as with the knot, it is the nature of the problem itself, not something external to it (something which would be required to convince or 'cure' others, for example), which places such demands on the person who would solve it or learn how it can be solved. And for this reason, I believe we should explain/justify the demandingness of McDowell's work not primarily by appeal to the therapy model, though that clearly has its place, but by thinking about what is required to unravel a knot. This is not to deny that producing conviction in others is part of McDowell's goal; nor is it to reject therapy as an apt model for explaining the character of his philosophizing.[30] It is to claim that there is an explanation/justification for McDowell's demandingness which is deeper and more philosophically satisfying because it would exist even if there were no others to convince: namely, that the challenge itself demands it.

This does not conclude the matter. For McDowell's writing style and presentation of arguments are closely allied to his conception of the philosophical task. They deliberately model that conception in formal as well as substantial terms, pursuing that conception right through from the deployment of arguments to their form and tone. And it is perhaps not immediately clear why this should be the case. After all, it might be said, the demands of unravelling philosophical knots could be placed on the unraveller alone; why should the reader be burdened with a style and approach that is demanding? Part of the problem with this objection is that it misses the point: the reader is no more exempt from the unravelling process than the patient is from treatment. The diagnosis might be made simple to grasp; but, however accessible, diagnosis alone will not cure.

The objection also misses an aspect of McDowell's style which is valuable independently of any potentially curative effect. It may be helpful to think of that style as an attempt, in part, to recapture the essentially peripatetic character of an oral discussion.[31] There is the same non-fortuitous but apparently casual arrangement of loosely connected but almost self-contained portions which, taken together, allow the reader to summon thoughts that circle around and centre on some major theme or problem. The purpose is strategically valuable, allowing McDowell to come at a set of interlinked problems from several directions, without according substantial priority to any by the accident of temporal priority in the discussion. Temporal ordering and the priorities determined by it are inevitable in any discursive form; McDowell's way of proceeding prevents one from according undue significance to it. The purpose is not to renounce continuous exposition; but nor is it the aim simply to hand out that exposition, flat and pre-packaged. The point is to make the exposition arise out of an encounter between author and reader, as between conversants. It is notoriously difficult to arouse and accommodate the mutually responsive and contributory roles of philosophical interlocutors in a writer–reader relationship, and it is tempting to give up wrestling with the problem. McDowell has resisted the temptation.

Unity vs diversity

Representing faith in the beneficial effects of being undeceived, the Default serves as a reminder to advocates of problematic positions like the crude theory: the very kinds of commitment which one must embrace even to engage in apparent rivalry are the commitments which annul such rivalry. So there may be infinitely many possible positions rivalling each other. But, in the light of the Default, the differences between them appear relatively superficial. Behind any particular manifestation, there must be a single genuine form of opposition: rejection of the reminder that the Default represents. For this reason, the challenge faced by those who offer the reminder, like McDowell, must be essentially uniform.

This is fortunate since manifestations of opposition are indeed multitudinous. The crude theory, for example, might be refined in all kinds of ways in response to attempts at correcting it. Suppose it could be shown that the theory gave a false account of language or of knowledge. Those aspects might safely be renounced, leaving the kernel of opposition: the accounts of experience and thought. Indeed, that kernel will offer the resources to re-model those accounts of language and knowledge in ways that escape the original criticism. Like Hercules facing the mythical Hydra, one might lop off many heads only to find them instantaneously re-grown in multiple and more resilient forms. The only effective response is to find and cut the one neck from which those heads sprout.

2

Response

In McDowell's view, there is indeed a uniformity to the positions which make the Default difficult or impossible to hold. Although each troublesome position has the unnerving ability cunningly to assume multiple forms and thus evade detection, constraint or dissolution, there is a basic and constant feature to all: they each proceed from false views about experience. And McDowell matches the uniformity in what he perceives with a uniformity in the way he responds: find the view of experience which is consistent with the Default, and see what it entails; dissolution of the problematic positions swiftly follows.

Thus McDowell's response has this basic form: there is experience; a necessary condition of the possibility of experience is the truth of some claim, that p; therefore the claim, that p, is true. Here, the claim 'that p' stands for both assertions of the sort to be described in a moment, which I shall refer to as McDowell's interdependence claims, and denials of the sort 'rival position A is incoherent'. This basic argument form is precisely that to which Kant's term 'transcendental' should properly be applied, given his official position (he himself was not always so austere).[1] It should be noted that this is quite the opposite to describing an approach as 'transcendent'. The transcendental is concerned with 'principles whose application is confined entirely within the limits of possible experience'; the transcendent with principles which 'profess to pass beyond these limits'.[2] The former aptly describes what McDowell's programme is, and the latter is equally suitable for describing what it is not. Indeed, McDowell rejects several positions simply and precisely because of their transcendent aspirations – either because they pursue the incoherent strategy of trying to go beyond all possible experience from within the viewpoint of experience itself, or because they assume some extra-sensory capacity on our part, or because they entail the existence of some super-sensible region of reality.

We should be cautious, however, in applying the label 'transcendental' to McDowell's response. For the main, perhaps paradigmatic, occasion for the use of a transcendental argument has been (perhaps continues to be[3]) epistemological, and particularly as a weapon with which to confront scepticism. And it is avowedly McDowell's purpose to ground his contentions in intentionality rather than epistemology, and to show how apparent rival positions like scepticism may be dissolved only if one refuses to confront them on the ground they choose. So 'transcendental' may be an unfortunate (because misleading) label for his response.[4]

It is important not to confuse matters here by supposing that McDowell *does* have scepticism directly in his sights. For it is relatively easy to see that his particular use of the transcendental argument form would not satisfy that bogey, the convinced sceptic. It is vital to any convincing anti-sceptical use of a transcendental argument that its first premise ('there is experience') be something that is agreed on all sides. The strategy is then to point out in the second premise what surprising anti-sceptical implications follow from this innocuous-seeming admission. But McDowell, as we shall see, packs a great deal into his view of what experience is – so much, indeed, that any convinced sceptic will simply reject the first premise as too demanding. 'If *that* is what you mean by saying "there is experience",' they will say, 'then no, I do not think that there is "experience", and I am not committed to the existence of any precondition for "experience".' But even if McDowell's application of the transcendental argument form is not anti-sceptical (it does not meet the convinced sceptic), it does not merely assume that scepticism is false. There is a third option: one consequence of McDowell's approach is that it becomes possible to purchase a licence to ignore sceptics.

'There is experience'; what follows from this depends on one's view of what experience is. McDowell answers that question by asking what view of experience is consistent with the Default. Such a view must secure the heart of that description: our openness to the world. That is to say: when things go well, our experiences are of the world, our thoughts are directed upon it, our uses of language refer to it; and, conversely, the world has a bearing on us in our experience of it, a bearing which informs what we think and say. Securing this openness leads to the view of experience which lies at the heart of McDowell's project, and it will be dealt with in detail in the rest of this book. But it is useful to have the basic elements in mind from the beginning. There are three points to highlight which may crudely be expressed as follows:

(i)   Concepts are the constituents of experience (so experience requires concepts and conceptual activity).
(ii) Concepts derive, either directly or indirectly, from experience (so concepts and conceptual activity require experience).
(iii) To possess concepts and engage in conceptual activity, at least for human beings, depends on mastering the use of words (so concepts and conceptual activity require language).

Of the various elements integral to this picture, none is more fundamental than concepts and the abilities conferred on those who possess and master them. So something must be said immediately by way of explanation.

Concepts and rational relations

It is customary to get at the meaning of 'concept' by asking what concepts do, what their function or purpose is, and (by extension) what conceptual activity involves. This approach has a nice degree of necessitation built into it; if φ-ing is what a concept does, then whatever else a concept is, it must be something which is capable of φ-ing. The original purpose of the 'concept' concept, introduced in something like its modern guise by Leibniz, was to provide a means of escape from the stranglehold on seventeenth-century philosophical debate exercised by the 'idea' idea. Being a generic term that covered *any* mental representation, 'concept', unlike 'idea', could not be unfairly reserved for naming the kind of item processed exclusively by any particular faculty, such as that of the intellect or of sensibility. (Mental representations need not be mental *images*, of course; for there are many other ways in which *a* can represent *b*, e.g. by being the word, sign or symbol for *b*.)

But 'concept' did not long enjoy the unrestricted use for which it was invented. *Any* mental representation would include what Kant called 'mere' appearances, which he described as 'nothing to us' –

fleeting mental goings-on so lacking in internal order or structure that it is dubious whether they might even count as potentially deceptive impressions of the world. And 'concept' quickly became reserved for certain mental representations: those which are necessarily drawn on, for example, in the kinds of organized, structured processes that count as *thinking*. Now thinking about something, giving it due intellectual consideration, tends towards – gets its purpose from; may even be essentially about – the disposition to find reasons for it, to believe it, to come to a certain judgement about it. So it was inevitable that reason, belief and judgement should turn out to provide the paradigm context within which concepts were to be understood as functioning; that was just a matter of teasing out what was implicit in the initial discomfort with, and modification of, Leibniz's definition.

McDowell makes this picture of concepts, together with what it implies, fundamental to his view (it owes much to Kant, Frege and Wittgenstein): we should elucidate concepts and conceptual activity by appeal to their exercise in beliefs (and judgements; but since judgements may be regarded as belief-type thoughts, we can phrase matters more economically). Beliefs are essentially linked to other beliefs in a structural way. Your belief that the weather is miserable at the moment would not be the belief that it is were it not responsive to other beliefs in various ways. It is established by some (you believe it is raining), supportive of others (you believe the match will be cancelled), and susceptible to yet others (you now believe it is not rain but a garden hose playing on your windows). This structure is rational, at least in the sense of being reason-sensitive: the beliefs you hold give you reason to form, retain or renounce other beliefs (i.e. whether or not you engage in that process, which depends additionally on your being sufficiently self-aware, reflective and careful). Concepts are then introduced as those items whose role it is to make these rational interrelations possible. Supporting a structured system of rational relations, like that exemplified by beliefs, there is a system of concepts; and those concepts are so structured as to determine the rational relations of the system they support.[5]

This descriptive definition of what concepts do will determine what they must be, of course, and working out these implications has given rise to considerable debate. It is very plausible to suppose that, in order to accomplish their task, concepts must be elements that can be combined and recombined in complex, structured contents; that they cannot enter into causal interactions independently of mental states; that they are classifiable. But this leaves various further questions, perhaps most pressingly whether concepts are mental representations (Locke, Fodor), abstract entities (Frege, Peacocke) or abilities (Wittgenstein, Geach, Strawson, Bennett). For our present purposes, however, it is only necessary to note the main implications for McDowell's view of experience.

The space of reasons

The structured system of rational relations determined by concepts plays a crucial role in McDowell's account and will often be referred to. So it will be useful to replace this complex phrase with a shorthand term. McDowell does so when he speaks of 'the space of reasons', a phrase borrowed from Wilfrid Sellars.[6] He employs the phrase often, so it is worth becoming familiar with it.

McDowell introduces the phrase 'space of reasons' in the following way:

> There is a special category of characterizations of states or episodes that occur in people's lives – for instance, characterizations of states or episodes as *knowings*; and, we might add, corresponding characterizations of the people in whose lives the states or episodes occur – for instance, characterizations of people as *knowers*. In giving these characterizations, we place whatever they characterize 'in the logical space of reasons'.[7]

'The space of reasons' is a metaphor like 'the realm of the senses' or 'a world of pain'. It is not a physical space, but it is like a physical space in some respects. A physical space might be regarded as the collection of physical items (objects, properties, etc.) with a layout appropriate to those items (size, shape, distance, etc.) which is to be thought of in ways that are appropriate to such items (physics, etc.). In the same way, the space of reasons collects rational items together (concepts, premises, conclusions, etc.) with a layout appropriate to those items (inference, justification, etc.) and is to be thought of in ways appropriate to such items (quite what that way is represents a substantive feature of McDowell's account; it will be dealt with in chapter 6).

One important feature of 'space' used in this metaphorical way should be noted since it has implications for what follows. 'Space' operates like 'world' when we say, quite consistently, that 'the world is a beautiful place' and 'the world is an ugly place'. The situation is ambiguous. We might be taking the same thing, the natural world, as being the subject of both sentences. We would then be saying that this one thing is beautiful in some respects and ugly in others. Alternatively, we might take two quite different things as our subject and yet describe them both as worlds. Asked to clarify, we might say, for example, 'the world of physical objects like mountains, lakes and blue skies, is beautiful' and 'the world of human relations, of suffering and anger, is ugly'. It is in this latter sense that the phrase 'the space of reasons' is used.

In brief, then, 'the space of reasons' denotes a logical space defined by relations of justification and implication. It is the space within which everything that involves rational-conceptual capacities and activities takes place. It does not compete with physical space; it is non-physical, not extra- or super-physical.

Dependency of experience on concepts

On McDowell's view, concepts are the constituents not only of beliefs (judgements) but also of experiences. Given our definition of concepts, that claim can now be glossed somewhat: experiences are essentially linked to other experiences and to other reason-sensitive states and abilities (like beliefs) in a rationally structured way. To learn more about what that way is, we need to think further about this part of the space of reasons: namely, the rational interrelations that obtain in our paradigm case, that of beliefs.

It is plausible to distinguish between two types of rational relation relevant to beliefs. The first connects beliefs with the world (its states, events, properties, etc.), and the second with other beliefs. When you believe that King John is eating a lamprey, for example, you might first point to some state of the world (the fact that King John is eating a lamprey) as giving you a reason for holding that belief, and then point to some further belief (that King John is eating an eel-like aquatic invertebrate with a sucker mouth) as finding its reason in that belief. Then it would follow from the definition of concepts described above that there must be a conceptual structure supporting these two types of rational relation.

To have a belief which is rationally grounded in another belief, one type of rational relation, it seems that concepts must have a logico-deductive aspect. To draw the conclusion that King John is eating an eel-like aquatic invertebrate from the belief that he is eating a lamprey, for example, it is not necessary to point to any state of the world. The one gives a reason for the other by virtue of those semantic properties which make those beliefs mean what they do and which, when combined in that way, instantiate a logically valid form. To deny that the King is eating an aquatic invertebrate while asserting that he is eating a lamprey is contradictory; and it is not contradictory (at least not in the first instance) of any state of the world.

To have a belief which is rationally grounded in the world, the other type of rational relation, it seems that there must be a referential or representational aspect to concepts. For applying the concept LAMPREY in such a way as to form genuine beliefs with 'lamprey' as a constituent, for example, one must be able to pick out instances of that concept in the world. And since the instance of the concept is what the concept refers to or represents, having a referential-representational function is part of the concept. Indeed, it is essential to the concept, for without such a function, the concept could not play its defining role of supporting the rationality of the particular belief formed in these particular circumstances.

McDowell himself takes these features of concepts to point towards a view that is controversial: concepts are unintelligible if either of their logico-deductive or referential-representational aspects are treated as basic, while the other aspect is treated as secondary. To treat one aspect as basic is to suppose that it characterizes what is essential to the existence and identity of concepts; to treat an aspect as secondary is to think of it as an implication of what is essential to concepts, something that is afforded by what is basic. In McDowell's view, neither the logico-deductive nor the referential-representational aspect of concepts is basic because neither can intelligibly be conceived of without the other. Instead, they are to be treated as in a local holism; the one requires the other if it is to be made intelligible. It is not possible to make sense of our capacity to assert statements which are (re-)combinable elements in deductive inferences only after we have made sense of the referential relation existing between them and extra-conceptual reality. So we cannot regard concepts as intelligible as such without appeal to their logico-deductive aspect. Conversely, concepts are not intelligible as such without appeal to their referential-representational aspect. It is not possible for us to make sense of the referential relation between concepts and the extra-conceptual world only after we have made sense of our capacity to assert and engage in deductive inference.[8]

On McDowell's view, concepts are the constituents of experiences as well as of beliefs. It does not follow, of course, that experience makes use of all (or only) those aspects of concepts which license the rational relations into which beliefs enter.[9] But it does suggest that those selfsame referential-representational and logico-deductive features of concepts which license different types of rational relation between beliefs are at least available to experiences also. It might be helpful, for example, if we were able to think of experiences as rationally supported by states of the world in a similar way to beliefs. This is to include experiences within the space of reasons. On this view, we would appeal to the subject's mastery of the concept RAIN and to the referential-representational aspect of that concept to account not just for the way in which his belief that it is raining is rationally grounded in his experience, but also for the way in which that experience is grounded in the fact that it is raining. Appeal to the logico-deductive aspects of the concept RAIN might be found unnecessary in the case of experience. Some, for example, deny that there is such a thing as deductive inference between experiences.[10] If that is correct, then there is no obvious problem; concepts make available more resources than experiences need (or in fact do) avail themselves of.

Dependency of concepts on experience

On McDowell's view, concepts and conceptual activities are unintelligible independently of experience, for they derive, directly or indirectly, from experience.[11] Given his contention that experience itself requires concepts and conceptual activities, this amounts to an interdependence claim. Indeed, it sometimes seems as if McDowell regards our experience and concept use as two aspects of what is essentially the same arrangement. This arrangement is thus part of the deep structure of the space of reasons.

The claim that concepts and conceptual activities derive ultimately from experience might appear to be a form of empiricism.[12] There are three different kinds of worry one might have about labelling McDowell in this way. First, if the claim is a version of empiricism, it is not empiricism in its usual form, which is epistemological – the assertion that all our knowledge, or at least our knowledge of non-necessary matters of fact, is dependent on experience. But suppose one were willing to say that any position which privileges experience with respect to some subject-matter counts as empiricism about that subject.[13] Thus one might be said to espouse empiricism about concepts, culture, cosmology, crop-dusting. As a price for being so liberal in our use of the term, we might exercise care in specifying the subject-matter; so we might say that claim (ii) amounts to 'concept empiricism' or 'semantic empiricism'.[14]

But – and this is the second worry – we should be cautious before saddling McDowell with a philosophical 'position' at all, no matter how vague, given the challenge he sets himself and his understanding of what it entails. This is a deeper point and perhaps annuls the first. For it is not that (concept) empiricist is the *wrong* label for McDowell; that makes it look as if another label would suit him better. (Concept) empiricism is the label of a position and instantly makes one think of rival positions, like rationalism, with which it can be contrasted. It is essential to recall that McDowell's purpose is not to enter the fray in this manner, to present a 'theory' of experience or concept use, but rather to recall shared conceptions which make it clear that there is no fray to be entered – that there can only be the appearance of competing views here, because what apparent rivals need to share just to count as rivals turns out to undermine any possibility of real rivalry. Since the 'empiricism' label tempts us to forget this central aspect of McDowell's goal in philosophy, it may be better to do without it, no matter how weakly it is understood.[15]

The final concern is that, given that particular sense in which McDowell takes experience as his subject-matter, it is simply incoherent to call him an empiricist. This point would annul the other two. It is not that there is anything lax about applying the label, or that it dangerously evokes the language of debates that should be dissolved and ignored; these worries make it look as if it might nevertheless make sense to call McDowell an empiricist. But recall the shape McDowell's response must take to meet the challenge set. There is experience; experience is openness to the world; certain claims follow, given what it means to characterize experience in this way. Since experience is what McDowell inquires into,[16] it can hardly be something he 'emphasizes' within that inquiry – surely the most permissive understanding of 'empiricist'.

Consider an analogy. Suppose you were trying to give an account of our ability to apply colour concepts like RED and GREEN. You will naturally emphasize the role of visual experience within the account – over aural experience or non-experiential forms of thinking, for example. But suppose you were trying to give an account of visual experience. Then it would be circular and nonsensical to describe you as 'emphasizing' the role of visual experience. Circular because your approach would boil down to 'visual experience is particularly important for having visual experience'. Nonsensical because anything that we could meaningfully describe as 'emphasized' must occur within your account as one more feature amongst others which counts – once the necessary contrasts have been drawn which make that feature of prime significance – towards an explication of the subject in hand. Naturally, visual experience cannot occur 'within' your account in this way if it is visual experience you are accounting for. Similarly, experience in general cannot occur 'within' McDowell's account since it is experience, and the conditions for its possibility, that he is accounting for. Given the nature of McDowell's inquiry, then, it would be circular and nonsensical to call him an empiricist.[17]

Dependency of concepts on language

McDowell argues that, at least for human beings, the possession of concepts and engagement in conceptual activity depends on mastering the use of words. This is not because he asserts that to grasp a concept just is to master the use of a word; if that were the case, there would be no need to add the cautious qualifier 'for human beings'. Rather, McDowell regards the ability to use concepts as something human beings have to be educated into by exposure to language-using communities.

The point depends directly on the view of concepts he espouses and his picture of the layout of the space of reasons. Conceptual activity accounts for rational activity. Human beings are not born rationally active but have to grow into people who recognize reasons as such, respond to them when produced by others, and produce them for others to respond to. To extend the metaphor, human beings are not born in the space of reasons but have to be initiated into it. Crucial to the child's development in this respect is its exposure to the community of rational agents in which it lives, a community which counts as such precisely by virtue of the rational relations binding it together, the myriad reasons for belief and action that it has managed to accumulate and store up over time. And what makes both exposure and community-bonding possible, for human beings at least, is a shared language. Hence, for human beings, entry into language is necessary for entry into those rational activities for which we need concepts to account.

Openness vs insulation

These claims of interdependence between experience and our capacities to conceive and use words neatly capture the interrelations expressed in the Default – that our experiences are of the world; our thoughts are directed upon it; our uses of language refer to it; and that the world has a bearing on us in experience which informs what we think and say. One question remains: how are these interdependence claims supposed to serve the Default? Specifically, do they offer a view of experience which secures the dissolution of problematic positions by recalling our essential openness to the world? To see what McDowell's line of reasoning might offer, by way of recollecting openness, consider some problematic positions – those which entail (whether explicitly or implicitly) that we are in some way closed off from the world.[18]

The crude theory, for example, makes our experience (thought, use of language) directly about mental images rather than about the world. We might find a way to relate those images to the world, perhaps by claiming that we are caused to have them by the way the world is. But if these images merely mediate the world to us, that will not open us up to the world; openness will not tolerate such go-betweens. And McDowell's interdependence claims help secure this conclusion. To recall: concepts are the constituents of experiences, as they are of beliefs; and, as with beliefs, it is the conceptual in an experience which explains its capacity for rational relations. The rational relation most relevant to the belief that some dog is barking, for example, is the relation between that belief and experience of the fact of the dog's barking. We appeal to the subject's grasp of the concept DOG and to the referential-representational aspect of that concept to account for the way in which his experience of the dog's barking is rationally grounded in the fact that it is barking. It is that fact, then, and not any intermediary (a mental image, for example), which rationally grounds the experience. And since the experience is constituted of those concepts which make this direct rational relation to a fact possible, the experience itself should be regarded as directly related to that fact.[19] Now any advocate of the crude theory, simply to engage with any apparent rivals, must allow for the possibility that rational relations exist between the subject's beliefs and his experience of certain facts. If this possibility makes the subject's experience directly about the world rather than any mental image, then the crude theory is incoherent (thus annulling any supposed rivalry with other positions).

Consider another problematic position. Suppose we put forward a theory which entails that our whole mental life (experiences, thoughts, desires, intentions, emotions, etc.) could proceed exactly as it does – indeed, as it *is* proceeding, in this present moment – even if there were no world at all.[20] If this were so, our mental lives would be insulated from the world and it would be highly unlikely that the world was exactly as our mental lives represented it as being. But the view would be just as problematic even if there were exact similarity. For on this view, any similarity could only be a matter of fortunate coincidence. This view is intolerable to openness and, again, McDowell's interdependence claims show why it need not be tolerated. For coincidence of this sort would not permit the kind of rational relations between our mental lives and the world which would enable the former to count as directed on the latter, or the latter to count as having a rational bearing on the former – those selfsame rational relations which make appeal to the conceptual constitution of experience necessary. Suppose that, when staring at a flat surface of water, you suddenly see what looks like a rough reflection of yourself. You might think that the image is 'of' or 'about' you. But when a small period of time passes and what you see turns out to be the reflection of a momentary cloud-formation, you will give up that thought. There was coincidence only between you and the reflection; the one was not 'of' or 'about' the other. In the same way, if we regard our mental lives as insulated with respect to the world, as proceeding whether or not the world exists and however the world exists, there may be the possibility of coincidence between them, but not intentional relations (relations where the one is 'about' the other).

Consider one final possible view. We might be impressed by the fact that, when we fall victim to hallucinations, we nevertheless suppose that our experience presents the world to us as it really is. We do not know that what we take ourselves to be experiencing is not in fact what is the case. It is possible that this condition afflicts you regularly, and that even though you are aware of the problem, you cannot tell when you are hallucinating and when you are not. When you are hallucinating, of course, the world is not exactly open to you. That is to say: your experiences may be of no worldly objects at all (this book you take yourself to be reading does not exist); your thoughts and words may be about nothing worldly (you think or say 'this book is heavy', but there is no such book); and, conversely, it is not worldly objects that are having a bearing on you, but your mental condition alone.

There are at least two conclusions one might be tempted to draw from this, one much stronger than the other. The first is that openness cannot characterize *all* our experience, thought and use of language about the world, for there must be more to each of these than openness could allow for. After all, one might argue, while you are hallucinating, and even though the world is closed to you, you are still having genuine experiences, entertaining genuine thoughts and uttering meaningful sentences. So some experiences, thoughts and uses of words genuinely count as such even though they are closed off from the world they are putatively about.

There is a fair point here, though exaggerated. There is a clear distinction to be made between asserting that our experience, thought and language-use are characterized by openness to the world, and claiming that every instance of these represents the world exactly as it is. It is difficult to see how one might uphold the latter view without giving so restricted a definition of 'experience' that the claim simply becomes truistic – 'experiences', being what they are, must be veridical. The former view is tenable, however, consistently with accepting that some experiences misrepresent the world to us. For this problem with experiences in the particular is just a hazard which accompanies and underpins the fact that experience in general is characterized by openness. The very possibility of the world's seeming to us as it is not on some occasions rests on its being the way it seems on (most) others. And so we need to develop an understanding of experience which keeps openness as the paradigm.[21]

One might draw a much more extreme conclusion from the possibility of hallucination: that openness cannot characterize *any* of our experience, thought and use of language about the world.[22] The thought goes as follows. If you are having genuine experiences, entertaining genuine thoughts and uttering meaningful sentences when you are hallucinating and the world is *not* as you take it to be, what essential difference could it make to your experience, thought and use of language when the world *is* as you take it to be? True, we may now describe your experiences, thoughts and sentences as being *veridical* and *true*. But that is like describing them as being *timely*. It is no more essential to the experience – something without which *that* experience (thought, sentence) would not be the particular experience it is – that it happens accurately to represent how things are than that it occurs at an opportune moment to satisfy some desire of yours. Whether or not the world matches the experience by making it true or timely is of no consequence to the experience. Being veridical, like being timely, is just a matter of the context in which the experience occurs. If circumstances affix veridicality or timeliness to an experience, so much the better; but the experience is still the same, unaltered in its content, the way it represents things as being.

There are many features of this line of reasoning worth scrutinizing, and we shall return to it. For the moment, however, it is enough to note the main line of response available to McDowell, given his approach. The extreme anti-openness conclusion about what an experience *is* derives ultimately from a premise about what we may be said to *know* about that experience. It is because experience can be either veridical or non-veridical *for all we know* that we should define experience as *being* what is common to them both. The argument assumes, then, that our view of experience should be grounded in epistemology. And McDowell can afford to accept the premise while denying the conclusion. For, as has often been remarked, he denies the assumption that epistemology is to be treated as basic here. The view of experience he explores is one grounded in intentionality instead. It is a view which, as we have seen, places experience at the heart of the space of reasons. This view has implications for what we know, of course; but it is not entailed by what we know. Instead, it derives from the Default, our common background conception that experience is openly 'about' or 'directed on' the world, and that the world has a 'bearing on' experience.

3

Implications

There is experience. A necessary condition for the possibility of experience is ... what? The emphasis so far has been on what unifies the variety of McDowell's contributions to contemporary philosophical thinking. Their point of origin has been located (the Default-centred challenge), and the direction in which they move has been indicated (the interdependence claims). These moves raise a host of different sorts of question.

Much of the framework making experience possible lies concealed and requires penetrating investigation. Suppose we find that experience is indeed the thoroughly conceptual affair McDowell presents it as being. What rival positions are dissolved by reminding us of this, and how? How is it that we are capable of enjoying experience? How is it that we have the opportunity to enjoy experience? What distinguishes us from those who lack the capacity or the opportunity? What implications do these claims have for our thought and talk about the world, particularly those thoughts we act on, i.e. judgements? These and other questions will be addressed in summary form here and the details filled in later. One aim of this summary is to give order and shape to the ensuing discussion by making its themes salient. But the more important purpose of the précis is to offset the inevitable singularizing effect of narrowing the focus on individual themes by making the interrelatedness of those themes clear while the view is still wide-angled.

Intentionality and experience

In McDowell's view, experiences *can* provide us with rational grounds for forming judgements about the world, and they can *only* do so if their contents are conceptual and if the world itself is composed of thinkable contents. To put the point in another way: experience has a place in the space of reasons and it takes on the conceptual structure of that space.

Concepts are the constituents of experiences. Since concepts are also the constituents of representational states relevant to thinking, believing, judging, and so on, experiencing the objective world is to be in a certain representational state where what is represented is what is available to be thought, believed, judged. Thinkable contents also belong to the fabric of the world, which is to say that it is in the nature of the world to be thinkable. These are, McDowell insists, direct implications of the Default and its picture of our openness to the world in experience. This account of experience is alone consistent with the directedness of experience, thought and language towards the empirical world. Certain implications follow, of which three are particularly important.

First, the directedness of experience and thought is unintelligible without regarding subjects as active and free. The reasons for this will become clear presently. Second, the intelligibility of directedness requires those experiences which purport to reveal facts about the world to operate within a conceptual structure that the subject already possesses. This structural point follows from the interdependence claims discussed above. Grasp of a concept depends on perceptual information about items in the world (in response to which concepts are constituted) and a background organizing conception (which organizes and permits the application of those concepts). Third, the directedness of experience and thought is unintelligible unless experiences of this sort disclose facts about the world directly. There is an unmediated openness between the experiencing subject and external reality: if our experience is not misleading, we are directly confronted by worldly states of affairs. The constitutive dependence of our most basic experiences on our environment implies that experience cannot be conceived of as bridging some gap between the experiencing subject and the world; as a series of exclusively subjective episodes occurring on one side, 'the inner', while the world goes about its business on the other side, 'the outer'.

Thus McDowell's position is a form of what has been termed 'externalism': the claim that the content of our thoughts is dependent on the world. Indeed, McDowell holds a particularly strong version of this claim for certain ('singular') thoughts: they depend for their existence and identity on the existence and identity of the objects they are about or directed on.

Spontaneity and receptivity

These observations lead to others, for example about what it is to be in states with conceptual content. We have seen that concepts and conceptual activity are linked intrinsically to the rational norms governing our thoughts, experiences and use of words. McDowell uses Kantian terminology to fix this account. He focuses on two kinds of feature which are distinguishable conceptually but whose contribution to experience is not even notionally separable. On the one hand, there are *intuitions* to which we are made *receptive* by our *sensibility*. On the other, there are *concepts*, which are organized *spontaneously* by our *understanding*. It is the combination of 'receptivity' and 'spontaneity' which explains what makes the potentially reflective responsiveness to rational norms characteristic of experience possible for us.

Kant defines spontaneity as 'the mind's power of producing representations from itself.[1] It is that faculty of self-awareness (apperception) which makes judgement possible by acting on the relevant materials (e.g. a sensory manifold, material delivered by our ability to sense the world), 'taking up' these elements and synthesizing them. McDowell emphasizes the active element represented by this synthesizing process. Spontaneity is what enables us to think actively – in the sense, for example, of being responsible for what we think, of reflecting on whatever it is in experience which we take to license or validate our beliefs. What underpins both approaches is the thought that experience cannot *just* be a matter of the causal reception and passive processing of sensory material. It must be possible to regard subjects of experience as sufficiently free and active to count as in charge of their thinking, at least on occasion; as able, for example, to adapt their response to what they take in perceptually as their experience itself changes. This spontaneity-based account leads directly to questions about the level of freedom presupposed by one's ability to engage in conceptual activity.

Humanism and naturalism

The account also directs us to ask about creatures which lack conceptual capacities. Spontaneity is necessary for concept use; conceptual capacities are necessary for experience of the objective

world. There are creatures which are incapable of engaging in conceptual activity, either because they do not have a faculty of spontaneity (probably most, if not all, non-human animals), or because
that faculty is not yet operational (human infants, for example).
Given McDowell's view, these creatures cannot *experience* the world,
and have no *world* to experience. This conclusion is no less eccen-
tric for being precedented (in the work of Heidegger and Gadamer,
for instance). McDowell might merely have defined 'world' in terms
of a conceptual exercise so that this conclusion would follow truis-
tically. But he uses 'objective reality' interchangeably with 'world'
and clearly means the implication to be taken as a substantial claim
and not a trivial terminological matter.

This raises the question of humanism – a polite way, perhaps, of
indicating anthropocentrism – in McDowell's account. It is necessary to disambiguate two very different senses of these terms. In
one sense, humanism about some particular subject-matter is the
claim that we should (or can only) view the topic from the perspective of human beings. (Someone might promote humanism
of this variety against those who think that there is a more 'objective' viewpoint from which things can and should judged – a non-
human view; perhaps even a view from nowhere.) But humanism
can also be the claim that, from whatever viewpoint, human or non-
human, human beings are central to that subject-matter. The distinction between types of humanism depends, in other words, on
whether human beings are taken to be the point of view or the point
of focus.

There are elements of both kinds of humanism in McDowell's
account. Together, they help explain why McDowell regards himself
as a naturalist. This has struck many as a surprising self-description.
What, for example, is 'naturalistic' about his championing of
the Kantian notion of spontaneity? The dispute reflects the fact that,
notoriously, 'naturalist' is used to describe widely divergent positions. This situation probably reflects a tension between (at least)
two lines of thought. For some, naturalism is closely related to pos-
itivism; the positive-naturalist takes the view that the organized
body of knowledge about matters of fact called 'natural science' is
all the knowledge there is. For others, naturalism is closely related
to humanism. Given the distinction above, we have two possibilities
here. Some humano-naturalists take what falls within the human
perspective to determine the limits to knowledge; others define
themselves by focusing their attention on nature as it is manifest in

human beings. McDowell appears to be a naturalist of the humanist type, and in both senses. The appeal to spontaneity, for example, is made legitimate on the grounds that it is proper to human beings. It is a faculty that we need to ascribe to ourselves if we are to explain those specifically human ways of engaging conceptually with the world which count as experiential – if we are to explain human nature, in other words.

Epistemology and externalism

McDowell's challenge and his response to it are not fundamentally epistemological, as we have discovered. Before we can say that our beliefs amount to knowledge of the world, we have to be sure that they can even be said to be about the world – a claim that we can easily lose the right to, given various tempting conceptions of the nature of our relationship to reality. But the characterization of experience in terms of the unmediated openness of the world to the experiencing subject has clear implications for epistemology. We seem to purchase the intellectual licence necessary to ignore most sceptical questions – those which are premised on a gulf between the perceiving subject and the world of ordinary facts, for example. This includes scepticism about the external world and about other minds (McDowell's views on the special case of testimony, believing the words of others, are particularly relevant here[2]).

McDowell's argument in the case of other minds rests partly on an interpretation of Wittgenstein's distinction between criteria and symptoms which has become influential in contemporary debate. If appearances are no longer conceived as in general intervening between the experiencing subject and external reality, we may distinguish between two kinds of case. On some occasions where things appear to be thus and so to a subject, that subject is perceiving what is the case. On other such occasions, the subject is misled and the appearances are simply that: *mere* appearances and not the way things are. This so-called 'Disjunctive' conception generates powerful rebuttals to arguments from illusion, scepticism about other minds, and causal theories of perception, amongst other things.

Openness, as mentioned above, entails a form of externalism: the claim that our thoughts, or some of them, are dependent on the world they are about or directed on. And McDowell adopts a strong version of that view, often called 'object dependency': certain thoughts, of which those expressed using perceptual demonstrative terms (e.g. 'That is *F*') are paradigmatic, are dependent for their existence and identity on the objects they are about. And the test-cases for this view are precisely epistemological. In cases where subjects hallucinate, for example, they might falsely take themselves to be having perceptual demonstrative thoughts – what can such subjects be thinking, after all, if the objects they are thinking about do not exist? This is a problematic description of what occurs because it impugns the intuitive authority persons have about what they think ('surely I know *that* I am thinking when I am, and *what* I am thinking . . . ?'). So deep questions are raised about what would constitute a plausible epistemology of self-knowledge, and about whether McDowell's views would be consistent with it.

These matters are, of course, deeply related to the question of what it is to think first-personally, and what abilities and opportunities are necessary to accomplish the feat. McDowell defends the claim that, although these thoughts are about worldly objects (their subject is the self; a corporeal object amongst others in the world), they are unlike other thoughts about such objects in an important respect: they are free from the need to identify the object they are about.[3]

Objectivity, value and ethics

McDowell regards perceptual experience as the correct model of how our claims to objectivity about value can be justified. So it is natural that he should draw on that position for an account of our evaluative thought in ethics and aesthetics. With his interdependence claims at the heart of the account, he has sufficient resources to explain how perceptual experience can justify our claims to objectivity about the world, and to argue for distinctive types of objectivity given different types of property.

McDowell agrees with others that objective thought is dependent on the existence of space-occupying matter and on our ability to distinguish between properties that are mind-dependent and mind-independent.[4] He maintains that our perceptual awareness of colours and tastes mirrors the role of reason in evaluative thinking. Values are objective in the qualified sense that colours are: an object's having the colour *F* is its being such as to look *F*. It is dependent not on actually looking red to anyone on a particular occasion, but on the possibility of perceptual experience, a world in which perceptual relations exist between subjects and the world of a sort that supports the possibility of objects looking red to those subjects. (There are differences between colours and values, but they are of lesser importance.)

As regards the specific case of moral and aesthetic properties, McDowell argues that they are real and objective (objects really are beautiful; people really are virtuous), but, unlike rocks and stones, their existence is simply not intelligible without appeal to the kinds of sensitivity characteristic of human beings. So for something to have value (e.g. actions, situations, persons, institutions), it must be internally related to some exercise of that kind of sensibility. And having sensibility of this sort depends on being educated in various ways, on acquiring habituated tendencies to be attracted towards objects or actions of various kinds.

McDowell is interested in the role reason plays in action – and particularly the place of character and its development – in a way that puts characteristic Aristotelian concerns to the forefront in his moral psychology. McDowell's contributions to ethics more generally persistently reveal the emphasis that his interdependence claims place on the significance of a background conceptual structure and the forms of life required to create it (he borrows the German notion of *Bildung* to describe this process). Combined with a strong Aristotelian influence, this intuition has provided, through McDowell's writings, much of the impetus behind the current interest in and respect for Virtue Ethics.

Trademarks and influences

Inevitably, focusing on the core of McDowell's philosophical contributions has done less than justice to those who have contributed to him. This will be remedied in the chapters which follow, since McDowell is a close reader of others whose writing reflects constantly on the workings of influence – whether benign or anxiety-inducing, supportive and salutary or constrictive and burdensome.

Certain names should be made salient alongside the basic theme which most clearly determines or dominates their relationship to McDowell. From the past: Aristotle (what is proper to human beings and hence natural);[5] Kant (the synthesis of understanding and sensibility in experience);[6] Frege (the conceptual structure underpinning rational relations);[7] and Wittgenstein (the openness of the experiencing subject; the tasks of philosophy).[8] Of McDowell's contemporaries, P. F. Strawson and Wilfrid Sellars stand out on the interpretation of the Kantian point;[9] Donald Davidson and Michael Dummett in connection with the Fregean and Wittgensteinian points;[10] and Gareth Evans on varieties of externalism.[11]

Most philosophers have peculiarities, traits, mannerisms, which stamp their writing with an identifiable mark. Five such characteristics of McDowell's work are worth remarking on. First, he is attracted by arguments of the form 'the only reason to adopt position *x* (which is bad) is if it is the only way to avoid position *y* (which is worse), and vice versa; it is not the only way (in either direction); hence we should reject *x* and *y*.' This methodology is ubiquitous in McDowell, unsurprisingly given his resistance to constructive philosophy; bad positions are destroyed on their own demerits rather than by advancing a new position.[12] Second, McDowell often finds an objectionable 'sideways-on' approach at the bottom of false theorizing. On this view, the proper account of some phenomenon cannot be given except from outside it. McDowell is particularly keen to undermine this approach in his treatment of language and of experience.[13] Third, he distrusts arguments which emphasize the first-person perspective. This was the route taken by Descartes: privileging subjectivity as an 'inner' region of reality leads to loss of the 'outer' world.[14] Fourth, McDowell inclines towards using perceptual experience as his model for a variety of cases.[15] To undermine scepticism about other minds, for example, he uses straightforward observations of material objects. Our responding 'I see him writhing in agony' to the question 'how do you know he is in pain?' does not adduce evidence but specifies a perceptual capacity which directly shows us how things are.[16] Finally, McDowell distrusts metonymy – that is, taking (substituting) the part for the whole ('the pen is mightier than the sword'). Foremost examples here are the tendencies to take subjectivity for reality itself rather than just a tract of it, and to treat the referent of the first-person pronoun *I* as an abstraction of the ordinary, corporeal person.[17]

Description and revision

Mindful, perhaps, of Marx's phrase about world-interpreters and world-changers, P. F. Strawson famously distinguished practitioners of philosophy into two basic types: the descriptive philosopher and the revisionary.[18] The first sets out to discover and throw light on the actual structure of our thought about the world, a conceptual structure with no history since its features are so general and fundamental that they are not subject to change but are shared with those in any age who have experienced and thought about reality. The second confronts the features of that conceptual scheme and rejects them, either piecemeal or altogether, in an attempt to improve our conceptual structure or replace it with a better one, a radically new vision of reality and of the place in which our ability to think and experience puts us.

Any response to the challenge McDowell sets himself which deserves to be called a response cannot fall wholly into either category, descriptive or revisionary.[19] For the aim is to secure the Default – our openness to the world in experience of it and thought about it – while dissolving the theories which make that view seem untenable. And this is very clearly not a revisionary aim; there are no new theories or world-views to be promoted. But it is also not a descriptive aim. The Default is indeed at the heart of our ageless worldview. But merely unfolding and elucidating that view would not show how theories that rival each other are in fact based on illusion and lack real power, any more than just stating the truth would.

Nevertheless, there must be elements of both approaches if the response McDowell offers is to meet the challenge set him. For the successful response must gain a clear sense of the myriad conceptual relations making up the Default, and then track down alleged rival positions to reveal and reject the illusory nature of their foundations. And that is not unlike running with the descriptivist while hunting with the revisionist.

Part II

A Naturalism of Second Nature

Central Elements

When will we be done with our caution and care? When will all these shadows of god no longer darken us? When will we have completely de-deified nature? When may we begin to *naturalize* humanity with a pure, newly discovered, newly redeemed nature?

Nietzsche, *The Gay Science*[1]

If the key challenge McDowell faces is securing our openness to the world, and his response is centred on unravelling the complex knot of illusions which tempt us to abandon that stance, then his views on nature are decisive. For, in his analysis, it is gaining the correct stance on the natural order which assures us of our openness to the world in experience, thought and talk. Conversely, all current illusions luring us away from openness ultimately resolve into a handful of views about nature. And these views are anyway ripe for revision. So we should gain a fix on this crucial intersection before exploring the various paths which lead to and from it.

> My proposal is that we should try to reconcile reason and nature, and the point of doing that is to attain . . . a frame of mind in which we would no longer seem to be faced with problems that call on philosophy to bring subject and object back together. If we could achieve a firm hold on a naturalism of second nature, a hold that could not be shaken by any temptation to lapse back into ordinary philosophical worries about how to place minds in the world, that would not be to have produced a bit of constructive philosophy. . . . In Wittgenstein's poignant phrase, it would be to have achieved 'the discovery that gives philosophy peace'.[2]

There are four central elements to McDowell's argument as it is presented or hinted at here; the coming discussion is structured around them. They are, respectively:

(a)   We should be naturalists even about nature and the natural order (naturalism can instruct us to revise our view of nature).

What, precisely, is meant by 'naturalism' is a matter of debate, one into which we shall enter. But the core idea of naturalism about some subject-matter (for example, naturalism about the mind, or about human beings) is that the subject in question forms a part of nature, and its existence, characteristics, behaviour (and so on) should be explained accordingly.

(b)   Naturalism instructs us to incorporate second nature into the natural order.

The 'second nature' of any being is what is proper to it, but also acquired by it. Walking, for example, is second nature to human beings. Our second nature is that set of capacities, abilities, habits and tendencies which we are not born with but pick up or attain through certain ways of living, and which become sufficiently fixed or essential to effect or explain quasi-instinctive patterns in our behaviour. Saying 'My leg hurts' when it does, for example, manifests a complex set of ingrained but acquired language-using abilities and capacities on our part, together with similarly fixed-acquired habits and tendencies to communicate verbally.

   McDowell places equal emphasis on the two parts of the phrase 'second nature'. He claims that our rational-conceptual capacities (those which, as we have found, he associates with the Kantian term 'spontaneity') are a paradigm case of the fixed-acquired capacities of second nature. They are the capacities which enable us to respond differentially to rational demands in rational ways. In McDowell's view, these capacities must be incorporated into the natural order, just as language-use must. For this is an essential truth about the natural lives of human beings: it is normal for human beings to be educated in ways that lead to their acquiring and making differential use of such abilities.

(c)   The current view of nature resists the incorporation of second nature, so we should adopt a revised view.

The argument for this claim quickly becomes complex and will be explored in some detail, but McDowell's central thought is relatively simple. The current view of nature tends to equate what is natural with what science alone makes comprehensible. Science alone cannot make our rational-conceptual capacities comprehensible. So the current view has difficulty finding the proper place for those capacities. Now rational-conceptual capacities are a paradigm case of second nature. They are essential to beings who form an integral part of nature, namely, human beings. Hence, if we are naturalists, we should revise our current view of nature.

(d) The current view of nature is responsible for making our openness to the world seem problematic. Suitably revised to incorporate second nature, our view of nature will no longer obstruct but express our openness to the world.

On McDowell's view, as we have seen, our openness to the world is dependent on the possession and use of conceptual capacities. Thus whether or not we find openness problematic will largely depend on whether we find conceptual capacities problematic. Given the argument under (c), we are drawn to the following conclusion. The way to dissolve the apparent problem with openness is to regard conceptual capacities as an essential part of human nature, a basic characteristic of our placement in the natural world.

The revised view of nature is not the only argument McDowell offers against positions that make openness seem problematic. As we shall see, he also finds certain of these positions internally incoherent, often in a self-defeating way. They cannot achieve the very ends to which they aspire and which alone would justify their establishment. But we are to regard the vindication of openness effected by the revised view of nature as dissolving a host of problems, familiar and less familiar. McDowell gestures at this with his reference in the extract to 'ordinary philosophical worries about how to place mind in the world'. Conspicuous among the mind–world problems we could expect to see dissolved would be the following familiar worries about how the mind could have a place in nature.

Surely matter is too dissimilar from mind to have been able to cause it; so how could mind have resulted or developed in a natural universe that previously contained only material things and nothing mental? The laws of nature, deterministically or probabilistically conceived, explain the behaviour of matter; so how could minds conform to nature, when their behaviour sometimes requires explanation in terms of ends instead (e.g. the goals for which minded agents act)? The natural world forms a deterministic and mechanistic system; so how can the mind be part of nature and yet free with respect to at least some of its operations? The natural world is material, a composite of ultimate particles which are conceived by physicists to be one and the same, without individual character; so how can minds be part of that order, given that they are essential to what in fact obtains: a plenitude of individuals with characters? If minds are mere bits of nature, how could their operations be structured by 'spontaneity', that Kantian term McDowell uses to denote 'the freedom that empowers us to take charge of our active thinking'?[3] If nature is what natural science aims to make intelligible without recourse to concepts like reason, understanding, meaning, how can it include such things as minds, things whose behaviour cannot be made intelligible except by appeal to those concepts?

McDowell argues that these problems can be dissolved by reconceiving nature so that it incorporates conceptual capacities. But he is careful to note that there is a sense in which the dissolution thus offered could not be a once-and-for-all matter.[4] Worries about mind–world relations take a particular form in current thinking, and his arguments are meant to be decisive when addressed to that form. But at some very general level of description, anxiety about how the mind takes its place in the world is perennial. The anxiety takes different specific forms at different times, and it is only in its specific forms that it can be addressed. There are specific forms that are not addressed, for example, by thinking of the anxiety induced by mind–world relations as essentially a problem of how to find a place for the mind in nature. Hence there are specific forms that are not dissolved by incorporating conceptual capacities into nature.

4

Naturalism

Man can only become man by education. He is merely what education makes him. [It] changes animal nature into human nature.
                                                        Kant, *Education*[1]

Nowadays, almost everyone aims to be a naturalist. Unfortunately,
it does not follow that there is one thing at which everyone aims.[2]

We need to clarify the issue somewhat if McDowell is to be adequately interpreted and his central claims are to be assessed.[3] Some
would deny that he counts as a naturalist at all, and hence assert
that he has no right to the very claim, which launches his argument,
namely, (a) 'We should be naturalists even about nature and the
natural order'. The following section makes a start by introducing
some crucial distinctions. The aim is partly elucidatory and partly
critical. By providing a kind of cognitive map within which
McDowell and his opponents can be placed and their interrelations
plotted, it is easier to see whether his position faces effective opposition from those who would deny that he is really a naturalist.

Varieties of naturalism

The existence of a bewildering variety of 'naturalistic' positions
owes something to a divergence, broadly understood, between
what is taken to be basic: (modes of) explanation or what is to be
explained. Some take a particular view of what items a naturalistic
conception of the universe would include, ask what modes of expla-

nation best explain them, and thus discover what modes count as naturalistic. Others begin with such modes, ask what items can be explained by them, and thus discover what is to be included in a naturalistic conception of the universe. The divergence is to be understood broadly because it is doubtful whether any actual naturalist has followed either path exclusively. That is almost certainly due to the fact that strong interdependence relations exist between the paths. These relations simplify matters in some respects (by creating uniformity) and complicate them in others (creating a need for foundations where none plausibly exist).

To clarify these points, consider an analogy with history. We might come to a notion of what it is for something to have a place in history by asking what kinds of thing are susceptible to historical explanation. To keep things simple, suppose one took the view that explanation requires (written) documentary evidence to count as historical. Then anything which pre-existed written evidence would not have a place in history. In this way, we create a certain uniformity by using a conception of appropriate modes of explanation to discover what is to be explained. But this might seem a bizarre conclusion, leading one to question one's view of what constitutes historical explanation in the first place; how is it, or should it be, arrived at? This appeal to a foundation might be answered if we run things in reverse. Starting with a conception of what it is for things to have a place in history, we work out how (best) to explain them. To be simplistic again, suppose one thought that only human affairs have a place in history. Then any mode of explanation which excluded human beings would not count as historical. In this way, we again create uniformity by using a conception of what is to be explained to discover the appropriate modes of explanation. But the result seems equally peculiar and one is forced to ask again for a foundation to the approach. How is one's conception of having a place in history to be arrived at? In practice, of course, historians tend to incorporate both procedures. Naturalists seem to follow suit. But this way of operating is not a particularly satisfying option. If it does not inherit all the problems of each procedure, it does not solve them either.

Most naturalists take their position to be monist about what is to be explained: they hold that the natural order is all there is or can be. Most are also reductionist about the modes in which what there is should be explained: they hold that natural explanation is all the valid explanation there is or can be.[4] It is theoretically possible to be a pluralist or non-reductionist naturalist, claiming that the natural order and natural explanation exist as one among many. But unless the natural is emphasized within the overall scheme proposed, there is no good reason to emphasize it by referring to the position as a whole as 'naturalist'. (So, for example, it would be very odd but not contradictory to describe as naturalists those who believe in the co-existence of natural and supernatural beings, or of types of behaviour whose explanation requires appeal to both natural and supernatural forces.)

The distinctions drawn so far reflect the basic state of things. They provide sufficient grounds for adopting different types of naturalism; hence the variety. And they suggest almost no grounds for adopting non-naturalism; hence the unanimity. Nevertheless, many naturalists feel that they are few in number or under attack. What explains this is an obvious aspect of our modern world-view to which McDowell often appeals: the great successes achieved by science in explaining the natural order.

Suppose one is a monist who tends to treat modes of explanation as basic. Impressed by the success of science, one might prioritize that mode of explanation among others which seek to explain the natural order. This priority might take different forms: an ideological form, a methodological form, a metaphysical form. And each of these forms might reveal itself in different ways: from the simple deference of other modes of explanation to the scientific, through re-modelling those modes to accord with the scientific, to excluding any modes that do not accord with the scientific. This last position is relatively close to another which changes the picture entirely: excluding any modes which are not actually scientific. To adopt that position is to move from deference to identity. For if there are no non-scientific modes of explanation that are naturalistic, and the only valid mode there is or can be is naturalistic, then that one mode must be scientific. This identity claim about modes of explanation has a direct effect on what is to be explained, of course, if the one is basic to the other. The one order there is or can be is the natural, which is now tantamount to saying the order that science is sufficient to explain. Call this final combined position 'scientism' (a label which is no longer assumed to be pejorative[5]).

The picture is further complicated by the fact that, just as there are many forms that deference might take, there are several different views of what is to be deferred to and what is to be identified with what. Is it only the so-called 'natural sciences'? If so, how broadly is that label to be taken? Does it include biology and the science of animal behaviour in respect to character-formation (i.e.

ethology; which, as defined, may include human culture, second nature and the kinds of acquired rational-conceptual capacities McDowell focuses on), or is it interpreted reductively so as to exclude all but what is universally applicable (i.e. physics)?[6] Is it what(ever) actually occurs under the name 'science', or what such investigations aspire to at a particular time, or what the ideal form of such investigations would be, whether or not that form is (ever) recognized? Is it any empirical investigation, or any inquiry whose goal is the discovery of objective empirical truth, or just those employing certain methods?

To see how these basic distinctions play out in practice, consider how to place a variety of different positions. Suppose we thought there was really no natural order – either because what so appears is in fact not natural but illusory, or because what so appears is in fact wholly supernatural. That would not necessarily make us non-naturalist, for we might think there were perfectly natural ways of explaining what is in fact the case. But since strong interdependence links exist between what there is and how it is to be explained, as mentioned above, it would be usual for the denial of one to follow the denial of the other. Alternatively we might adopt naturalism, claiming that the world and its occupants form a part of nature, and its behaviour should be explained accordingly. Taking this view, we might nevertheless think, as the Plato of the middle dialogues seems to have done, that ordinary natural things get their nature by being imitations of 'forms', which are independent of and transcend the natural world. Then our very attempt to account for the natural order will lead us to posit the existence of things outside that order. We would then be naturalists but not monists. Suppose that, like Locke or Kant, we added to this kind of theory the claim that, if we were entirely to understand these non-natural items underpinning the natural order, we would require non-natural modes of explanation. Then we would be naturalists but neither monists nor reductionists.

Although it might seem that a naturalism of the monist and reductionist type would be restricted, in fact much is left still to play for. We might conceive of a large spectrum with the tightest scientism at one end: the natural order and natural modes of explanation are to be identified with science narrowly conceived as physics. Relatively close to it would be forms of scientism that conceived of science more broadly, for example in such ways as to include biology and ethology. In the centre would be non-scientistic views that were nevertheless deferential to science, however conceived.

And at the other end would be the loosest monist and reductionist non-scientism: even when broadly conceived, science is just one among many modes of explanation that count as natural, and there is more to the natural order than what it describes. Moreover, these other ways of describing what there is and explaining it need not defer to science.

Monist, reductionist non-scientism

So naturalism itself, as opposed to its many sub-types, is a relatively unrestricted field. To claim that the topics with which one is concerned form a part of nature and should be explained accordingly, one need not adopt even the loosest non-scientism; indeed, one might reject both monism and reductionism. Hence we can appreciate how difficult it would be to exclude McDowell from the naturalist camp, on any plausible understanding of that position. In a moment, we shall look in detail at the precise kind of naturalism he embraces. But McDowell's position, and the positions of those from whom he explicitly distinguishes himself, can briefly be sketched in relation to the foregoing taxonomy.

McDowell tends to approach the question of naturalism by treating what is to be explained, rather than modes of explanation, as basic. He argues that the abilities of second nature are among those essential items a naturalistic conception of the world must include. Paradigmatic of those abilities are our rational-conceptual capacities. The modes of explanation which best explain these capacities are proper to reason. Hence these modes of explanation have as good a claim to count as naturalistic as those associated with the natural sciences. McDowell is apparently monist and reductionist about what is to be explained. Certainly, he does not admit non-natural explanations of what there is into his account, and he rejects those theories (like the platonic[7] or the Kantian) which posit a non-natural order in order to account for human experience and thought. On the other hand, McDowell does not identify naturalistic modes of explanation with scientific modes, or the natural order with the order that science is sufficient to explain. This is because, in his view, our rational-conceptual capacities exceed science and scientific explanation, even when 'science' is broadly conceived.

So, if we abstract for a moment from the very many possible alternatives our taxonomy offers to McDowell's position, there are two basic alternatives within naturalism for him to combat: pluralism and scientism. To put it in other terms: suppose we accept that room must be found for our rational-conceptual capacities. Then we might either regard those capacities as non-natural and requiring a non-natural explanation (pluralism), or we might regard them as fully explained by science and by appeal to the scientific order alone (scientism).[8] Before we can assess McDowell's attack on these alternatives, however, we must gain a firmer grip on his positive project, the so-called 'naturalism of second nature'.

It helps to have a guiding question while examining the specific passages which clarify what precise position McDowell actually holds, and needs to hold, in order for his central argument (outlined in the synopsis above) to go through. So we will focus on this: what sub-types of naturalism are consistent with the basic elements of his position, (a)–(d), as outlined in that synopsis?

Second nature

As we have already seen, the basic elements of McDowell's position depend heavily on the notion of 'second nature' and the acquired-but-fixed features that phrase refers to, particularly rational-conceptual capacities.[9] So that is where we should begin.

> If we generalize the way Aristotle conceives the moulding of ethical character, we arrive at the notion of having one's eyes opened to reasons at large by acquiring a second nature.[10]

McDowell introduces 'second nature' by appeal to Aristotle's *Nicomachean Ethics*, particularly book II. His suggestion is that we should treat one aspect of our rational-conceptual capacities, the aspect which Aristotle exposes in our ethical dealings, as a model for the whole: 'Moulding ethical character, which includes imposing a specific shape on the practical intellect, is a particular case of a general phenomenon: initiation into conceptual capacities, which include responsiveness to other rational demands besides those of ethics. Such initiation is a normal part of what it is for a human being to come to maturity.'[11]

So the rational-conceptual capacities included in our second nature and necessary for our (open) experience of the world constitute the general case. The particular case is our capacity for ethical thinking: our ability to recognize ethical reasons for action in situations that the world sets up for us, for example; our capacity for connecting them up with other such reasons so as to justify various possible courses of action; and so on. All these abilities count as natural because it is normal for certain natural beings (human beings) to acquire them: 'what is specifically human is surely natural (the idea of the human is the idea of what pertains to a certain species of animals).'[12]

These comments leave us with various questions. What is it to 'have one's eyes opened to reasons at large' or to have a 'specific shape' imposed on one's practical intellect? Why should our ethical dealings be a good model for our acquisition of rational-conceptual abilities? What is 'specifically human' about human beings? The appeal to Aristotle's ethical views helps clarify McDowell's position on these points.[13] Much depends on the question of how 'first' and 'second' nature are to be distinguished.

Aristotle on powers, abilities, capacities

Aristotle presents a crucial aspect of his own view in a way that is immediately available for generalization: 'None of the virtues of character arises in us by nature . . . virtues arise in us neither by nature nor contrary to nature, but nature gives us the capacity to acquire them, and completion comes through habituation.'[14] What is true here of virtues in particular holds in general for second nature abilities. The contrast Aristotle is making is not between the natural and the non-natural, but between those natural abilities that we simply *have*, like the ability to sense things,[15] and those that we *acquire*, like the virtues, or the ability to build houses or the skill of playing musical instruments. Those abilities that we simply have, the abilities of 'first' nature, 'arise in us by nature'. But nature also plays a part in regard to those (second nature) abilities that we acquire; it provides the opportunity for their acquisition by the subject and for the subject's habituation.

There is a further distinction, in Aristotle's view, between those natural abilities that we have and those that we acquire. The former exist prior to their exercise by us, whereas the latter are acquired in their exercise, 'since what we need to learn before doing, we learn by doing'.[16] The route by which a subject or agent gains these natural abilities, therefore, does not have a two-stage structure: acquisition of the ability followed by its exercise. There is instead a single process; one in which it is impossible to extricate implementation of the ability from its achievement, putting the ability into effect from gaining purchase on it. So the term 'habituation' is appropriate, with its related terms 'education', 'training', 'breaking in', 'conditioning'. Unlike a staged procedure with abilities that pre-exist their exercise, there is no expectation of clear temporal boundaries on the habituation process, of signs which decisively mark off the subject's attainment of an ability from their earlier lack of it.

In his *De Interpretatione*, Aristotle makes a further remark about abilities and capacities which will be relevant to McDowell's use of the notion of second nature:

> It is evident that not everything capable either of being or walking is capable of the opposites also. There are cases of which this is not true. Firstly, with things capable non-rationally; fire, for example, can heat and has an irrational capability. While the same rational capabilities are capabilities for more than one thing, for contraries, not all irrational capabilities are like this. Fire, as has been said, is not capable of heating and of not heating, and similarly with everything else that is actualized all the time. Some, indeed, even of the things with irrational capabilities are at the same time capable of opposites. But the point of our remark is that not every capability is for opposites – not even all those which are capabilities of the same kind.[17]

Leaving aside for the moment the question of which capacities count as rational, the passage indicates a useful distinction. Some capacities must be exercised by the agent who has them, given the opportunity to do so; the ability to heat things, for example, is something that fire must exercise if it has the opportunity. Other capacities incorporate a certain degree of freedom. The ability to walk, for example, is something that I usually may or may not exercise if I have the opportunity to do so. Following Aristotle's description of the distinction, it might be called one between non-contrary and contrary abilities and capacities. The distinction is important for the notion of second nature. As we shall see, some of the abilities and capacities involved in second nature incorporate the kind of freedom characteristic of the contrary type; others are non-contrary and lack that freedom.

Habituation and language

The rational-conceptual capacities McDowell focuses on are secondary. The animals who manifest them (and human beings are the paradigms) are not born with them, but only with various abilities to acquire them, given the right opportunities. Abilities and opportunities are inextricably linked: abilities can only be exercised when opportunities to do so present themselves; opportunities can only be taken by those with the appropriate abilities.[18] McDowell claims that nature provides the opportunity to acquire and exercise our rational-conceptual abilities. So we can learn more about what McDowell means by calling our rational-conceptual abilities 'natural' by asking what opportunities their exercise requires. 'You cannot walk without legs', for example, indicates a certain kind of opportunity condition on our ability to walk, which tells us something in turn about that ability. The opportunity condition which McDowell sets on our rational-conceptual capacities is one that follows from Aristotle's remark: 'it is not unimportant how we are habituated from our early days; indeed, it makes a huge difference – or rather all the difference.'[19] The idea is that we are conditioned to rationality, educated to appreciate and grasp concepts; that this habituation is an integral part of the normal process by which certain animals naturally develop, 'grow up'; that this single process of learning and doing has no clear boundaries; and that the abilities and capacities conferred by it are integrally part of their animal nature. McDowell speaks of habituation in terms of 'proper upbringing', which recalls the links Aristotle draws between education and leisure (*scholé*). The opportunities required for such growth include leisure, sufficient freedom from necessity in areas of one's life relevant to and made significant by what is being learned. McDowell develops the Aristotelian line here. Growth of the kind necessary for the acquisition of rational-conceptual capacities requires that the person is not compelled solely to secure the means to stay alive or to satisfy his most immediate desires just because they are present. Self-control is required, and a willingness to sacrifice advantage in the short term for greater gains in the future. The correct use of leisure, then, is the mark of the civilized, educated and 'properly brought up' person. Those who satisfy immediate desires though they seem to have the freedom not to do so are not exercising true leisure; they are to be regarded as slaves to their appetites. And those who lack the opportunity for true leisure, like most animals, lack the opportunity to develop rational-conceptual abilities.

According to McDowell, 'pride of place' in the habituation process must go to learning the sort of language into which human beings are first initiated, that is, natural language.[20] This is because 'a natural language . . . serves as a repository of tradition, a store of historically accumulated wisdom about what is a reason for what';[21] and therefore, 'In being initiated into a language, a human being is introduced into something that already embodies putatively rational linkages between concepts, putatively constitutive of the layout of the space of reason, before she comes on the scene. This is a picture of initiation into the space of reasons as an already going concern.'[22] 'The space of reasons', we may recall, is a Sellars metaphor which McDowell adopts.[23] It is meant to denote that logical space defined by relations of justification and implication; the space that encompasses everything that involves rational-conceptual capacities and activities.

According to McDowell, human beings enter into this space of reasons because it is in their nature to do so. The actualization of a child's second nature depends on an ability (to take the opportunity to mature and learn) which is offered by habituation within a language community. Although it enables entry to the space of reasons, that ability is not itself a rational ability, of course; for the child cannot even recognize reasons as reasons at this stage. So the habituation process does not justify or in any way recommend itself to the child. Indeed, it is precisely part of the purpose of the process to enable the child to do what it could not at birth: recognize reasons and justifications as reasons and justifications.

The ability to take the opportunity to become habituated is also not a contrary ability, one that the child may or may not exercise when it has the opportunity. The chance to develop concept-using and rational powers is not invited by upbringing, but is in a sense forced on the child. The sense of force which describes the child's exercise of its ability to be conditioned/educated is similar to that which describes fire and its ability to heat; in both cases, the ability must be exercised when, and whenever, the opportunity to do so is present. So the exercise of that ability is not the exercise of the child's freedom, at least in the positive sense of choosing what abilities it is going to develop. Later, of course, this freedom is offered; the child might decide to add a second language to its first, for example. But the condition for that possibility is that the child has matured sufficiently to have acquired new abilities and is fortunate enough to have been granted new opportunities for their exercise. And that requires that those first abilities have been exercised. So there is a considerable degree of unfreedom about the way the whole habituation process gets going and becomes established. We will return to this feature of McDowell's account.

Summary

McDowell's overall view on these matters is as follows. To acquire rational-conceptual capacities, one must be initiated into the space of reasons – which is to say that one must become capable of recognizing reasons and the relations between reasons (i.e. what is a reason for what) *as* reasons and rational relations. That is an opportunity condition on rational-conceptual abilities. Natural languages are used by people to formulate, express and communicate reasons; over long periods of time, they have come to embody the traditions of the people who have used them in these ways. So initiation into a natural language is initiation into the process by which one comes to recognize reasons and rational relations *as* reasons and rational relations. This is one way of meeting the opportunity condition on rational-conceptual abilities. The process is open-ended and ongoing; the layout of the space of reasons is not revealed in all its detail in a moment. The space of reasons into which one is initiated exists prior to one's initiation, and independently of one.

It is in these ways that McDowell's view of this space and of initiation into it deliberately recalls his own interpretation of Aristotle on 'the ethical'; it is

> a domain of rational requirements, which are there in any case, whether or not we are responsive to them. We are alerted to these demands by acquiring appropriate conceptual capacities. When a decent upbringing initiates us into the relevant way of thinking, our eyes are opened to the very existence of this tract of the space of reasons. Thereafter our appreciation of its detailed layout is indefinitely subject to refinement, in reflective scrutiny of our ethical thinking. We can so much as understand, let alone seek to justify, the thought that reason makes these demands on us only at a standpoint within a system of concepts and conceptions that enables us to think about such demands, that is, only at a standpoint from which demands of this kind seem to be in view.[24]

So the capacities and tendencies described by the phrase 'second nature' – ethical abilities like the virtues on Aristotle's view; rational-conceptual abilities like experience on McDowell's view – legitimately count as natural. They form a proper and essential part of the natural lives of the (human) animals who manifest them.

5

Reasons

We have preliminary answers to certain of our questions – how second nature differs from first; how Aristotle's view of the ethical relates to McDowell's view of the rational; how we recognize the rational; what is normal about human beings that makes their acquisition of rational-conceptual abilities natural; and so on. Thus we now know enough about McDowell's position to compare and contrast it with those of others. There is some pressure to exclude McDowell's position from the naturalist camp. So the main question concerns those forces: what are they; what is their source?

Rational abilities and natural abilities

Consider the varieties of naturalism. It might be thought that only the adoption of the most extreme sub-types (such as the very narrowest forms of scientism) would prevent admitting rational-conceptual capacities and explaining them within an order and a mode that counts as natural, for these capacities figure as some among many cases of non-genetic learning. To reject rational-conceptual capacities from the natural order would thus require either of two basic moves.

One might reject rational-conceptual capacities along with all types of non-genetic learning from the natural order. But this would require adoption of something like the narrowest scientism, for non-genetic learning is a mode of acquiring abilities whose role plausibly needs to be acknowledged and accounted for as essential if we are to understand the behaviour of all animals and some of the major distinctions between animal kinds.

Alternatively, one might reject rational-conceptual capacities from those types of non-genetic learning which are regarded as essential to explaining the natural order. But, again, this would require adoption of an implausibly narrow view of that order. For suppose someone claimed that we need only appeal to certain types of genetic learning to explain the natural – call them 'purely instinc- tual' types; and, further, that rational-conceptual capacities do not count as purely instinctual. Then we should ask whether the class of 'purely instinctual' types includes those modes of non-genetic learning required to explain the behaviour of human beings and what distinguishes them from other animals. If it does, then it should include rational-conceptual capacities after all; if it does not, then we are back with a very narrow conception of the natural order. To summarize then, it seems that McDowell might admit rational-conceptual capacities into the natural order and still be left free to adopt naturalism in almost any of its sub-types: from a broader scientism, through deferential non-scientism, to non- monist and non-reductionist forms of naturalism.

But this claim supposes that McDowell is correct, among other things, to consider a subject's conceptual and rational abilities as his natural powers. And there is perhaps a problem with this view. Following Aristotle, as we have seen McDowell do, it is usual to contrast natural powers (the power of acid to dissolve metal, for example) with rational powers (the ability of Athenians to speak Greek, for example). It is not entirely clear what criteria are in oper- ation here to distinguish 'the natural'. But Aristotle's strategy seems to reflect one that is still very common amongst naturalists and which Bernard Williams has labelled the 'creeping barrage' approach. Since it is difficult – perhaps illegitimate – to decide in an antecedent way what nature is, and hence what a naturalist can invoke in explaining things naturalistically, it is better to set about the inquiry in a more open-ended way. A naturalist is one who explains some given phenomenon in relation to the *rest* of nature. Whether a power counts as natural and how it should be explained, for example, depends on whether and how we need to ascribe it when explaining the rest of nature.[1] Whatever kind of power the human ability to speak Greek is, it is not the kind we need to ascribe to non-human nature. So, perhaps, it is not a natural power at all.

There are two kinds of response. First, this application of the approach which generates the reason/nature distinction is problematic. Intuitively, the abilities to breathe, blink, snore and digest are natural powers, yet they also are not shared with *all* the rest of nature; and the abilities to brachiate and to grapple with objects using opposable thumbs are shared with very *little* of the rest of nature. Our task as naturalists may be to ask about human life in relation to the rest of nature. But, evidently, this should not be taken as meaning that we must exclude from consideration anything that is found in the latter and not in the former.

Second, the reason/nature distinction is not necessarily harmful to McDowell's position even if it can be soundly made. For if the natural is to be contrasted with the rational, it does not follow that they are two different types of power altogether. It might only be that the one is a sub-type of the other, or that the two sets overlap. Undoubtedly not all natural powers are rational powers; it is no part of McDowell's claim that they are. This is sufficient to generate a contrast. Nevertheless, it may still be that some or all rational powers are natural. Consider an analogy with colours. The colour *Oxford Blue* should be distinguished from *Blue* since not all *Blues* are *Oxford Blue*; but it is still the case that anything coloured *Oxford Blue* is *Blue*.

The notion that rational powers might count as a natural sub-type is made more plausible by a further feature of powers that Aristotle himself made much of: that they nest within each other in various ways. Thus the ability to understand sentences like 'Ich bin Berliner' is the actualization or exercise of another ability, to understand German; this itself is the exercise of the ability to learn languages, which is the exercise of the ability to learn anything. This last is a natural power, both intuitively and on the creeping barrage approach. It may be that we should think of those rational powers which exercise natural powers as themselves natural. On this approach, the rational-conceptual powers McDowell focuses on count as natural.

A naturalism of human nature

We get closer to a real challenge for McDowell's position by modifying the creeping barrage approach somewhat, so that one remains a naturalist if one explains aspects of human life in relation not to the rest of nature as a whole, but to the rest of *human* nature. There are various options available to one who would take this approach. Consider, for example, Bernard Williams' version as he applies it to ethics:

> If we can make sense of this undertaking, of explaining the ethical in terms of an account of human beings which is to the greatest possible extent prior to ideas of the ethical, then there is a project of ethical naturalism which is intelligible, non-vacuous, and not committed to a general physicalistic reductionism that is (to put it mildly) dubious and anyway ought to be a separate issue.[2]

Suppose we replace Williams' 'the ethical' with McDowell's 'the space of reasons'.[3] The strategy then plays out as follows. We first ignore the space of reasons and inquire instead into the rest of human nature, finding out whatever features are natural to human beings in these other areas, and whatever modes of explanation account for them. Then we apply these features and modes of explanation as a kind of measure to the space of reasons. Whatever features we find in that space that we already have, we retain in that space; and whatever features we find which can be explained by modes we already have, we also retain; but everything else, we reject. The question is then whether we would have anything recognizable as 'the space of reasons' at all. If we think not, are we excluded from the naturalist camp?

McDowell answers both questions in the negative. He rejects the notion that we could somehow reconstruct an ersatz space of reasons from materials that belong elsewhere, for, as we shall see in a moment, he regards that space as autonomous, or independently regulated. Moreover, McDowell rejects the priority aspect in Williams' naturalistic strategy which would lead to building that ersatz space in the first place. There is no need to find some antecedent account of the natural and then apply it as a measure to that space, excluding whatever does not fit that account. Given the autonomy of the space of reasons, we could not achieve that end anyway – any more than we could build a real castle using only the materials used to construct a sandcastle. And as we have seen, it is enough to count as a naturalist about the space of reasons, on McDowell's view, that we show it to be a space into which human beings are initiated naturally, and within which it is natural for them to live.

The autonomy of the space of reasons

What is to be made of McDowell's claim that the space of reasons is autonomous? In arguing for what he called 'the nomological irreducibility of the mental', Donald Davidson drew attention to one way that we might come at the claim.[4] (We might replace talk of the 'autonomy of the space of reasons' with the 'nomological irreducibility' of that space, for the idea is essentially the same. The laws operating inside that space are proper to it, peculiar to it, and could not be replaced by other laws without changing or destroying it.) Davidson is concerned to distinguish 'the disparate commitments of the mental and physical schemes', and he does so by appeal to features which precisely distinguish the space of reasons from those other aspects of human life which Williams' strategy would make prior:

> It is a feature of physical reality that physical change can be explained by laws that connect it with other changes and conditions physically described. It is a feature of the mental that the attribution of mental phenomena must be responsible to the background of reasons, beliefs, and intentions of the individual. There cannot be tight connections between the realms if each is to retain allegiance to its proper source of evidence.[5]

Davidson is alluding here to a vital distinction between laws as they operate inside and outside of the space of reasons. Suppose we notice remarkable uniformities of sequence between certain physical events – the striking of a match and its lighting, for example. Given a sufficient number of sufficiently determinate cases, we might even say that we expect the match to light if struck, and that, in this sense, the match *should* light if it is struck. This enables us to state a law: 'whenever a match is struck, it should light.' This law allows us to anticipate, to make predictions. It enables us to say in a specific case, for example, that, if

(1)   that match is struck

then

(2)   that match will light

We notice something essential about the character of this law of physical change when we ask about the kind of support which it gives to the conclusion (2). In particular, if anything is to be revised, it is the law rather than the conclusion. It is possible, for example, that the match does not light; perhaps because it is damp. If (1) is nevertheless true, we should then correct the law, perhaps simply by limiting its application – 'whenever a dry match is struck, it should light.'

Contrast this law of physical change with the nature of the support offered by two other kinds of law. An example of one type of alternative law is this: 'Whenever one strikes a match, it should be the case that a match is struck.' This allows us to say, in a specific case, that if

(3)   Abelard strikes that match

then

(4)   that match is struck

Another kind of alternative law is exemplified by this statement: 'Whenever anyone believes that they strike a match, they should believe that a match is struck.' In a specific case, this might be used to support the claim that if

(5)   Abelard believes that he strikes that match

then

(6)   Abelard believes that that match is struck

For brevity's sake, call the three types of law 'physical', 'logical' and 'rational', respectively. All three types have something in common: in each case, given the law and the first premise, the conclusion 'should' follow. But notice how the sense of 'should' differs from case to case.

As we have seen, the support that (2) gains from premise and law is the support of certain kinds of regularity and the inductive principle. But (4), clearly enough, follows from the premise alone, given the laws of logic and the meaning of the terms used. Unlike (2), (4) could not be false, given its premise. Unlike the physical law invoked for (2), the logical law relating to (4) is redundant; (4) follows anyway. Unlike the physical law, the logical is a tautology; it is unrevisable while the terms used have their meaning; it does not rest on probability; and its function is not to support expectation or prediction but simply to remind us of what follows from logic and meaning – that is the sense of 'should' in operation here.

What of the sense of 'should' in the third case of rational law? Like (2), the conclusion (6) could be false, given the premise – perhaps Abelard is confused about the passive voice. And like (2), the conclusion (6) could be false given both premise and the law invoked – perhaps Abelard is confused even though he should not be. Like (4), however, the law is redundant in (5)–(6); whatever support (6) gains, it gains from (5), together with the laws of logic and the meaning of the terms involved. (6) may be false while (4) cannot be because logical law and meaning do not offer sufficient support in this latter case.

So the sense of 'should' employed by the rational law is not a matter of definition alone, as with the logical law. But neither is it a matter of expectation or prediction, as with the physical law. To suppose otherwise would be to claim that, whenever (6) turns out to be false, it is the law we should correct rather than Abelard. Of course, there is a sense in which, given regularities in Abelard's use of the active and passive voices, we can predict what he will say. If Abelard always misuses the passive, for example, we might say: 'If Abelard believes that he has struck this match, he *should* deny that the match has been struck.' But in this same case, there is the other sense of 'should' which puts us into a position to correct Abelard: 'If Abelard believes that he has struck this match, no matter what we *expect* him to believe, he *should* believe that the match has been struck.' And it is this sense which is referred to in the rational law relating to (6); one that appeals not to an impressive regularity, or to logic and meaning alone, but to something about the person with the belief – for it is that person, after all, who stands to be corrected.[6]

The constitutive ideal of rationality

To what, then, does this rational law appeal? In Davidson's view, and McDowell's also, it appeals to a rational constraint on anyone who has beliefs that they check to see what follows from them, and revise them where necessary in the light of such checking. Davidson calls this 'the constitutive ideal of rationality'. Those who entertain beliefs and other propositional attitudes, like desires, must 'stand prepared' to adjust those beliefs in the light of other beliefs that they have and in the interests of 'overall cogency'.[7] The kinds of evidence relevant to (5)–(6), for example, are precisely the considerations relevant to (3)–(4). Given the laws of logic and the meanings of the terms used, anyone who has beliefs about someone striking a match should have beliefs about matches being struck.

Moore's paradox may offer one way to reinforce these points. Suppose one were to say 'It is raining, but I don't believe it' or 'I believe that it is raining, but it is not.' We know there is something very wrong with these statements. But we cannot appeal to logic alone to explain this, since there is certainly no contradiction in them – it may be true at the time of utterance both that it is raining and that I do not believe it. If I *should* believe it is raining when it is, that is not because it is logically or even physically impossible for me to do otherwise. And for someone to say that this is what I should believe given their observation of past regularities in my behaviour is to miss the point; I should believe it no matter what my past behaviour has led someone to expect of me.

The statement 'It is raining, but I don't believe it' nevertheless has an unmistakeable air of incoherence about it, and that is perhaps a clue, for we can ask what it fails to cohere with. Not with itself or the possible facts, as we have discovered. A further clue is offered by the ineliminably self-referential character of the incoherence; the statement is both by and about the person whose belief is described. This is crucial; if we invented a word like 'misbelieve' meaning 'to believe falsely', its use would only be problematic in the first person, not the second or third.[8] This leads us to focus on the following question: what is incoherent about ascribing to oneself a belief which is contrary to something one regards as a fact? And the answer then seems plain. Simply by entertaining beliefs, we make ourselves answerable to evidence for and against them; and this feature of what it is to be a believer runs so deep that it is simply incoherent to both have beliefs and ignore or flout that responsibility. So Moore's paradox highlights the constitutive ideal of rationality. It is not merely problematic but simply unintelligible to describe anyone as having beliefs who is yet exempt from the attempt to achieve coherence between those beliefs and what is the case (given others of those beliefs, or given other facts).

The constitutive ideal of rationality is proper and peculiar to the space of reasons; it is not found in relation to the physical or logical laws. It would be nonsensical to claim that the match is bound by the ideal of rationality, and that is why it 'should' light when struck. The rational law is simply not of a type that is captured by, or reducible to, the laws called 'physical' and 'logical'. And since it is laws of this type which regulate and structure the space of reasons, that space may be regarded as nomologically irreducible – or 'autonomous', in McDowell's own usage, which comes to the same thing. According to McDowell, 'the fundamental point' of concepts like belief 'is to subserve the kind of intelligibility that is proper to meaning, the kind of intelligibility we find in something when we place it in the space of reasons . . . we cannot reduce those concepts to concepts governed by a different "constitutive ideal", or, to put it in Sellarsian terms, concepts whose home is a different logical space.'[9]

The constitutive ideal of rationality is used by Davidson (as the first quotation from him indicates) to argue for the nomological irreducibility of the mental. This claim then functions as a premise in his more extended arguments for anomalous monism, the claim that each particular mental event is also a physical event, but that there are no laws bridging those instantiated by mental events and physical events. It is because Davidson regards the mental as 'responsible' to the background space of reasons that the points made so far lead him towards the first claim, and from there to his theory of mind; the nomological irreducibility of reasons leads to the nomological irreducibility of the mental.

McDowell, on the other hand, need not take this step or any that are said to follow from it. That the space of reasons is autonomous is sufficient for his claims at this point. For any theory – any sub-type of naturalism, for example – which implies that the space of reasons is not autonomous must then be rejected; such a theory could only mistake or ignore the nature of that space. This holds not just for sub-types of naturalism, but for the views of nature from which they spring. And, so McDowell argues, our current view of nature must be revised for precisely this reason.

Meaning

Before moving on to this revision, one feature of the foregoing McDowell quotation should be noted: that the kind of intelligibility appropriate to the space of reasons is also to be described as the kind that is proper to meaning.[10] For this is a controversial claim in itself, since it has seemed to some that a world-view entirely characterized by the vocabulary and methodology of inquiries appropriate to discovering truths about the natural world must have difficulty accommodating meaning. And it would be helpful to our overall grasp of McDowell's position to examine the forms of response open to him on this specific question.

What is it for sentences to mean anything at all? What is it for some particular sentence to mean what it does in particular? These questions dominate the theory of meaning. Certain forms of naturalism awaken doubts and concerns with the enterprise. The usual way of drumming up worries is to ask 'by virtue of what does any ("mere") mark or sound, or sequence of them, come to have a given meaning?' This might strike one as a bogus question, given that it is precisely not as 'mere' marks or sounds that we apprehend words, sentences and other tokens of meaning. A more compelling question is this: 'how it is even possible that facts about physical systems and natural animals might be facts about meaning?'

One response to the question is to deny that there are such facts to accommodate. This claim, though often called 'meaning scepticism', is not a form of scepticism at all but meaning eliminativism – it does not say 'we have no way of knowing whether there are facts about meaning' but asserts straightforwardly 'there are no facts about meaning.' Quine famously took this view, and we shall examine it in a moment, since it throws light on McDowell's position.[11] Another, more moderate, answer to the original question is to accept that there are semantic facts, but to give them a functional analysis in terms of the underlying and purely physical facts realizing them. This may mean that 'the kind of intelligibility proper to meaning' is that kind offered by the physical laws science discovers or formulates. And we are in the process of discovering why McDowell rejects this option. Yet another response is to claim that there are genuine facts about meaning, and that they can be accommodated by facts about physical systems and natural animals; this is precisely because they are facts about a certain special set of natural animals – i.e. human beings with the appropriate education. This last view, of course, is the one McDowell wishes to promote, and we have seen something of how he goes about doing this. For the moment, however, consider the more extreme response: meaning eliminativism.

Quine's aim is clarity and simplicity about the kinds of thing to be admitted into what we regard as existing, our ontology. Anything abstract or ill defined, or lacking clear identity conditions (what is it for some x to be precisely the thing it is and not some other thing?) is suspicious. Meanings are to be eliminated from our ontology, for example, because they are not clearly individuated, one from another. The most well known of such arguments for semantic eliminativism is Quine's so-called 'argument from below'.[12] It contains a number of assumptions which McDowell must reject; so it is worth examining in some detail.

Quine's argument can be reconstructed as follows. For any given language, we should be able to construct a translation manual. It would contain statements like the following: '"mein Pferd ist hübsch" means the same as "my horse is pretty".' Now in Quine's view, clarity and simplicity insist that

(1)   If there are facts of the matter about the meaning of any sentence in any given language, there must be facts about whether any given translation manual for any given language is correct.

They will be facts like the following. 'Mein Pferd ist hübsch' is a sentence of a natural language meaning that the speaker's horse is pretty. In uttering the sentence, the speaker said that his horse was pretty. What the speaker said is true if and only if the speaker's horse is pretty. The instance of 'mein Pferd' refers to a particular horse belonging to a particular person. The sequence 'ist hübsch' applies to, or is true of, some particular thing if and only if that thing is pretty.[13]

Quine then asks what would constitute facts of this sort. In his view, if they exist, facts about meaning must be constituted by conventions amongst speakers of the language. And these conventions are observable facts about the speakers' dispositions to behave in various circumstances – when they utter the sentence, why, with what effect, expecting what kind of response, and so on. Now if these dispositions are what constitute facts about meaning, and those facts are indeed sufficiently clearly individuated for us to admit meanings into our ontology, then those dispositions themselves had better be sufficiently clearly individuated. This puts certain constraints on our construction of translation manuals. Suppose two groups of people set about constructing a translation manual for some language independently of each other. It had better not be the case that their results conflict with each other but are equally justified by the evidence (observable facts about the speakers' dispositions to behave). So

(2)   If there are facts about whether any given translation manual for any given language is correct, it will not be possible to construct an indefinitely large number of translation manuals such that both

(a) all fit all observable speakers' dispositions to behave and (b) any two will be incompatible with each other.

But suppose that the two teams of translators are completely ignorant of the language – ancient Romans, perhaps, confronted by German-speakers on the banks of the Rhine for the first time. Given long observation of the speakers' behaviour (what they say; how they act in response; and so on), the two teams might both come to the working hypothesis that 'ja' is 'yes' and 'nein' is 'no'. They might then use that information to work out what other utterances might mean. One set, for example, notes that 'Pferd' and 'Ah, a horse' are said in the same circumstances and evoke the same response. So they duly note down that ' "Pferd" means "horse" '. But the other set, working independently but with exactly the same evidence, might translate the utterance with equal justification in a number of ways; as 'Ah, horse-behaviour is going on', for example, or as 'Ah, the horse', a use of the general term as in 'the horse is a solid-hoofed herbivorous quadruped.'

Manuals constructed on these hypotheses would all fit all the observable speakers' dispositions to behave (i.e. (2a)), and any two would be incompatible with each other (i.e. (2b)). We might well prefer one manual over another, but this could only ever be a purely pragmatic matter. It certainly could not rest on some overt or tacit appeal to any fact since there are none such available – the thought is that, since all are equally justified in this matter, none are. So, given that

(3) It is possible to construct an indefinitely large number of translation manuals such that both (a) and (b) hold,

it follows from (1)–(2) that

(4) There are no facts of the matter about the meaning of any given sentence in any given language.

There are various ways to respond to this argument. (1), for example, might be rejected on the grounds that Quine has confused two different sorts of enterprise: constructing translation manuals with constructing a theory of meaning.[14] That is to say: there may be no facts about whether any given translation manual for any given language is correct (i.e. there may be indeterminacy of translation); but this does not imply that there are no facts about the meaning of any sentence in any given language. We might deny (2), claiming that facts about meaning are not constituted by speakers' dispositions to behave; the issue is not susceptible to a behaviourist analysis.

Finally, (3) might be rejected on the grounds that viable and legitimate forms of evidence available to the Roman translators have been ignored. In Quine's view, the observable facts which the translators experience and have to go on when attempting to uncover the conventions of the German speakers is a matter of 'stimulus meaning'. The stimulus meaning of a sentence like 'mein Pferd ist hübsch' is an ordered pair consisting, on the one hand, of experience, conceived as various 'stimulations' to the subject's 'sensory receptors',[15] and, on the other, of what those stimulations typically prompt or cause, considered as assent to or dissent from that sentence.

There are, broadly speaking, two ways to reject Quine's claim that evidence is restricted in this way. The first is to claim that evidence *does* not consist of what Quine says it does. Perhaps what the stimulations prompt is more than assent to or dissent from sentences. In which case, the Roman translators have more to observe; their working hypotheses can justifiably be enriched to include more than guesses at the words for assent and dissent. The second response is to argue that evidence *could* not consist of what Quine says it does. Perhaps if experience is conceived of as merely the stimulation of sensory receptors, it is quite unfit to offer reasons for anything – in no condition, for example, to stand in the kind of rational relation to the translators' hypotheses that would be necessary if it were to count as 'supporting' or 'offering evidence of' those hypotheses.

This final response is McDowell's, and we are beginning to see how the resources for it are being gathered. Experience *does* give us reason to ascribe particular meaning to the utterances of others. So the kind of intelligibility that is proper to meaning is the kind we find in something when we place it in the space of reasons. Experience *could only* give us reason to ascribe particular meaning to the utterances of others if it were regarded as occurring within that space; and that means regarding experience as always already conceptual. Part I of this book sketched details of this crucial aspect of McDowell's view, and part III will fill in the details. For the moment, it is enough to concentrate on the implications for naturalism.

It is not difficult to see why, as naturalists, we would be tempted to think of experience in Quine's way, the way which makes meaning eliminativism itself tempting. We are intent on explaining matters consistently with our conception of nature and natural modes of explanation. That conception identifies nature and natural modes with science in its various guises and with what science makes intelligible. We need to find a place for experience in our ontology, since experience is all we have to go on, ultimately, in arriving at our account of what there is.[16] And to conceive of experience as the stimulation of sensory receptors is to conceive of it as something that science is not only able, but also best able, to make intelligible.

In McDowell's view, of course, this picture is hopelessly compromised. It appoints experience to a task (giving rational support to our view of the world) which experience, so conceived, could not possibly accomplish. Experience must be irreducible to a purely causal story of the sensory reception of material and its series processing as information if it is to provide rational justifications and play a role generally in the space of reasons. So where does the story go wrong? With our current conception of nature. Once we revise that conception, we are free to conceive of experience in a way that is consistent with its appointed task and with naturalism. On this view, as we have seen in the sketch included in part I, experience is the distinctive mode by which concept-users endowed with spontaneity receive and process sensory material. So experience is peculiar to some beings and denied to others. But those to whom it is peculiar are all, so far as we know, animals; and the abilities exercised in experience are actualizations of the second nature of those beings. So the view remains naturalist, of the monist, reductionist, non-scientistic sub-type.

6

Nature Revised

The current view of nature McDowell wants to revise is one which supports all scientistic sub-types of naturalism (i.e. whether 'science' is broadly or narrowly conceived). To put matters crudely for the moment, McDowell seeks to undermine this position and the view of nature supporting it by showing that science in its various guises deals only with first nature and those aspects of second nature which fall outside the space of reasons.[1]

Nature and the space of reasons: various options

McDowell's argument that we should revise our current conception of nature begins with the following claim about that conception: it identifies nature with what science aims to make intelligible. But, on his view, science does not have the resources to make intelligible the autonomy of the space of reasons. The kind of intelligibility scientific resources offer is exemplified by the sense of 'should' in the physical law and its use in supporting claims (see the previous chapter). So, given those resources alone, we cannot make intelligible the sense of 'should' exemplified by the rational law.

At this point, then, we are faced with various choices. First, we might simply reject the notion that there is a space of reasons to be made intelligible. Second, we might acknowledge such a space but reject its autonomy, attempting to make it intelligible by appeal to scientific resources. Clearly neither is a viable option on McDowell's view. There is a sense of 'should' captured by the rational law; that sense is made intelligible within a logical space of reasons governed by the constitutive ideal of rationality; and that sense is only made intelligible in that space governed by that ideal.[2]

If we retain the autonomy of the space of reasons, we are left with two further basic options. The third option is to retain the identification of nature with what science makes intelligible, and thus set the space of reasons outside nature. Again, McDowell regards this option as unacceptable. This is not simply because, if it counts as a sub-type of naturalism at all, it renounces the monist and reductionist forms. The main problem with this third option is that it cannot deal adequately with any animal who inhabits the logical space of reasons – and human beings are the paradigm here, of course. For on this option, nature is augmented with a non-natural realm, and human beings somehow have to be regarded as living in both. This may not seem immediately problematic. The space of reasons and the natural realm might be regarded as two different types of space altogether (one logical and the other physical, perhaps), so there is no problem about our fitting into both; since they are different types of space, being in one does not exclude being in the other. But the spatial metaphor is misleading at this point; the problem can be expressed in a simpler way. Being animals, what we are and do should be made intelligible by appeal to nature. But that is not possible if what we are and do is largely characterized by our capacity for forming beliefs and other propositional attitudes, together with the constitutive ideal of rationality to which having those attitudes commits us. For so long as we identify nature with what science makes intelligible, these capacities put us outside nature.

The final option is then obvious: reject the identification of nature with what science aims to make intelligible. This is McDowell's own position. On his view, as we have seen, it is natural for certain animals to inhabit the space of reasons; the notion of second nature made that claim legitimate. So our view of nature should be revised accordingly. Nature is to include the space of reasons; we are to regard the items in that space as natural, as well as the modes of explanation necessary to make that space intelligible.

The space of reasons and the realm(s) of law

A terminological interlude. When McDowell himself discusses these issues, he distinguishes 'the space of reasons' from 'the realm of law', identifying the latter with what science aims to make intelligible. So another way to put his opening claim that our modern view identifies nature with what science aims to make intelligible is to say that our modern view identifies nature with the realm of law.

McDowell prefers 'law' over 'causality', the more familiar way of designating the focal field of science, because of reasons offered by Bertrand Russell. Insofar as we can make sense of a principle of causality, it is false, and scientists do not in fact use it; they may and in fact do use the notion of laws, however.[3] McDowell uses 'law', therefore, to discourage a certain false impression of what science is about.[4] Unfortunately, this use may encourage a false impression of his own view. For McDowell's terminological contrast between 'the realm of law' and 'the space of reasons' makes it look either as if the space of reasons is entirely without laws, or as if that space is precisely what science aims to make intelligible – since science is thought of as being precisely that form of inquiry which makes law-involving structures intelligible. These are misapprehensions of his view whose significance can best be appreciated in the light of certain remarks of Aristotle:

> When the objects of an inquiry, in any department, have principles, causes, or elements, it is through acquaintance with these that knowledge and understanding is attained. For we do not think that we know a thing until we are acquainted with its primary causes or principles, and have carried our analysis as far as its elements. Plainly, therefore, in the science of nature too our task will be to try to determine what relates to its principles.[5]

Our terminology should leave clear space for the following view (which is, after all, McDowell's own). The space of reasons is the object of law-invoking and law-revealing inquiry no less than is the 'realm' investigated by science. It is by appeal to laws and principles that both regions are made intelligible. These laws will be of different sorts, of course, since they make matters intelligible in different ways. The distinction is akin to that captured in Greek thought by *physis* and *nomos*, but akin only, since it is tempting to think of that as a distinction between laws relating to nature and laws relating to convention.[6] The rules which regulate the space of reasons are to be regarded as no less natural than those governing the realm investigated by science, for both kinds of law count as occurring within nature, and both are to be accounted for by natural modes of explanation.

Pre-modern, modern and revised views of nature

McDowell's position leaves us with various questions. What would stand against his proposed revision of our view of nature? Why do we hold our current view? What implications would the revision have? These queries can be treated together as aspects of a single question.

According to McDowell, our current conception of nature is a reaction to the view held before the Scientific Revolution of the seventeenth and eighteenth centuries. It is enough for his purposes, and ours, to have a crude idea of the distinction, one which ignores complex debates over the historical details. The earlier view exaggerated the kind of intelligibility proper to the space of reasons and came close to identifying nature with what the constitutive ideal of rationality makes intelligible. On this view, there is a rational order underpinning the 'should' in 'that match should light when it is struck', for the match is regarded as an element of a cosmic order each part of which is striving to achieve the rational coherence of the whole and somehow sees in that goal the reason motivating it to act.

In understandable reaction to this anthropomorphic exaggeration of the competence of rational law, our current conception of nature exaggerates the kind of intelligibility proper to its alternative, physical law, and identifies nature with what science makes intelligible. The only sense of 'should' operative in the natural order which we could then make intelligible to ourselves is that of prediction and explanation, given observed regularities and the inductive principle. The natural order is not meaningful or purposive but mechanical and determined; its laws do not govern it but describe it, since it is the laws rather than the order which stand to be corrected if there is some discrepancy between them.[7]

On this way of looking at things, with exaggeration characterizing the two views of nature which McDowell wants to resist, his suggested revision looks like equilibrium, a return to common sense. It is natural to find meaning and purpose in the world – when we look to the beliefs and actions of subjects and agents, for example. And it is equally natural to find mechanism and efficient causal relations – when we look to the neurology of those same subjects and agents, for example. So the kind of intelligibility proper to the space of reasons should be given a place in nature, together with that proper to science; neither should exclude or dominate the other.

If an analogy might help clarify the issue, consider the case of religious people who are legally married to each other during a church service. The secular and religious institutions within which they marry each have a structure and system of relations with their own authority and perspective on the event (ways of making the act intelligible) which exist completely independently of each other. Notwithstanding this division, it may be equally natural to the couple to find religious significance in their single action of marrying each other, given the religious institution within which it takes place, as it is for them to find secular (legal) significance in that same action, given the secular institution which sanctions it. Indeed, they may think of the religious institution as making it the one particular action which it is, and of the secular institution as having no less a role. In that sense, they may think of 'the' marrying action while resisting the temptation to suppose there must be one mode which is 'the' mode for making it intelligible. They recognize two very different ways of making what they are doing intelligible: one that is proper to the law of the land, and one that is proper to religious law and convention.

McDowell's revised view of nature is simply a starting point, compatible with various very different further positions – if beliefs are not intelligible in the way neural events are, must they be distinct, or is it possible to regard some particular belief or mental event as ontologically identical with some neural event? The point is simply to think in terms of 'the' natural order while resisting the temptation to suppose that there must then be one mode which is 'the' mode for making it intelligible. We should not ignore or destroy the distinction between two very different ways of making intelligible what is natural: one that is proper to science and physical law, and one that is proper to the space of reasons.[8]

Being at home

McDowell's proposed revision allows us to regard nature as encompassing both what science makes intelligible and what is made intelligible by the autonomous space of reasons. The former will appeal to such things as physical laws, the instantiations of those laws, the inductive principle supporting those laws, the experimentation required of scientists, the degrees of probability which ground their predictions, and so on. The latter will appeal to such things as judgements, the inferential relations between them, the conceptual structure supporting such relations, the constant search for coherence required of thinkers by the ideal of rationality, the spontaneity which grounds their use of concepts, and so on.

It follows that human beings are 'at home' in the logical space of reasons: which is to say that the exercise of rational-conceptual capacities pertains to the proper activities of this particular species of animal. Human beings enter this space because it is their nature to do so (thus there is nothing super- or extra-natural about their rational-conceptual capacities). The space is autonomous, regulated in a way that makes it peculiar, independent, irreducible to the kinds of law-governed process science makes intelligible to us. Human beings are not born in the space of reasons; they acquire rational-conceptual capacities by exercising capacities they are born with, making use of the opportunities provided by language-using communities and their reasoning-imbued traditions.

These claims leave us with a host of queries, particularly about how McDowell's overall project, as described in part I, can accommodate these remarks about nature, our rational-conceptual capacities and the space of reasons. We shall tackle these matters in part III, investigating the main elements of McDowell's project – openness and the Default; conceptualism and the space of reasons; the mutually supportive roles of spontaneity and receptivity. But, before moving on, two rather shadowy features of McDowell's views and approach should be remarked on and made salient.

First, there are hints of humanism about McDowell's particular brand of naturalism. Humanism comes in various forms, depending on whether what is emphasized is the particular human perspective on things, or whether the emphasis lies in giving human beings centre place. Human beings undoubtedly function as paradigms in McDowell's account. As we have discovered, we are the sort of animal whose second nature forces us to revise our view of nature. The question is whether McDowell's inquiry takes its point of view as well as its focal point from human beings, and, if so, whether this is legitimate. To put the point another way: is the focus on human beings a merely accidental feature of McDowell's account and usefully illustrative of its claims, or is it a necessary feature, given the way he establishes his inquiry? And if the latter is the case, is McDowell's inquiry innocent or prejudiced, stimulated by an appropriate interest in human beings or directed by an inappropriate disregard for other animals?

A second theme to be made salient concerns relations between reason, experience and freedom. As the human child is brought to maturity, it learns to use various conceptual capacities. Its exposure to the traditions of a language-using community alerts it to the requirements characteristic of reasons and justifications. This actualization of the child's second nature consists in a suitably enriched notion of habituation. Now this habituation process cannot offer reasons or justify itself to the child, or at least not initially. For the process is the designated precondition of the child's so much as appreciating something as a justification or as any other kind of rational ground for belief, judgement or action. So the role for free will is severely limited here. It is not just that engaging initially in the crucial educative process which actualizes one's second nature is not an act of conscious choice. The process itself will inevitably involve disciplinary features of constraint and external inconvenience that the child does not choose (and many even fight against), at least at the time they are experienced. Balanced against this lack of freedom in the child's exercise of its abilities (to take the opportunity presented by habituation, for example) is the freedom that comes with being at home in the space of reasons. This freedom is required for the active employment of concepts which being at home there involves (a freedom that McDowell denotes by the Kantian label 'spontaneity'). It is through the unfree habituation process, then, that the child comes to enjoy one of the greatest freedoms: experiencing the world.[9] For experience is a rational-conceptual ability whose exercise depends on opportunities only afforded to individuals endowed with spontaneity. So there is a straightforward sense in which, on McDowell's view, those who experience the world have been forced to be free.[10]

Part III

An Intentionality of Second Nature

Central Elements

What makes my image of him into an image of *him*?
Wittgenstein, *Philosophical Investigations*[1]

If McDowell is right to characterize revised nature as 'the discovery that gives philosophy peace', it should offer a return to the Default and secure our openness to the world in our experience, thought and talk of it. For, in his view, it is the inducement to abandon openness for some other form of relationship with the world that is the crux of philosophy, the deep cause of deep disquiet. And, conversely, it is securing our openness to the world that constitutes the decisive move in philosophy. As we have seen, revised nature allows us to regard rational-conceptual capacities as natural and yet autonomous, irreducible to what science alone makes intelligible. If this is the solution, what precisely was the predicament? There must be facts about our experience, thought and talk which are revealed as open to the world once nature is revised and our rational-conceptual capacities are thereby made an essential part of it, made basic to our position in the natural world. So we should now discover what those facts are and explore the path from revised nature to the Default.

In a particular experience in which one is not misled, what one takes in is *that things are thus and so*. *That things are thus and so* is the content of the experience, and it can also be the content of a judgement: it becomes the content of a judgement if the subject decides to take the experience at face value. So it is conceptual content. But *that things are thus and so* is also, if one is not misled, an aspect of the layout of the world: it is how things are. Thus the idea of conceptually structured operations of receptivity puts us in a position to speak of experience as openness to the layout of reality. Experience enables the layout of reality itself to exert a rational influence on what a subject thinks.[2]

All the major features of the coming discussion occur in this passage, implicitly or explicitly. It will be useful to comment on the six central elements collectively before dismembering the body for analysis.

The central topic is intentionality. Our experiences, thoughts and words can be about, directed on and mean particular objects in the world (and not some mental surrogate for such objects, for example). What must be the case, given that this is possible?

(a)   Experience is a two-way and rational intentional relation; subjects of experience and the world bear rationally on each other.

Subjects bear on the world in their experience of it; which is to say that their experience is about the world in ways that give them reasons for what they then think and say about the world. And, conversely, the world bears on subjects in their experience of it: which is to say that the way the world is determines how it appears to experiencing subjects to be in ways that rationally constrain what they then think and say about the world. In the attempt to secure this two-way rational directedness of intentionality, McDowell is led to various conclusions about what experience must be and what it requires.

(b)   Experience is passive, a matter of receptivity in operation.[3]

The world exists for all subjects and is therefore independent of any of them. Conceived in this realist way, the world nevertheless has a rational bearing on experience, thought and talk. Hence, in McDowell's view, there must be an element of passivity in the way subjects experience the world. The world constrains the subject's experience of it to the way that it is, and the subject, who desires that his thoughts and judgements about the world be rationally grounded in the way the world is, allows himself to be so constrained. This receptivity is one facet of our 'openness to the layout of reality'.

(c) Experience is the exercise of capacities that belong to spontaneity; experiences themselves are already equipped with conceptual content.[4]

Experiences are to be treated as occurrences within the space of reasons. For they engage in rational relations, being supported by states of the world and supporting judgements about those states. On McDowell's view, only what has conceptual content can play such a justificatory role in relation to beliefs, judgements and statements.[5] So the contents of experience must be conceptual. And the subjects who enjoy experience must be endowed with spontaneity, that faculty without which there could be no such exercise of conceptual abilities.

Claims (b) and (c) amount to the following view. The exercise of our conceptual capacities (spontaneity) is subject to constraint imposed by the world itself (receptivity); and since that imposition of the world occurs *within* the exercise of our conceptual capacities rather than as a causal impact on them from beyond their exercise, the constraint itself can be regarded as genuinely rational and justificatory.

McDowell makes three claims in the quoted passage about the content of an experience, the way the world appears to its subject to be (for example, 'that things are thus and so'). First, as we have seen, it is conceptual. Second,

(d) The content of an experience can also be the content of a judgement.

So it may appear to the subject of experience that things are thus and so ('this computer screen before me is flickering'), and, on the basis of that experience, he may judge that precisely this is how things are. The content of experience can be what the subject commits himself to if and when he endorses as true or correct the way in which the world appears to him to be.

McDowell's third claim about the content of experience is that it can also be the state of the world. This last claim is a truism, in McDowell's view, as we would expect of a claim that merely returns us to the Default.[6] The fact that the claim itself is obvious and unexceptionable does not mean that its implications cannot be startling, however. And McDowell does indeed draw from it a further claim with deep ontological significance, significance for the question of what there is:

(e)   There is no ontological gap between the sort of thing one can experience or think or mean and the sort of thing that can be the case.[7]

Claim (e) is a second facet of our openness to the world. When one is spontaneously receptive to the world in one's experience of it (sense one), what one experiences or thinks is what is the case (sense two). We shall call the former 'receptive openness' and the latter 'ontological openness'.

(f)   Structurally basic to intentionality are thoughts whose existence and identity is dependent on the existence and identity of the worldly objects they are about or directed on.

The thoughts in question are so-called 'perceptual demonstrative' thoughts; they are grounded in perceptual experience and expressed by demonstrative terms like *This* and *That*. (For example, 'that pen is shoddy'; thought while looking at a particular pen.) In McDowell's view, such thoughts are ontologically dependent on the aspects of the world they are about or directed on (not the other way around). And so they fall into the class of 'object-dependent' thoughts.

Such thoughts are structurally basic for two reasons. First, they are peculiarly directly connected with experience in a way that many are not. Unlike the thought 'shoddiness is a characteristic feature of pens today', which is available whether or not one is experiencing any pen at all, 'that pen is shoddy' could not be thought (on this view) without experiencing some particular pen. The second reason for counting such thoughts as basic is that they bear on the world and the world bears on them in the strongest sense; a particular thought of this sort would not exist if the object it was about or directed on did not exist. So these thoughts are the purest product of the two-way rational intentionality of experience.

These six central claims (a)–(f) are supposed to answer our original question, 'what does revised nature offer that McDowell can describe it as giving philosophy peace?' Revised nature is designed to return us to the Default and secure that view of intentionality according to which we are open to the world in experience, thought and talk; but how?

The answer is that, if (a)–(f) are true, then our experience, thought and talk are fundamentally the exercise of rational-conceptual capacities. If these capacities are to be associated with the autonomous space of reasons, then there is a strong temptation to regard them as separated from the natural world, closed off from it. And it is revised nature which shows us how to resist this thought. If rational-conceptual capacities engage second nature, we can regard them as both natural and associated with an autonomous space of reasons.

So this is the path by which McDowell proposes to move: from the naturalism of second nature to the naturalism of intentionality, which is nothing other than the Default. To express the point slightly differently: the openness of human beings to the world in experience, thought and talk is an intentionality of two-way rational directedness; and, given revised nature, that intentionality is a natural fact about the world, one that naturally places beings of this natural kind within the natural order.

7

Experience

McDowell's starting point is that of a traditional transcendental argument: there is experience. What follows from this claim, of course, depends on one's view of what experience is, and this is a notoriously controversial matter.[1] We might see McDowell as coming at the question with the strategy that is the founding insight of functionalism. When it is difficult to see what something is, ask what it does or can do, what function it has.[2]

McDowell does not court much controversy on the question of experience's function. He does not attempt to offer a complete answer, but highlights certain features which most are content to acknowledge. When things go well, experiences are of the world, are directed on the world. Conversely, the world has a bearing on subjects in their experience of it. A subject's capacity for experience of the world puts the world into a position where it can provide reasons and other rational grounds or warrants for the subject's judgements. Experience has the function of enabling the world to offer reasons for what is thought and said.[3] In experience, therefore, subjects are rationally directed on the world just as the world is rationally directed on those subjects. Their experience is about the world in ways that give them reasons for what they then think and say about the world. Conversely, the way the world is determines how it appears to experiencing subjects to be; and that in ways which then rationally constrain what subjects think and say about the world. This is what is meant by characterizing the intentionality of experience, its 'aboutness', as a two-way and rational intentional relation. In experience, subjects bear rationally on the world and the world bears rationally on subjects.

If this is the function of experience, or part of the function of experience, how is it possible? What are the necessary conditions and preconditions for such two-way rational intentionality? McDowell's view follows directly from the attempt to answer this question. The view, in a nutshell, is this. Given the receptivity of experience, the world imposes constraints on subjects; given the spontaneity of experience, that imposition is applied to the exercise of capacities which are conceptual and hence of the sort capable of sustaining rational relations; and neither of these features, receptivity and spontaneity, even counts as such without the involvement of the other.

Receptivity

In McDowell's view, experience is passive, a matter of receptivity in operation.[4] Subjects are acted on, in ways made possible by their ability to be receptive. This ability or power is akin to the passive powers described as such by Aristotle. Fire has the active power to burn wood; wood has the passive power to be burned by fire. Objects without these passive powers cannot be acted on in the relevant ways. Water is without the passive power to burn; so it will not burn when fire is brought to it, no matter how much active power fire has to cause burning. Similarly, some animals are without the passive power of receptivity; so they will not experience the world no matter how much active power the world has to give rise to experiences.

One reason why McDowell insists that the subject's experience of the world should be treated as passive, the engagement of a passive power, is that he is a realist about the world. In his view, the world exists for all subjects and therefore independently of any particular subject; it is something of which such subjects can truly and knowledgeably have experience, think and speak; it is not an artefact or construction of the thoughts or experiences of subjects. What appears to be the case to subjects may not actually be the case; what is the case may not in fact be known by subjects. The world conceived in this way nevertheless has a rational bearing on experience, thought and talk. In McDowell's view, this combination of two-way rational intentionality in experience with realism about the world, its independence from subjects in their experience of it, entails that there must be an element of passivity in the way subjects experience the world. The world constrains the subject's experience of it to the way that it is; this constraint is necessary if the subject's thoughts and judgements about how the world is are to be rationally grounded in how the world is; hence the subject must be regarded as something acted on by the world in experience.

Indeed, part of the appeal of describing experience using the phrase 'openness to the layout of reality' is precisely that it conveys this element of passivity. Here, emphasis is given to the sense in which being open is being receptive or accessible; the sense in which openness has to do with transparency, immediacy, penetration and disclosure is relegated to the background. The phrase 'subject of experience' also conveys this sense; one in which there is something to which a person is subject. Call this sense of openness 'receptive openness'. (We shall examine the other sense in a moment.)

There are several senses of passivity. On occasion, the phrase 'being passive' is used synonymously with 'being unreceptive' or 'inert'. That this cannot be the sense McDowell means is clear. The passivity of the subject must be of a type which is nevertheless receptive to the world if that passivity is to make it possible for the subject to experience the world. The sense of passivity to which McDowell appeals is the passivity, for example, of having one's eyes open rather than closed; the latter position would make visual experience impossible. The passivity of the subject in receptive openness is also quite inconsistent with the subject's being inert. Being receptive to something is more than just being present to it or being presented with it. Receptivity carries the sense of potential engagement, of impending response. The subject must be open to possibilities, more or less attentive, ready if not actually prepared to take action. That this is the relevant sense of passivity becomes clearer when we focus on another feature of experience.

Spontaneity

McDowell regards experience as the exercise of capacities that belong to spontaneity; he claims that experiences themselves are already equipped with conceptual content.[5] Concepts are, as we have discovered, to be thought of in terms of the structure behind systems of intentional states like experiences and beliefs which determine the rational (e.g. inferential) properties of those states. As McDowell notes, 'the capacities that are drawn on in experience are recognizable as conceptual only against the background of the fact that someone who has them is responsive to rational relations, which link the contents of judgments of experience with other judgeable contents.'[6]

Experiences are states or occurrences in McDowell's view.[7] They are rationally supported by states of the world, and rationally support beliefs, judgements, statements, and so on, in their turn. This is to place experiences within the space of reasons. And, as the sketch in part I indicated, on McDowell's view, only what has conceptual content can play such a justificatory role in relation to beliefs, judgements and statements.[8] The contents of experience must be conceptual if they are to sustain the rational interrelations which conceptual structure alone makes possible. Moreover, the subjects who enjoy experience must be endowed with that faculty necessary for the exercise of conceptual abilities, namely, spontaneity. In McDowell's usage, 'The faculty of spontaneity is the understanding, our capacity to recognize and bring into being the kind of intelligibility that is proper to meaning.'[9]

The inextricability claim

McDowell claims that experiences should be regarded as combining receptivity and spontaneity inextricably: 'We must not suppose that receptivity makes an even notionally separable contribution to its co-operation with spontaneity.'[10]

His reasoning in support of this inextricability claim is as follows. We need to describe experience in a way that can recognize its two-way rational intentionality. This requires that we form a view of experience on which it is intelligible for particular instances to stand in rational relations with the world and with the subject. Such relations with the world are only possible if experience is passive and the subject receptive. Such relations with the subject are only possible if they are relations with the subject's exercise of his reasoning powers, those conferred by his understanding, 'the faculty of spontaneity'. So we need 'a conception of experiences as states or occurrences that are passive but reflect conceptual capacities'.[11] On this conception, the subject is made receptive (potentially responsive) by the fact that his spontaneity is already operative. So, even though we can distinguish what receptivity is from what spontaneity is, we cannot look at the properties of experience and divide out those which come from one and those which come from the other.

Consider an analogy with the fluidity of water at room temperature. We can distinguish hydrogen from oxygen; they can and do exist prior to their combination in water. And we can divide up some of the properties of water according to whether they derive from hydrogen or from oxygen. But there are some properties of water – and fluidity is an example – to which these elements do not in fact make separate contributions. Fluidity derives from the combination. McDowell's claim about experience is stronger still, of course. It would not be false, but simply unintelligible, to separate out the properties of experience into those which derive from spontaneity and those which derive from receptivity. And this combinatorial model applies not to certain particular properties of experience, but to experience as a whole.

McDowell's terminology is an explicit recognition of his indebtedness to Kant in this area, and examining this background provides greater insight into the inextricability claim. Kant introduces his usage in the following way: 'If the *receptivity* of our mind, its power of receiving representations in so far as it is in any wise affected, is to be entitled sensibility, then the mind's power of producing representations from itself, the *spontaneity* of knowledge, should be called the understanding.'[12] Sensibility should be described in terms of receptivity (i.e. a potentially responsive passivity or vulnerability) because it deals with intuitions. Intuitions are the representations of which the mind is sensible given its capacity for receptivity; the possibility of being impressed or impacted on by objects in the manner of intuitions is to be identified with being receptive. The understanding should be described in terms of spontaneity (i.e. a certain type of freedom) because it deals with concepts, which operate in the space of reasons, and that space is to be identified with the realm of freedom.[13]

Kant goes on directly to make the inextricability point:

> Our nature is so constituted that our intuition can never be other than sensible; that is, it contains only the mode in which we are affected by objects. The faculty, on the other hand, which enables us to *think* the object of sensible intuition is the understanding. To neither of these powers may a preference be given over the other. Without sensibility no object would be given to us, without understanding no object would be thought. Thoughts without content are empty, intuitions without concepts are blind.[14]

So McDowell works within the Kantian picture; that concepts are 'based on the spontaneity of thought, sensible intuitions on the receptivity of impressions'.[15] The view may be represented as follows:

Faculty/Power	The Understanding	Sensibility
Faculty/Power to be described in terms of	Spontaneity	Receptivity
Representations the faculty /power works with or on	Concepts	Intuitions

The passage from Kant appeals implicitly to a distinction he makes between the kind of representations to which the mind is receptive, called 'intuitions', and what he calls 'mere sensations'.[16] It is not objects which are 'given to us' in mere sensation, so it is not such as to yield knowledge of any object. The taste of wine, for example, belongs merely to the special subjective constitution of the manner of sensibility in the subject that tastes it. In intuition, however, the subject is put in touch with the 'objective determinations' of objects, such as the wine. And intuitions give objects to us and yield knowledge of them precisely by virtue of the engagement of spontaneity in the manner of their reception. This is one reason why, in Kant's view, we should not 'give one power preference over the other'.[17]

McDowell's reason for defending this inextricability of the powers of spontaneity and receptivity is that, unless we treat spontaneity and receptivity equally as making a not-even-notionally separable contribution, we will lose the claim that our experience rationally warrants our judgements about the world. Exaggerate receptivity, and our empirical thinking will appear unwarranted, non-rational – in which case, our judgements will not be justified by the way the world is, for we will have insufficient resources. The most that could be said is that we are blameless ('exculpated') in having the empirical beliefs or making the empirical judgements we do.[18] Exaggerate spontaneity, and our empirical thinking will appear unconstrained or ungrounded by the world (reality external to thought) – in which case, we will not in fact even be 'exercising concepts' at all, for concepts derive directly or indirectly from rational relations with the world.[19] (So the notion of a coherent but self-contained 'conceptual scheme' which is not rationally constrained by the world would be simply unintelligible on McDowell's view.)

The inextricability claim forces us to reject a picture in which conceptual capacities are exercised 'on' what receptivity delivers;

instead, they are exercised 'in' receptivity. It is the involvement of conceptual capacities, the fact that they are already drawn on and are in play in receptivity, that makes receptivity what it is: passive without being inert. In experience, one takes in that things are thus and so, which is also the sort of thing one can judge – i.e. a conceptual content. Given McDowell's definition of concepts and their exercise, we could not suppose that the capacities at play in experience are 'conceptual' at all if they were only manifested in receptivity and not in active thinking – 'active thinking' being, minimally, what makes it possible to decide whether or not to judge that things are (or are not) as one's experience represents them to be.

The contents of experience

The phrase 'content of a subject's experience', used about some particular occasion of perception by a subject, means the way that things – aspects of reality, of the world – then and thereby appear to him to be. Take any such moment and consider the content of your experience, of all the ways things appear to be that are made available to you by your ability to see, hear, touch, taste, smell; of all the ways that you yourself appear to be that are made available by your ability to sense your balance, the position of your limbs, the fatigue in your joints, the temperature of your skin, the hunger in your stomach, and so on.[20] Experiential content at any particular moment is so staggeringly rich and variegated that giving a full and satisfying description of the way things appear to a subject to be in experience would stretch a Proust with inexhaustible writing materials, even if that subject were locked into a tiny isolation cell. This is an important feature of experiential content and we shall return to it. For the moment, however, it is sufficient to take one aspect of how things appear to the subject to be and let what is true of that part of experiential content stand for the whole. In McDowell's usage, experiential content is presented under the phrase 'that things are thus and so'. So let the part of it we shall concentrate on have a similar form: 'that this computer screen is flickering', for example.

Experiential states are often supposed to be kin to propositional attitudes. Both have intentional content of some kind; both represent objects, properties, events ('facts', the totality of which constitutes the world) as being a certain way;[21] both have truth conditions – the truth conditions relevant to the representational content of experience will be specified in terms of how the external world would have to be for the experience to be veridical. McDowell makes a more extreme claim about how the world is represented in experience. If the contents of one's perceptual experience can be the content of judgements, then perceptual states must have intentional content of a very particular kind: that is, content of the kind that is judgeable – conceptual content. So McDowell claims that the contents of experience are always already conceptual. Call this 'conceptualism about experience'. Perceptually experiencing the world is to be in a certain representational state; the representational content of that experience is the way the experience presents the world as being; that way is conceptual. On this view, experience is essentially a concept-employing exercise. Experiences are the impacts of the world on our senses; and those impacts already have conceptual content.[22]

Conceptualism about experience is, in McDowell's view, the only way to secure the two-way rational intentionality of experience. For the world to bear rationally on subjects, it must constrain their experience. And for subjects to be directed rationally on the world, that constraint must be exercised over conceptual capacities. It is only because the imposition of the world in experience occurs *within* the exercise of our conceptual capacities (rather than as a causal impact on them from beyond their exercise, for example) that the constraint such imposition offers can be regarded as genuinely rational and justificatory. We must adopt conceptualism if we think experience can provide us with rational grounds or warrants for forming judgements about the world.

Conceptualism comes in different versions, as we shall see. It may serve to clarify the version McDowell proposes to note the following three sub-claims. First, as part I described, an account of concepts for McDowell is an account of those capacities the possession of which is constitutive of engagement in judgement and in reasoning. It is an account of concept possession – just as a theory of meaning has been taken to be a theory of understanding. The vital question is 'what is it to grasp F?' And grasping a concept consists in certain abilities of the subject – abilities to use F to represent or refer to things in the world (objects, states of affairs, properties, and so on); to form statements with F as a content; to use F-containing statements to assert things and to combine with other statements in reasoning, particularly of a deductive kind. Second, experiences provide ways of telling what is the case that, in certain circumstances, warrant judgements or count as evidence for them (albeit of the kind that can be defeated; things may not be as they appear or as they are judged to be). Third, evidential support between experiences and judgements or other experiences requires that they stand in rational relations to each other – that relations of a (merely) causal kind, for example, would not suffice. In McDowell's view, it is these three claims which above all entail conceptualism. If experience is to provide support for our judgements, support that is intelligible as rational, its contents must be conceptual.[23]

Conceptualism is a complex set of propositions which requires close examination. In the next chapters, we shall be concerned with the negative reasons McDowell offers for rejecting alternatives, the positive reasons he offers for regarding conceptualism as true and well motivated, and the direct forms of defence he provides against criticism.

8

Conceptualism

Conceptualism stands out more clearly in relief. So we shall first consider how the arguments McDowell offers in support are supposed to count against the main group of opponents; those who regard the contents of experience as non-conceptual.[1] Non-conceptualism considers experience to be, ultimately, an impact of facts, unfiltered and uninfluenced by concepts, on the sensory apparatus of a subject.

Conceptualism is a controversial view; its advocates have faced strenuous opposition.[2] Many argue that the contents of experience must be, or at least must *partly* be, a kind of *non-conceptual* content. 'After all', so the non-conceptualist characteristically argues, 'conceptualism implies that the perceiver's experience is constrained by the concepts and conceptual capacities in his possession. And this should seem straightforwardly false. How things appear to a perceiver is certainly restricted by his sensitivity to the world. But that sensitivity is not dependent on whatever concepts the perceiver has.' If the non-conceptualist view is correct, then conceptualism is false: the content of one's experience cannot be a thought; it must first be put through a process of 'conceptualization'.[3]

There are, broadly speaking, two alternatives for non-conceptualists. On the one hand, they may reject McDowell's claim that it is the function of experience rationally to support our beliefs, judgements, statements, and so on. On the other hand, they may try to accept that claim, and show how it is consistent with non-conceptualism. The first strategy is associated by McDowell with the coherentism of Donald Davidson, and the second with the so-called 'Myth of the Given'.

The Myth of the Given

Consider first the non-conceptualist who affirms the possibility of a genuinely rational relation of justification between the concept-using subject and experience as it would then be conceived, a set of non-conceptual impacts on the subject. We shall examine this view more closely in a moment. But it may be helpful to know the basic form of McDowell's response immediately and figuratively.

To support genuinely rational relations, the contents of experience must count as one side or 'term' of a relation that can be considered as genuinely rational. So the non-conceptualist who affirms the possibility of rational relations must find a way of showing that the contents of experience occur within the space of reasons. What complicates matters for non-conceptualists of this type is that they are also obliged to say that the contents of experience occur beyond, or outside, the space of concepts. For this is precisely their position: that the contents of experience are non-conceptual. So this kind of non-conceptualist must show how we can make sense of the following interrelated claims: that the space of reasons extends beyond, or outside, the space of concepts; that non-conceptual impacts on the experiencing subject act as justifiers in the intentionality of experience and empirical knowledge; that such impacts, though non-conceptual, are sufficiently epistemic to ground forms of knowing; that we can compare our best beliefs (and other attitudes for which concepts are essential) with a physical or mental reality that lies beyond them. In McDowell's view, these claims are simply incoherent. We cannot make sense of the rational relations constituting the space of reasons except as supported throughout by conceptual structure. That is why we should regard the conceptual as unbounded.

McDowell's discussion of the non-conceptualism which affirms the possibility of direct rational relations is centred on what Davidson calls 'the dualism of Scheme and Content'. McDowell himself prefers to talk of the dualism of Scheme and Given or the Myth of the Given. 'Content' suggests what is given in a 'that' clause (i.e. representational content), whereas the dualism of concern to both McDowell and Davidson is one that sets a conceptual scheme over and against intuitions or experiential intake.

And since this intake is regarded as simply what is 'given', independently of the conceptual scheme, the word accurately depicts the position which is at issue. Both Davidson and McDowell reject the Myth. But, as we shall see below, McDowell thinks Davidson 'contrives' to be ignorant of what is right about it (its 'lure'), and hence falls into an opposed position that goes too far in the other direction (i.e. coherentism).

The Myth of the Given may be described in various ways, depending on one's focus. So one might concentrate on the conditions for the possibility of knowledge, for example. Then the Myth is the idea that some kind of non-epistemic facts about knowers could entail epistemic facts about them. Or the Myth is a blurring of the distinction between sentience and sapience. Or the Myth is the claim that there can be a form of awareness that has two properties: being in such a state both entails having the knowledge that one is in that state, and is possible without the acquisition of any concepts. But these knowledge-based formulations point to a deeper expression of the Myth; one with explicit relevance for intentionality. The Myth is thinking that anything could (intrinsically, naturally, necessarily) possess a particular significance for the space of reasons (that of entitlements to claims, commitments, endorsement, justification) independently of the acquisition of concepts by the one for whom it has that significance. In case this position seems like a straw man, note that the British empiricists, Locke, Berkeley, Hume, all took for granted that the human mind has an innate ability to be aware of certain determinate repeatables or sorts, like the colour whiteness, and that it is aware of them simply by virtue of having sensations.[4] C. I. Lewis endorses the following more sophisticated version of such empiricism: 'There are in our cognitive experience two elements, the immediate data such as those of sense, which are presented or given to the mind, and a form, construction, or interpretation, which represents the activity of thought.'[5] The version is more sophisticated precisely because it attempts to recover as much of the root Kantian position as possible while preserving the notion of the Given (datum) in experience:

> If there be no datum given to the mind, then knowledge must be altogether contentless and arbitrary; there would be nothing which it was true to. And if there be no interpretation which the mind imposes, then thought is rendered superfluous, the possibility of error becomes inexplicable, and the distinction of true and false is in danger of becoming meaningless.[6]

The Given theorist and the Kantian can agree that both intuitions and concepts are required for experience.[7] What the former affirms and the latter denies is that intuition, or the sensuously Given, makes a separate (or at least separable) contribution; that it is a stand-alone component; that a non-conceptual content might function as the (ultimate) grounding for our empirical beliefs; that, being non-conceptual, intuition's impact on our beliefs is causal only, and yet, being the (ultimate) grounding, that impact on them is also somehow justificatory.

There are idealist versions of the Myth also. So Bradley, for example, denies the empiricist claim that what is given is anything 'for the intellect', as 'data' would have to be. His grounds are that what is given is apprehended sensuously but passively, and only what is associated with the activity of thought can be truly regarded as 'data'. But he nevertheless affirms that something is given: namely, immediate experience, whose ineffable non-conceptual character can only be captured by a kind of gestural 'this': 'all our knowledge, in the first place, arises from the "this". It is the one source of experience, and every element of the world must submit to pass through it.'[8]

As this quotation makes clear, versions of the Myth are often closely associated with foundationalism.[9] On this view, there is a structure of particular items (e.g. beliefs) such that each one is non-inferentially arrived at, each one presupposes no other items, either particular or general, and each one (or the structure as a whole) is the ultimate ground or justifier for all factual claims. But it would be a mistake to concentrate too much on this connection, for there is a two-way independence between the Myth and foundationalism.[10] One can be a foundationalist about justification but reject the Myth by rejecting the notion that anything which might count as ultimate in the order of justification could also be non-conceptual or in some other way exist outside the space of reasons. Alternatively, one might accept the idea that there are non-conceptual justifiers of this sort while rejecting the claim that any count as structurally ultimate or grounding.

Epistemology and intentionality (I)

What is tempting about the Myth, in McDowell's view, is that it is after the right thing – it wants to allow us to acknowledge a rational restraint on our freedom to employ empirical concepts.[11] The problem with it is that it assumes such a restraint can only come from *outside* the realm of concepts; and that move undermines its claim to providing a *rational* constraint. The root claim of the Myth, according to McDowell, is this: empirical justifications depend on rational relations; their ultimate foundation is in entities outside the realm of concepts. And the root problem with the Myth is to do not with epistemology but with intentionality.

To see why this must be so, consider the following case. On the basis of my current experience, I judge that 'this computer screen is flickering'. One question for the non-conceptualist is how this judgement could possibly count as knowledge on their conception of the experience to which I am appealing. How is merely pointing to some non-conceptual impact supposed to confirm that my judgement counts as justified and true?

But there is a deeper question for the non-conceptualist concerning the same judgement that I make on the basis of my current experience: how could this judgement even count as meaningful? The question is deeper, obviously, because a judgement has to be meaningful to constitute knowledge. Simply to count as false even, or unjustified, judgements must have a meaning. My putative judgement in the present case has a meaning, and has the meaning I take it to have, only if it counts as about, or directed on, this particular computer screen before me. If it cannot count as about any such object at all, it has no meaning, and is hence disbarred not only from knowledge but also from the class of judgements. On the basis of my current experience, I take myself to be making a judgement about a particular object, this computer screen. And this is precisely where the deeper question for the non-conceptualist arises. For it is difficult to see how this putative judgement could count as meaningful on their conception of the experience to which I am appealing. How is merely pointing to some non-conceptual impact supposed to confirm that my judgement counts as about or directed on this particular object, and hence counts as a judgement in the first place, a significant item whose meaning is partly dependent on its being about this object? How do these or any concepts employed in similar judgements acquire intentionality, the ability to represent or be about or directed on the world, if the experience to which they appeal is non-conceptual?

So we can distinguish broadly between two kinds of task that pointing to non-conceptual impacts is supposed to accomplish for the Myth theorist: justifying our claim to judge at all, which is to say meaningfully; and justifying our claim to judge truly and justifiably, which is to say knowledgeably.[12] To judge meaningfully in cases like that described requires that the concepts used in the judgement count as intentional, as about the world. And, in McDowell's view, the non-conceptualist has as much difficulty explaining how this is possible as he has explaining the possibility of judging knowledgeably. For it is in virtue of the subject's experience that the concepts used in judgements of this type acquire their warrant to be about the world. And if experience is conceived as the non-conceptualist conceives it, this warrant is unobtainable.[13]

For further clarification, consider Bertrand Russell's discussion of these matters while addressing the question whether there is any knowledge in the world so certain that no reasonable person could doubt it.[14] He takes knowledge of the reality of the table before him to be the most likely candidate. The fact that the table appears differently to different people shows to Russell's satisfaction that 'the real table is not the same as what we immediately experience'; rather 'it must be an inference from what is immediately known.' The question then arises whether, given Russell's view of what the real table is and what experience of it amounts to, he has a right to the notion of inference or of warrant at all at the relevant stage. For, broken down, there are four stages to his account, and one of the steps is illicit in precisely the way that opponents of the Myth describe.

Russell has us begin with the following claim: there are physical objects in front of me (in his case, a brown, smooth object with an oblong facing surface). As a result, in his view, I have sensations of sense data (a collection of sense contents: 'brown colour, oblong shape, smoothness, etc.'). As a result, I form an immediate non-inferential belief (that there is a brown smooth object with an oblong facing surface before me). And as a result of this immediate belief, I form a mediated, inference-based belief (that there is a real table before me).

We should ask at each of the three steps what supports the phrase 'as a result'. The step from first to second stage is supported causally and non-epistemically; the step from third to fourth is supported inferentially and epistemically; in neither case is there a problem. But to what might we appeal to support the crucial second step, from sensation to 'immediate' belief? It is non-inferential; that is the point of the immediacy claim. But is it nevertheless epistemic? If it is not, then we should ask how the immediate belief acquires its capacity for epistemic relations from the sensation of sense data; for that belief certainly counts as an inferential premise – it is by inference that it supports the step to the fourth stage. If the support is to be regarded as epistemic, it must be that having a sensation of some sense datum *a* just is to *believe* it has some characteristic *F* (e.g. that it is smooth, brown in colour, oblong in shape). But the notion of sensing the datum is avowedly non-epistemic. So, even if we ignore the fact that epistemic support here has simply been pre-supposed rather than accounted for,[15] the problem remains: with what right could epistemic support be claimed here, given what sensing data is conceived as amounting to? And the problem here arises again at the level of intentionality. If we cannot see how the immediate belief is knowledgeable, given the kind of links available to experience conceived in terms of sense data, that is because of a deeper problem. Given this sort of conception of experience, how is it that the immediate belief could claim to be about or directed on the world at all?

The Myth should be judged on what it sets out to achieve: to account for the intentionality of experience by explaining how our use of empirical concepts (their capacity to represent or 'be about' the world) is justified, and to account for empirical knowledge by explaining how our experience-based judgements are justified. The Myth entails that the space of reasons (of justifications, warrants) extends beyond the conceptual sphere – to a brute impact of the non-conceptual, an alien force, a causal impact of the world. The effect of this picture is to constrain our spontaneity in the exercise of our judgement – the only way it leaves it open for us to 'explain' how our concepts may justifiably be regarded as representing the world, or how the combination of those concepts in our judgements about the world may justifiably be regarded as knowledge, is by appeal to operations outside the control of our spontaneity. So, in McDowell's phrase, the best that appeal to the non-conceptual can offer is 'exculpation' for our use of concepts and our judgements when what we were after was justification.[16] That is to say: it would not be right to regard our usage or our judgements as blameworthy, but nor would it be right to regard them as warranted or validated. Hence the Myth fails in its own terms – it does not offer an explanation of justification. We cannot understand the relations in virtue of which a concept represents or a judgement is warranted except as relations within a conceptual sphere.

Defeating the Myth raises a challenge for McDowell. How, then, is the world to be regarded as exercising rational constraint over our experience? How are the judgements we make about the world in virtue of our experience of it rationally constrained by the world?

McDowell is keen to recognize this challenge; it distinguishes him from the alternative kind of non-conceptualist.

Coherentism

The Myth is one route that the non-conceptualist might take. The alternative route is taken by those who, in McDowell's view, see what is wrong with the Myth but ignore what is right about it. These are non-conceptualists who deny the possibility of genuine, direct rational relations between the concept-using subject and the world in experience. This position is immediately suspicious, since it offers what seems to be too easy a way of defeating the Myth. Theorists who support the Myth insist on the need for a rational constraint on experience and go to great lengths to try to provide for that constraint. To say that we do not need such a rational constraint, as the non-conceptualist alternative has it, is to discard such arguments as those discussed above. All one would need say is that the Myth is there to do a job that does not need doing; so get rid of the Myth.

What non-conceptualists of the alternative type correctly see as wrong with the Myth is the notion that such rational relations could exist if the contents of experience are regarded as non-conceptual. What they wrongly ignore about the Myth, in McDowell's view, is its perfectly correct appreciation of the fact that such rational relations are (must be) possible, and that showing how they are possible is a necessary goal for any account of our experience, thought and talk about the world.

The solution McDowell proposes is to give up thinking that the contents of experience are non-conceptual. Non-conceptualists go wrong either because they completely give up the goals set for any account of our experience, thought and talk about the world (by denying the possibility of genuinely rational relations), or because they make the goal impossible to achieve (by making the scope of spontaneity less extensive than that of the conceptual, and that of the conceptual less extensive than that of reasons). Instead, we should retain the possibility of rational relations as our goal, and achieve it by regarding the capacities belonging to spontaneity as inextricably implicated in the operations of receptivity. Our current view of nature blinds us to the possibility of this move; revised nature awakens us to it.

McDowell regards the non-conceptualist alternative to the Myth as equally incoherent and self-defeating. The alternative denies the possibility of genuine rational relations with the world in experience but nevertheless tries to retain a role and place for rational relations in our systems of belief and judgement, together with related concepts that have to do with truth and knowledge. If experience cannot provide a rational ground for the application of such concepts, what could? The preferred answer is to suppose that rational relations, together with the concepts that have to do with truth and knowledge, depend ultimately on relations of coherence and consistency internal to systems of belief and judgement. The best-known and developed version of this position is the coherentism of Laurence BonJour and Donald Davidson; McDowell concentrates his adversarial attention on the latter.[17]

One problem with coherentism is that it cannot help but create the kind of gap between us and the world which is inconsistent with the Default. But this is an aspect of a deeper problem that makes coherentism self-defeating. The goal of the theory is to provide for rational relations and the warranted application of concepts that have to do with truth and knowledge while remaining non-conceptualist about experience. Central to our belief-judgement systems are concepts and claims that purport to be about the world. So part of the goal is to find a way of providing for this intentionality. And, in McDowell's view, this goal cannot be achieved without appeal to that to which the coherentist categorically cannot appeal, namely, experience (conceptually conceived). Like the Myth, then, the alternative form of non-conceptualism fails in its own terms; there is no need to counter it by advancing a separate and preferable position.

If rational relations and the application of the relevant concepts depend ultimately on relations that are internal to a belief-judgement system, and that system is regarded as existing in rational independence of the world itself, then the world could have no rational bearing on us. It is the rationality of the relation which is the key here. For the coherentist is free to claim that certain other kinds of relation between belief-judgement systems and the world can and do exist. The world could be depicted as exerting a causal impact on our sensibilities, for example. So any such possible or actual system of beliefs and judgements need not be portrayed as entirely detached from the intake of facts. But in the coherentist picture, experience of the world could not be conceived as giving rational support to our belief-judgement systems; conversely, our belief-judgement systems could not be regarded as rationally bearing on the world. And without rational support of this sort, we have no warrant to regard our concepts or judgements as about the world or directed on it. So we are left with the intolerable picture of belief-judgement systems spinning frictionlessly in a void, to use McDowell's own memorable phrase.[18]

Epistemology and intentionality (II)

This may seem to be a thoroughly epistemological point, about how our judgements about the world may justifiably count as knowledge; but, as with the Myth, it is really concerned with the deeper problem of intentionality, and particularly of how judgements, and the concepts of which they are constituted, may justifiably be said to be about the world or directed on it. If the coherentist picture is correct, in other words, it certainly puts in doubt our ability to make judgements about the world that constitute knowledge of it. But, much worse, it puts in doubt our very ability to make judgements about the world at all, even erroneous ones – for example, those that misrepresent it in some way. For a judgement cannot even count as misrepresenting, as getting 'it' wrong, unless the judgement can count as in some way about 'it'. That is why, even though a chance pattern in the sand might have the same form as a bad drawing of Napoleon, we would say only of the latter that it misrepresents him; it is only the latter that is about him. And the problem with the coherentist picture, in McDowell's view, is that it puts the 'aboutness' of our judgements in question. For if the world acts only causally upon us, it is not just that we cannot be said to know anything about it; we cannot even make sense of our experiences or thoughts as being about the world or directed on it.

This claim has epistemological implications, undoubtedly. If our experiences and thoughts are not about the world, then they cannot accurately represent the world in such a way as to constitute knowledge. They could not even be said to represent the world, but inaccurately. Equally, any concept we could form that purported to be about the world could not be measured against the world. But the fundamental claim is about intentionality. For if non-conceptualists deny the possibility of any genuine, direct rational relation between subjects and the world, then they must deny the possibility of any particular such relation. And the intentional relation is one such particular relation; it is that relation in virtue of which a subject's concepts (or the assembly of such concepts, the conceptual scheme) may justifiably be said to be about the world. Unless that relation occurs within the space of reasons, a subject's concepts and conceptual scheme may not be said to be justifiably about the world. The world would exist independently of, 'beyond', whatever conceptual scheme it would be possible to construct (*if* it were possible to construct one at all under such circumstances).

It might be thought that causation could recover the necessary links between subjects and the world to sustain intentionality. The idea would be that, if world-independent experiences of a given type (call them E's) are regularly caused by worldly things of a given sort (call them W's), then those E's will be of, about or directed on those W's. By appealing in this way to facts about causal relationships, so the response goes, it is possible to show how an experience of a certain type can count as an experience *of* the world. There are two related problems with this response. First, it remains to be seen why the mere fact of causal correlation between an experience and some state of the world is sufficient to claim one is *of* the other at all. Second, the kind of intentionality manifested by experience is a two-way rational directedness. So even if causation were shown to sustain intentional relations of a certain sort, that move would be of no use to McDowell's opponents. By restricting the rational to the conceptual and then denying that experience of the world is conceptual, such adversaries render themselves incapable of claiming that whatever intentional relation with the world causation makes available is also rational. To put it briefly, if experience is non-conceptually of the world, and the non-conceptual cannot be rational, then experience cannot be rationally of the world.

So McDowell regards his conceptualism about experience as secure against non-conceptualist opponents. Unless the contents of experience are conceptual, experience cannot be regarded as a two-way rational intentionality. Indeed, it is only because experience makes essential use of the subject's conceptual faculties, his spontaneity, that it counts as awareness (or even *apparent* awareness) of aspects of the world at all. And, in keeping with the strategy dictated by the Default, the security of conceptualism is attained not through advancing a separate position and using it to combat alternatives (by showing how comparatively preferable it is, for example), but by showing that the alternatives are self-defeating.

Either the non-conceptualist opponent sets experience a task which, so conceived, it could not possibly accomplish – of providing for a two-way intentionality that is rational. Or the opponent accepts that experience, so conceived, could not possibly accomplish this particular task. But, by denying experience the possibility of rational relations to the world, the adversary also denies experience the possibility of accomplishing its lesser task of providing for some form of intentional relation between subject and world.

9

Judgement

The contents of a subject's experience on those occasions where his perceptual capacities are exercised are the ways that aspects of the world then and thereby appear to him to be. Central to McDowell's account are three claims about such experiential content.[1] We have begun to examine the first, that such content is conceptual. This claim, which we have called 'conceptualism about experience', is strongly related to the other two. The second claim is that the content of an experience can also be the content of a judgement. The third claim is that the content of an experience can also be a state of the world.

These three claims are closely interrelated in a way that captures the Default. For, plausibly, this is a view we would need to be argued out of rather than into: the way things appear to a subject to be in experience is what the subject commits himself to in judgement (when he is trusting) and what is the case in the world (when he is right). The second and third claims are explicit here, but the first is also present implicitly. We shall investigate the point more closely below, but the basic idea is simple. The content to which the subject commits himself in judgement is conceptual. If the second claim is correct and that content is the content of the subject's experience, it follows that experiential content is also conceptual.

The relationship between the first and third claims also depicts the Default view of openness to the world in experience. If the content of a subject's experience can be some state of reality, some aspect of the world, then, in McDowell's view, there is 'no ontological gap between the sort of thing one can mean, or generally the sort of thing one can think, and the sort of thing that can be the case'.[2] This is the stance we have called 'ontological openness', to distinguish it from the related stance of 'receptive openness', which McDowell also holds. And it is precisely the first claim, conceptualism about experience, which relates the two stances. What we experience or think is what is the case (ontological openness) when we are spontaneously receptive to the world in our experience of it (receptive openness).

The interrelations between these three claims give rise to various questions. What are the differences between experiencing and judging if they are both modes in which the subject's conceptual abilities are engaged, and if they both have, on occasion, the very same contents? What are the differences between experiencing the world and the world of which we have experience if the content of the former can be a state of the latter? If ontological openness is correct, does that mean we should identify those things which give rise to experiences (states of the world) with those things to which experiences give rise (thoughts, beliefs, judgements)? Attempts to answer these questions provide helpful clues to the heart of McDowell's account, so we shall examine them more closely in this chapter and the next.

Experiencing and judging

In McDowell's view, experiencing the world is one mode in which the subject's conceptual capacities are engaged.[3] But the paradigmatic mode of this sort is judging.[4] Indeed, McDowell holds that the content of experience 'is essentially a fragment of judgmental content'; the subject has the opportunity to experience the world only if he has the ability to make judgements.[5] So the interrelations between experience and judgement are crucial to his account.

The basic elements are these. According to McDowell, the contents of an experience and of a judgement can be the same. But judging itself differs radically from experiencing, in his view, for the latter is passive while the former is not. The subject 'has' experiences but 'comes to' judgement; experience is what happens to the subject, while judgement is what the subject makes of what happens. The subject is free to exercise control over his judgements in ways that are not open to him in experience; he is, to some extent, responsible for what he judges. These elements of freedom, control and responsibility necessarily enter into the subject's use of his conceptual capacities when the move from experience to judgement is made.

If judgement and experience are different but intimately linked, we need to know more precisely how that linkage operates. A significant clue is offered by McDowell's denial of the claim that everything a subject thinks as the result of experience is subject to the exercise of control associated with judgement. Suppose the subject has some reason to distrust how things appear to him to be – it appears to him that this computer screen is flickering, for example, but he doubts whether he is awake, or whether his eyes are functioning normally, or whether there is sufficient ambient illumination. Before endorsing how things appear to him to be, the subject will then naturally try to engage the various checks and controls available to him. Generally speaking, however, subjects have no such reason to doubt, and their experience therefore leads them to form beliefs about the way the world is without engaging the checking procedures.

This leaves us with the possibility of taking various alternative positions on the nature of judgement. We might say, for example, that to count as judging at all on some occasion, a subject must actively engage checking procedures on that occasion; forming beliefs about the world in experience of it does not require the active exercise of control in this way; so this is one way in which judgements and beliefs should be distinguished. McDowell takes this view:

> more typically, perceptual belief acquisition is not a matter of judging, of actively exercising control over one's cognitive life, at all. Unless there are grounds for suspicion, such as odd lighting conditions, having it look to one as if things are a certain way – ostensibly seeing things to be that way – becomes accepting that things are that way by a sort of default, involving no exercise of the freedom that figures in a Kantian conception of judgement.[6]

This view will be clearer if it is contrasted with an alternative which preserves much of what McDowell picks out as essential to judgement: namely, the exercise of control over one's cognitive life.

The exercise of control

On McDowell's own view, judgement is associated with the active exercise of explicit checks by the person judging on the occasion of judgement. But we might think of the association between judgement and the exercise of control as looser than this. For we might plausibly regard the subject as 'in control' of his cognitive life, to the extent that he is capable of being in control of it, even if he is not actually checking it, so long as he does so when necessary.

More specifically, the exercise of control may be regarded as a matter of being capable of checking on one's cognitive life when necessary or appropriate, of recognizing when it is appropriate, of being attentive so that occasions when it is necessary do not pass by, and of actually checking it when necessary. So, in the situation where one has no reason to doubt how things appear to be, the subject may nevertheless be regarded as judging that the computer screen is flickering. This might be so for various reasons that are consistent with the more relaxed view, but most obviously because the subject has checked on the veridicality of this very appearance regularly in the recent past and has no reason to do so again now.

This more relaxed view agrees with McDowell that judgement is to be regarded as a use of the subject's conceptual capacities over which he exercises control, and that the exercise of such control is to be regarded as a matter of the engagement of various checking procedures. The views disagree over whether or not these procedures need actually to be engaged. Thus one way to characterize the divergence is over the status of what McDowell calls 'a sort of default' in the passage quoted above.

Let us stipulate that accepting appearances by default does not involve engaging one's checking procedures. On McDowell's view, that is enough to show that it cannot count as an exercise of the subject's control, and therefore cannot count as judging. If this seems too strict a view of what it is to be in control generally, let alone in this specific case, there is an alternative. On the more relaxed view, accepting appearances by default is consistent with the exercise of control. The subject may be described as exercising control over what he thinks, even on occasions where he trusts how things appear and does not check before endorsing that appearance with his judgement that how things appear is, in his view, how they are.

This relaxed view is not in any immediate danger of being too relaxed, so that just anything in any mode can count as exercising control. For we might still plausibly hold the following: that it is precisely because the subject is capable of engaging such checking procedures, sees the relevance of so doing, and recognizes occasions on which it must be exercised, that he may be described as exercising the kind of control over his cognitive life necessary for his 'accepting appearances by default'. The contrast here is with someone who, on some occasion or through some condition, simply lacks the ability or the opportunity to engage such procedures and hence to exercise control over his cognitive life. While subjects are engaged in dreaming, for example, or in feverish hallucinating, there is little sense to be made of describing them as 'accepting' appearances at all, let alone 'by default'.

Passivity and activity

It is perhaps puzzling that McDowell does not take the more relaxed view. The notion that there is no control worthy of the name that is not the continuous engagement of checking procedures is oddly extreme, and not just when applied to the political arena. But it is certainly one way to keep the distinction between experiences and judgements sharp within the conceptualist picture.

That picture threatens to confuse the two: an experience is something whose content is conceptual; its content can be just what one judges; in such cases the content of the one is the content of the other. If the contents are the same, is not the experience the judgement? No; and McDowell's views on judgement and the exercise of control afford him the resources to say why. Even if the contents of experiences and judgements are the same, they are two very different ways in which the subject uses his conceptual capacities. Experience is passive, and the subject's conceptual capacities are merely engaged thereby; judgement is active, the exercise of control through the engagement of checking procedures.[7] McDowell describes the view from this position in the following way:

> An ostensible seeing that there is a red cube in front of one would be an actualization of the same conceptual capacities that would be exercised in judging that there is a red cube in front of one, with the same togetherness. This captures the fact that such an ostensible seeing would 'contain' a claim whose content would be the same as that of the corresponding judgement. As actualizations of conceptual capacities with the appropriate togetherness, the judgement and the ostensible seeing would be alike. They would differ only in the way in which the relevant conceptual capacities are actualized. In the judgement, there would be a free responsible exercise of the conceptual capacities; in the ostensible seeing, they would be involuntarily

drawn into operation under ostensible necessitation from an ostensibly seen object.[8]

The mention of necessitation is crucial here. Conceptual capacities are freely exercised in judgements and necessitated, or unfreely actualized, in experience. Given McDowell's position on the exercise of control, it is possible to regard judgements as free because they necessarily involve the subject's engagement of checking procedures for whose outcome he is responsible. In experience, on the other hand, the subject is not free but imposed upon; and since this deprives the subject of the opportunity to engage whatever checking procedures are at his disposal, the notions of control and its exercise have no application.

McDowell's portrayal of what is similar and dissimilar between judgements and experiences has various benefits; the next two sections provide an example of each.

Non-conceptualism

In McDowell's view, the way things appear to a subject to be in experience is what the subject commits himself to in judgement when he takes the way things appear for the way they are. This is what it means to say that the contents of a subject's experience may be the content of his corresponding and ensuing judgement. The benefit of this view is that it captures something intuitively plausible about the character of judgement in such cases: namely, that what the subject endorses is precisely the way reality, aspects of the world, appear to him to be. And it is conceptualism about experience which provides for the possibility of this intuitively compelling description, the claim that experiential content, like judgemental content, is conceptual.

Opponents who regard the contents of experience as non-conceptual cannot present matters in quite this way. For they must regard the contents of experiences and the contents of judgements as wholly different and dissimilar, the one as non-conceptual and the other as conceptual. What the subject endorses (the content of his judgement) is not, cannot be, the way the world appears to him to be (the content of his experience).

Moreover, such opponents have to find room for (and tell) a story about how the way in which the world appears to a subject is then processed into conceptual form. One such non-conceptualist,

Gareth Evans, recognizes this: 'The informational states which a subject acquires through perception are *non-conceptual*, or *non-con-ceptualized*. Judgements based upon such states necessarily involve conceptualization: in moving from a perceptual experience to a judgement about the world (usually expressible in some verbal form), one will be exercising basic conceptual skills.'[9] Our intuitions may support McDowell's theoretical considerations against non-conceptualists like Evans here. Ordinary perceptual experience, of tables and chairs, for example, does not seem to have room for the subject first taking on non-conceptual information and then working it up into conceptual shape. Don't we just see tables as tables?

There is undoubtedly a complex story to be told about the non-conceptual doings in the overall process of perceptual mechanisms, for example those grouped under the label 'the visual system', which are associated with the having of visual experiences. These sub-personal systems may, perhaps should, be regarded as taking on raw, non-conceptual information. But we are concerned at present not with information processing at this level, but with what such processing helps produce: what McDowell is referring to by 'the content of experience' and what Evans describes as 'states which a subject acquires': namely, the way in which things appear to the subject to be, the contents of states of a conscious subject. And there is something strongly counter-intuitive about the non-conceptualist proposal that even when the information has passed through the sub-personal levels of processing to the level at which it is something for the subject, it is still non-conceptual.

Does not my seeing the arrow give me a reason to take cover – when that action is not a mere autonomic reaction? Not, strictly speaking, on the non-conceptualist view. My experience of seeing the arrow is non-conceptual; it must first be processed into a different kind of content altogether, a conceptual one, if it is to be endorsed by the subject or provide him with something that could count as a reason for his action. Evans explicitly recognizes this:

> Although the subject's judgements are *based upon* his experience (i.e. upon the unconceptualized information available to him), his judge-ments are not *about* the informational state. The process of concep-tualization or judgement takes the subject from his being in one kind of informational state (with a content of a certain kind, namely, non-conceptual content) to his being in another kind of cognitive state (with a content of a different kind, namely, conceptual content).[10]

The notion that experiences and judgements are directed at two different kinds of content is not just counter-intuitive on McDowell's view, of course, but simply unintelligible. Rational links do not extend beyond the conceptual in ways that would provide for the possibility of judgements being rationally grounded in experience conceived non-conceptually. To think otherwise is to fall for the Myth of the Given.

The content of a judgement – that this computer screen is flickering, for example – is something to which the subject commits himself in judging. In cases where the content of a subject's experience is the content of a judgement he makes, the subject commits himself to taking the way things are for the way they appear to be. Judgements of this sort may be said to endorse experiential content, the way the world appears to be in the course of some experience. So the connection between the first and second claims smooths the path between the way things appear to be and the way they are judged to be. For judgements must be conceptual. So, if experience is always already conceptual, we need not regard judgement as involving or based on or presupposing a conversion process by which experiential content is turned into conceptual form or given conceptual structure.

This, then, is one way in which McDowell's portrayal of what is similar between judgements and experiences benefits his overall view. In the next section, we examine a case in which his description of what is dissimilar is equally supportive.

Judgement independence

There is something intuitively compelling about the claim that there is and should be no difference in kinds of content between experiential content and judgemental content when the subject's experience is veridical and does indeed just represent the way things are. But it can seem equally tempting to distinguish the two kinds of content, given the possibility of certain kinds of non-veridical experience, namely, illusions. For these are precisely occasions where what the subject judges to be the case, and what appears to him to be the case, differ. McDowell, as we shall see, has the resources to acknowledge illusionary cases while resisting the temptation to distinguish at the level of content between judgement and experience in the veridical case. It is sufficient to recall distinctions between the different ways that experience and judgement involve the subject's

conceptual capacities. Judgement is the active use of such capacities, being the exercise of control through engaging checking
procedures; experience is passive and merely a matter of the
engagement of the subject's conceptual capacities.

There are various ways to be a conceptualist about experience. It
is possible, for example, to hold that the contents of experience are
always already conceptual because experiences either are, entail or
are reducible to judgements. According to Thomas Reid, for
example, my smelling a rose counts as my *perceiving* the rose in the
following sense. I enjoy a certain olfactory 'sensation' (a sensation,
in Reid's terminology, 'can be nothing else than it is felt to be'); I
am led by 'nature to conclude some quality to be in the rose, which
is the cause of this sensation'; 'and that act of my mind by which I
have the conviction and belief of this quality is what in this case I
call perception.'[11] Thus 'perception implies an immediate conviction
and belief of something external – something different both from
the mind that perceives and from the act of perception' – namely, a
belief that the cause of a sensation is such and such.[12] The nature of
'implies' here is not clear; it may signify material implication or –
as seems much more likely – a conceptual connection. Say the latter
is indeed the case. Then it seems that Reid is claiming states of
affairs will appear to the subject as that F is G if, and only if, that
subject judges that that F is G.

The problem with this view is that we are subject to perceptual
illusions of various sorts. In some cases, we find it difficult to believe
what we are experiencing perceptually; in others, we find it actually impossible, since the one contradicts the other. By checking a
Müller–Lyer-type illusion with rulers and a non-arrowed comparison line, we may be wholly persuaded to *believe* that a line terminated at each end by outward-pointing arrows and one terminated
by inward-pointing arrows are the same length as the comparison
line even though we continue to *perceive* the first as being shorter
and the second as longer.

Most critics of conceptualism appear to suppose that regarding
perceptual experience as logically independent of judgement is dev-
astating to that position.[13] That is the nerve of a deep-rooted objection. It may be said, for example, that if illusion cases of this sort
are possible, perceptual experience cannot be governed or norma-
tively constrained by rational relations in the ways McDowell
requires. Accounting for such cases is only possible if it is acknowledged that, even in *non*-illusory cases, our perceptual experiences
exhibit a lack of responsiveness to reasons. We should appeal

instead, perhaps, to automatic psychological associations between perceptual experiences. The basic point is just this: whatever relations *do* explain these cases, they cannot be rational or (quasi-)inferential relations. That, at least, is the tempting thought.

Any viable form of conceptualism must acknowledge that conflicts between perceptual experiences and beliefs occur, and that illusion cases reveal perceptual experience to be logically independent of judgement. States of affairs in the world may appear to me as if 'that F is G' although I believe that it is not the case that that F is G. As I watch films in which wheels revolve at certain speeds, I cannot help it appearing to me that the wheels are turning in one direction, even though I may fully believe and judge that they are actually moving in the other direction. If the exercise of control over one's cognitive life leads one to seek an explanation of the illusion, even that may not affect the way things continue to appear in this and other similar cases. If, sometimes, we do not, and cannot, judge that the ways things appear in experience is the way things are, then Reid's version of conceptualism – always supposing he has been interpreted correctly – must be false. This is so because it mistakes a contingent link between experience and judgement for a necessary or constitutive link.

But acknowledgements of this sort are welcome; they serve only to deepen the conceptualist analysis, not to undermine it. It is quite compatible with conceptualism in general and McDowell's variety in particular to deny that experiences are, entail or can be reduced to propositional attitudes in general, or judgements in particular – or even that any particular experience is, entails or is reducible to a particular judgement. Certainly, concepts are essential constituents of judgements. And, according to conceptualism, they are also essential to the content of experience. But this does not amount to the claim that experiences are judgements, or to the entailment claim that states of affairs will appear to me as if p if, and only if, I judge that p. Conceptualism in general and in McDowell's particular form can preserve the logical independence of experience from judgement. States of affairs in the world may seem to me as if p without my necessarily judging *that* p. Indeed, experience and judgement may be two different kinds of mental state altogether. The conceptualist need only claim that they are two attitudes to the same kind of content – conceptual content.

The logical independence of experience and judgement is consistent with McDowell's insistence that the content of experience 'is essentially a fragment of judgmental content'; that the subject's ability to make judgements is necessary if he is to be granted the opportunity to experience the world.[14] What cases of illusion reveal at work is precisely the subject's exercise of control over his cognitive life, the control that McDowell regards as essential to judgement. In the case of the filmic wheels, for example, the subject restrains himself from endorsing the way that things appear. Such cases reveal logical independence, but they do not support the view that what one experiences is to be entirely distinguished from judgements as such. The conceptualist is free to press the point that the very ability and opportunity to restrain one's endorsement or affirmation of the way things appear in experience presupposes the exercise of control over one's cognitive life. And this brings us, seemingly quite naturally, to the conceptualism McDowell proposes. Experiences, both veridical and illusionary, are the engagement of capacities whose paradigmatic actualization is in judgement. Seeing is not necessarily believing, still less judging; but it is being always already in a position to judge.

This kind of response may be thought to place McDowell in a dilemma of another sort. For it entails that states of affairs will appear to a subject as if *p* (that this computer screen is flickering, for example) if and only if that subject is in possession of the concepts necessary for believing that *p*, for judging that *p*. Thus no subject can be accredited an experience with a given representational content unless he possesses the concepts of which that content is composed – COMPUTER SCREEN, for example. And it may be thought quite implausible that a subject has as many experience concepts as there are sensibly discriminable features of the world made accessible to him in experience. Our ability to speak about and fully articulate experience is clearly constrained by concepts; but it is not obvious that the same applies merely to the having of experience.[15] Objections of this sort take seriously the repleteness and specificity of our experience. We shall return to the problem in the next chapter, having first assembled the resources McDowell uses to answer it.

10

Openness

McDowell makes various claims about the content of an experience, the way the world appears to its subject to be ('that things are thus and so').[1] Each spells out a different central feature of his explanation of how it is possible for experience to manifest a two-way rational intentionality. We have begun to examine the first two of these claims: that the content of experience is conceptual, and that this same content of experience can also be the content of a judgement, what the subject commits himself to in endorsing the way the world appears to him. By making it possible to identify the contents of experiences and judgements, but distinguishing what it is to be engaged with such contents, as we have seen, McDowell is able to reflect a compelling picture: that the subject's move from experience to judgement is effortless in cases where he trusts the way things appear, but that in cases where he does not, the subject has the ability to resist making the move at all.

McDowell's third claim about the content of experience is that how things appear to the subject to be can be a state of the world. When the subject is not mistaken, how things appear to him to be can be how things are. This claim captures certain features of the Default, as we shall see. It is intuitively compelling to regard the way things appear to a subject as what is the case in the world, certainly in cases where the subject is sufficiently trusting to endorse the way things appear as, in his view, the way things are. And it is precisely conceptualism about experience which allows us to take this position. When we are spontaneously receptive to the world in our experience of it, what we experience or think is what is the case.

Various questions are raised by the interrelations between the first two claims and the third. If the content of experience can be a state of the world, how are we able to make a distinction (if we can) between experience of the world, on the one hand, and the world of which we have experience, on the other? The distinction is crucial if McDowell is to retain his claim that our experience, thought and talk about the world are as the robust realist conceives of them. For the objectivity of our experience, thought and talk about the world depends on our being able to distinguish them from the world in various ways. We shall explore the problems arising after examining McDowell's third claim more closely.

Ontological openness

There is something truistic about the claim that how things appear to the subject to be can be how things are, of course. As noted earlier, McDowell is keen to point this out; it is in line with his belief that he is pointing out obvious features of our experience, thought and talk which return us to the Default.[2] But, in McDowell's view, it is not sufficiently recognized that the third claim has ontological significance, significance for the question of what there is and how it is. He argues that the truism implies the following: 'There is no ontological gap between the sort of thing one can mean, or generally the sort of thing one can think, and the sort of thing that can be the case.'[3] This claim expresses one facet of our openness to the world which is different from that facet we have examined earlier: the claim that we are receptive to the world in experience of it. When we are spontaneously receptive to the world in our experience of it (first sense), what we experience or think is what is the case (second sense). The first sense was called 'receptive openness'; and the second 'ontological openness'.

McDowell follows the early Wittgenstein in regarding the world as 'everything that is the case'.[4] And, given ontological openness, when what one experiences or thinks is true, what one experiences or thinks is what is the case. So McDowell concludes that 'there is no gap between thought, as such, and the world'.[5] McDowell regards ontological openness as a gloss on the following passage in Wittgenstein's *Philosophical Investigations*:

'Thought must be something unique.' When we say, and mean, that such-and-such is the case, we – our meaning – do not stop anywhere short of the fact; but we mean: *this – is – so*. But this paradox (which has the form of a truism) can also be expressed in this way: *Thought can be of what is not the case.*[6]

This is the translation McDowell uses. A more accurate translation of the crucial phrase (*'das und das – so und so – ist'*) might be: *such-and-such – is – thus-and-so*. For the German leaves open the possibility that the 'is' connects two statements rather than the sub-sentential expressions 'this' and 'so'. It is perhaps odd that McDowell does not adopt this translation since it neatly brings out the concurrence with his own position as that features in the quotation cited in the introduction to this part of the book, for example: 'In a particular experience in which one is not misled, what one takes in is *that things are thus and so.*'[7]

As the sentence opening the previous extract indicates, Wittgenstein is interested in what gives rise to the notion that there is something odd or remarkable about thought. Elsewhere, he remarks that thought does not strike us as strange while we are thinking, but only when we reflect on it and ask 'how was that possible?' So there is a clear link here with the transcendental form of McDowell's argument: experience and thought and meaning are possible; what are their preconditions? We should ask first what they involve. And this is the point at which the strangeness seems to arise: spelling out and accounting for the possibility of intentionality. For, in Wittgenstein's own terms, thinking about an object, just like experiencing an object or meaning an object by some word, 'deals with the very object *itself*'; 'goes up to the object', points right at it, contains it, so that it is as if 'we had caught reality in our net'.[8] This is what it is for thought, experience and meaning to be intentional; they are 'about' objects, and do not 'stop short' of them. And yet thought, experience and meaning are quite ordinary; so we should find a way to dispel the sense of mystery.

McDowell's way of capturing what Wittgenstein notes as apparently remarkable about the intentionality of thought, experience and meaning is to claim that there is 'no ontological gap' between them and what they are directed on. Like Wittgenstein, he regards this as an ordinary feature of our relations with the world; dispelling the mystery merely returns us to the Default. But his position raises a host of questions.

McDowell's discussion of conceptualism, in the context of this third claim, is clearly designed to undermine that sharp dichotomy between 'mind' and 'world' effected in the title of his 1994 book by what Nietzsche called 'the sublime presumption of the little word "and" '.[9] The contents of our experience and of our thoughts need not be regarded as 'falling short of' the facts (the totality of which constitutes the world); the facts are literally things that we can think. But by undermining a dichotomy between mind and world, is McDowell not thereby in danger of just *collapsing* the one into the other?

If we are to answer this question, we need to know what kind of relation is being spoken of in the 'no gap' claim, and what the terms of that relation are. So we might say that there is 'no gap' between two items and mean that they are literally identical, or that they conform to one another in some strong sense, or that they are onto-logically dependent on each other, for example. And we might say that there is 'no gap' between the sort of thing one can think and the sort of thing that can be the case and mean that there is no gap between thought as such and the world, or between the engage-ment of mental-conceptual capacities and the behaviour of physi-cal reality, or between what is experienced or thought and what is the case.

It matters a great deal what relation the third claim has in mind and what the terms of that relation are. For suppose McDowell is claiming identity. Does he then identify 'that which is the case' with the engagement of the subject's conceptual capacities? 'That which is the case', facts, might be conceived as occupants of the world or as mental representations of the world or some form of substitution for worldly objects. If facts are conceived as worldly objects and identified with the employment of the subject's conceptual abilities, then the claim suggests idealism. The independence or autonomy of the world is being undermined; it is being constructed so as to fit the mind; it turns out to be mind-like, a reflection of mental capacities. Alternatively, McDowell might be identifying 'that which is the case', conceived as a set of worldly objects, with the (conceptual) contents of experiences and judgements. This position runs the equal and opposite risk of constructing the mind so as to fit the world. It suggests what might be called spatialization of the mental, because it seems that the contents, properties and structures of the mind are being turned into spatial entities, like other worldly objects.

McDowell is undoubtedly fond of using spatial terms to repre-sent the relation between thoughts and the world; it is by appeal to the spatial that phrases like 'the space of reasons' get their meaning. His way of describing what we have called ontological openness depends especially heavily on picturing mind–world relations – between what he calls 'the realm of subjectivity and the world of ordinary objects'[10] – in spatial terms; they are relations between an 'inner' and 'outer'.[11] We should, on his view, regard each term of the relation as 'interpenetrating' the other, not 'separated by a gulf' that experience would have to 'bridge'. Perceptual experience of the world, properly conceived, is the immediate 'presence to consciousness' of 'tracts of the environment', not 'images' of that environment, 'mere appearances' of the way things are. This goes for perception-based knowledge of the 'inner' states of others. When we are not misled, there is no 'interface' between ourselves and others; their thoughts and experiences lie open before us.[12] We have been assuming that these forms of expression are merely metaphorical. But if the third claim is to be interpreted as identifying worldly objects with conceptual contents, then it seems that these forms of expression are to be taken literally.

If the 'no gap' claim is to be interpreted in terms of a strong conformity between mind and world, rather than identity, we should ask which conforms to which. If some item, A, conforms to another item, B, then B is the dominant item, the model which A fits. Suppose McDowell advocates conformity; then what is the direction of fit? Does the world conform ontologically to thought as such, or does thought as such conform ontologically to the world? The former still runs the risk of becoming some form of idealism, the literal conformity of the ontological structure of the world to the structure of our experience and our thoughts. And the latter suggests some form of spatialization of the mental, literally rather than metaphorically taking mental properties and their interrelations to reflect the interrelations existing between spatial structures.

If McDowell's 'no gap' claim is meant to reflect ontological dependence between mind and world, we should ask which is to be treated as the basic item and which the dependent. And when we have addressed the question of which direction the dependency operates in, similar questions will arise as with the conformity interpretation. Depending on what, precisely, the terms of the relation are taken to be, McDowell's third claim may court either idealism or spatialization of the mental.

We should be guided by some relevant, basic features of McDowell's position when looking more closely at these questions. McDowell is a conceptualist about experience. He regards the conceptual as 'unbounded'; if we ask for the justification of some belief and obtain another belief and go on repeating the question until we arrive at an experience and a point at which we cannot ask the question, that point will still be conceptual, a feature of the way things appear that is thinkable, judgeable.[13] Finally, and crucially, experience is to be regarded as passive; an engagement of the subject's conceptual capacities which is quite unlike his active exercise of them in judgement. So there is nothing so far in this radical world-experience conceptualism *per se* to prevent the direction of fit between mind and world being robustly realist (there is a world which exists for all – and therefore independently of – any-minded subjects; it is something of which we can speak and think knowledgeably and truly). Indeed, states of affairs may be regarded as determining the content of judgements about them, and not vice versa. That such states are intrinsically *thinkable* does nothing to undermine this point. For experience is passive; one can decide how and where to place oneself in experience, but 'it is not up to one what, having done all that, one will experience.'[14] McDowell is clear about this. 'How things are' is independent of any one subject's thinking.[15] There is no guarantee that the world is completely within reach of a subject's system of concepts at any one point in time.[16]

Fregean background

A fair judgement on McDowell's third claim depends on accurately representing the context in which it figures. That requires some degree of acquaintance with three interdependent notions, each of which can be traced back to Gottlob Frege: sense, the identity theory of truth, and object-dependent thoughts.[17] So these notions will be briefly introduced here.

According to Frege, thinking is a two-place relation between the subject and a proposition – a thought – which is 'grasped'.[18] A thought/proposition is a structured entity with senses as its constituents.[19] Frege introduced the notion of sense to account for the fact that we may think about the same object in sufficiently different ways that it is possible, for example, quite rationally to hold views that actually contradict one another. Consider two propositions:

(1)   Queen Elizabeth reigned in twentieth-century England.
(2)   Elizabeth Windsor reigned in twentieth-century England.

It is possible for someone who understands both propositions correctly to take coherently different attitudes to them. If I didn't know that Queen Elizabeth II is Elizabeth Windsor, for example, I might regard (1) as true and (2) as false. Now what is different about (1) and (2) that would explain the possibility of taking such strikingly different attitudes to them? Not what the sub-sentential expressions 'Queen Elizabeth' and 'Elizabeth Windsor' refer to, for they refer to the same person. In Frege's view, the difference lies in the 'mode' under which this person is 'presented'; either as 'Queen Elizabeth' or as 'Elizabeth Windsor'. We can make the same point while preserving clear continuity with the intentionality theme being pursued here. In the Fregean view that McDowell adopts, 'Queen Elizabeth' and 'Elizabeth Windsor' indicate different ways in which it is possible to think about this same person. So to say that a thought/proposition is a structured entity with senses as its constituents is to explain the difference between propositions like (1) and (2) that refer to the same worldly objects. They are composed of different ways of thinking about those same worldly objects.

In McDowell's Fregean view, senses are not only what words (like the sub-sentential expressions 'Queen Elizabeth' and 'Elizabeth Windsor') express. They are also what the mind 'grasps' when the subject enters into that two-place relation with a thought/proposition. Senses are objective; they may be grasped by all subjects, but are independent of any.[20] When one grasps a sense, its reference is presented to the understanding in a certain way; it is this 'mode of presentation' or of 'representation' which grounds intentionality, the fact that one is thinking about that reference.[21] Indeed, the truth-value of the thought/proposition which the mind grasps is determined by its relation to the object it is about.

These Fregean claims might naturally lead to two more that are of crucial importance to the representation of McDowell's views. The first such claim is one that Frege himself certainly saw as implied by the overall position: that true thoughts/propositions are identical with facts, or that which is the case. This is the claim called 'the identity theory of truth'. A thought/proposition is true if and only if it is identical with a fact. So true thoughts/propositions are facts.[22]

The second such claim is only controversially attributable to Frege himself, but it can easily seem to be motivated by the overall position.[23] The sense of a proposition like (1) is composed of the senses of its constituents, one of which is a singular term (the title-name 'Queen Elizabeth'); the sense of a singular term is a way of thinking of the particular object it is about or directed on; if there were not that same object, there could not be that same way of thinking about it; hence the sense of a singular term, and the sense of any proposition in which it occurs, is dependent for its existence and identity on the existence and identity of the particular object it is about or directed on. This is the claim called 'object dependency'.

In this Fregean context, it will be possible to represent McDowell's rethinking of mind–world relations more clearly. Though he accepts the basic Fregean position, he never espouses identity theory explicitly. So we may legitimately ask whether he does so implicitly or in fact, what the cost of doing so would be, and what, outside identity theory, could be the meaning of the claim that there is 'no ontological gap' between what one thinks truly and what is the case.

The fact that McDowell does explicitly adopt a version of object dependency will help answer these questions. To anticipate somewhat, it will turn out that McDowell need not, and should not, adopt an identity theory of truth. For the constituents of true thoughts (senses) need not be identical with the constituents of facts (worldly objects) to be open to them; not if they are essentially dependent on them. And, since McDowell is free to advance this object-dependent account, his openness thesis can escape both idealism and the charge of 'spatializing the understanding'. We shall first see why this must be so, and then examine more closely the claim on which so much is then made dependent, namely, object dependency.

Identity and dependency

According to an implication McDowell draws from his third claim about the contents of experience, there is no ontological gap between the sort of thing which is the case and the sort of thing one can think. If this is meant to be understood as an identity claim, then McDowell holds a version of Frege's identity theory of truth. McDowell certainly adopts a Fregean approach to propositions, identifying them with Fregean thoughts – items which contain only 'senses' as constituents.[24] But the Frege connection raises a significant problem of interpretation: how are we supposed to conceive of the 'facts' with which true thoughts are supposed to be identical?[25] Facts are abstract even if their constituents are concrete. Call an identity theory 'strong' if facts are conceived as identical with items whose constituents are particular worldly objects and properties. A theory, correspondingly, will be 'weak' if those constituents are conceived as non-worldly items. Thus, if McDowell *is* a Fregean identity theorist, he has a choice between two theories:

- *Strong Fregean identity theory:* a true proposition/Fregean thought (with senses as constituents) is identical with a fact (with particular worldly objects and properties as constituents).
- *Weak Fregean identity theory:* a true proposition/Fregean thought (with senses as constituents) is identical with a fact (with non-worldly items as constituents).

If true thoughts are identical with facts, then their constituents are identical too. So the strong theory makes senses identical with worldly objects, and the weak theory makes them identical with non-worldly items.

Although Frege himself adopted the weak theory (conceiving of senses as denizens of a 'third realm'), we know that McDowell does not. He identifies the totality of facts with the world ('the world is everything that is the case'). But he cannot afford to adopt the strong theory either. For the world itself will then be conceived as composed of Fregean senses. McDowell claims that 'facts in general are essentially capable of being embraced in thought'.[26] To portray thought in the Fregean way as the 'grasping' of such worldly contents would then spatialize the mind, making mental properties and structures take on the spatial forms of the objects they are about or directed on. McDowell evidently needs to avoid this result.

So there is an apparent dilemma here, which takes the following form. If McDowell *does* adopt the identity theory of truth – in either of its two Fregean forms – so much the worse for him. But if he does *not* adopt the identity theory, how are we to understand his reconfiguring of mind–world relations, his attempt to recapture the Default? For that reconfiguring is based on ontological openness, the openness of facts to the contents of acts of thinking. And this thesis is not available unless we suppose that the world is made up of 'the sort of thing one can think'. Without this claim, a gulf (or 'ontological gap') immediately opens up between the constituents of facts and thoughts 'as such'.

But there is a way to advance the openness thesis and to escape the dilemma; and, I suggest, it is the way taken by McDowell. We should distinguish between the view that there is no ontological gap between the constituents of true thoughts and facts (the openness thesis), and the view that those constituents are identical with each other (identity theory). If McDowell embraces the former while rejecting the latter, then mind–world relations may be reconfigured without spatializing the understanding (strong theory) or violating ontological economy (weak theory).

This distinction is made available to McDowell by the very Fregean approach to thoughts/propositions he espouses. A sense is a mode of presentation of an object in thought; there are any number of different ways for an object to be presented to a subject or identified by him; so no sense can be identical with its object. After all, as we have seen, the motivation for claiming that thoughts are composed of senses is to explain how it is possible rationally to hold conflicting attitudes towards the same object. On the other hand, there need be no ontological gap between any one of those senses and the object presented. For the existence and identity of each sense may be considered as essentially dependent on the existence and identity of its object. And if a particular object figures in a thought under a mode of presentation exclusive to it, a mode that would not be available if that object had not existed in that particular way, then the content of the thought does not 'fall short of' the facts. Consider an analogy: the way in which a present is given is not identical with the fact of its being given; but there has to be a present for it to be given in some way.

It is well known that McDowell favours just such an 'object-dependent' account of sense.[27] And it is surely in the light of this account, rather than identity theory, that the phrase 'no ontological gap' should be read. For identity theory places McDowell in the dilemma posed above. The object-dependent account, on the other hand, escapes the dilemma, for it is compatible with the openness thesis without constructing the world out of Fregean senses. Now, in conceiving of the world in this way to avoid idealism and in nevertheless continuing to acknowledge the fact that it exercises a rational constraint on subjects, McDowell's position may be thought to collapse into a form of the Myth. For rational relations must then exist between what the subject experiences or thinks and what is independent of that experience or thought, namely what is the case (the totality of which is the world). And is this not to say that rational relations exist between items of which some are nonconceptual? This is a mistake that trades on ambiguity in the phrase 'what the subject experiences or thinks'. It might mean the experiencing or thinking of some object, the object experienced or thought about, or the way experience or thought represents the object as being. In McDowell's view, the last of these three is always already conceptual, which allows us to regard the first as manifesting a two-way rational intentionality. This blocks any collapse into the Myth. The second of these three is thinkable but need not be thought, just as it can, but need not, be experienced; so it exists independently of both the first and the third. This blocks the way to idealism.

To conclude. In the attempt to rethink mind–world relations in ways that it is necessary to do to recapture the Default, McDowell claims that there is 'no ontological gap' between what one thinks truly and what is the case. But this view need not entail an identity theory of truth. If the constituents of true thoughts (senses) are regarded as essentially dependent on the constituents of facts (worldly objects), then they are open to them, and that is all the openness required. The identity theory is not only to be avoided but is quite unnecessary.

This gives us an answer to the central question raised by this chapter: what kind of relation does (ontological) openness denote, and what are the terms of that relation? The relation is one of onto-logical dependence (not strong conformity or identity), and the terms of that relation are the contents of acts of thinking (not the acts themselves), on the one hand, and facts conceived as worldly objects (not mental proxies), on the other.

11

World Dependency

Crucial to McDowell's account of our openness to the world is his claim that there is 'no ontological gap' between the world and the contents of our experience, thought and talk about it. Elucidation of this claim has depended heavily on appeal to the notion of object dependency, a form of world dependency since the items in question (they may be properties or states of affairs as well as objects) are worldly items.[1] So we should examine that notion more closely and find out what motivates it. This research will turn out to be worthwhile for other, deeper reasons. An understanding of what it is for thoughts to be object-dependent turns out to be basic to an understanding of what it is for our experience, thought and talk to manifest two-way rational intentionality.

One source of support for object dependency, as we have seen, is the Fregean account of thoughts/propositions as being composed of senses, or ways of thinking about objects. For it may seem simply inconceivable that there should be such a way of thinking about an object if there is no object to be thought about, a mode of presentation of an item if there is no item to be presented. And if a statement expressing a thought/proposition contains a singular term putatively about an object but whose object does not exist, then the thought/proposition itself may be considered as empty as the sense to which the singular term corresponds.

This way of putting things does not distinguish between the ways that thoughts/propositions may be about or directed on objects. In particular, it does not depend on any special features peculiar to some singular terms embedded in the statements that express such thoughts/propositions.[2] A second argument for object dependency does rest on such a distinction, and it appeals directly to features of McDowell's account of experience that we have already encountered.[3]

Perceptual demonstrative thoughts

There are some thoughts/propositions which are expressed using singular terms that refer directly to objects experienced by the subject, and of these thoughts it is most especially plausible to claim that their existence and identity depend on the existence and identity of the object they are about or directed on.[4] These thoughts/propositions belong to a kind often called 'perceptual demonstrative', because they arise out of perceptual experience and are expressed using demonstrative terms like *This*, *That*, *This F* and *That F*.

So suppose a subject, Abelard, is searching through the contents of a drawer and thinks 'this pen [the one I am now looking at] is shoddy'; that is an example of a perceptual demonstrative thought. In McDowell's view, such thoughts are ontologically dependent on the aspects of the world they are about or directed on (not the other way around). And this claim of ontological dependence is to be spelled out in the following terms. They are only available to a subject in thinking about a particular object, *O*, if *O* exists and the subject is appropriately related to *O*. Consequently, any thought/proposition expressed by a statement containing such perceptual demonstrative terms is object-dependent.

Consider a case in which a statement containing such a term is intended to express a certain thought/proposition entertained by a subject on some particular occasion: the case in which Abelard thinks 'this pen is shoddy', for example. Whether or not what the statement expresses is indeed a genuinely significant and meaningful thought/proposition will depend on whether its constituent senses are significant or empty. The singular term 'this pen' putatively refers to a particular experienced pen and corresponds to a particular sense, namely, the way in which that pen is thought about by Abelard or presented to Abelard. If there is in fact no pen before Abelard (he is hallucinating, perhaps), then there is no such 'way' in which it is thought about or presented; indeed, there is no 'it' to be thought about or presented in such a way. So the sense corresponding to that particular sub-sentential expression is empty.

There is nothing to be contributed to the sense or significance of the whole thought/proposition by what corresponds to that part of the statement. So the whole thought/proposition lacks the meaning or significance imputed to it by Abelard in the statement he expresses.

There are, as we are beginning to see, particular reasons to think of thoughts expressed using perceptual demonstrative terms as object-dependent; these reasons are peculiar to such thoughts. The point needs closer examination, so consider first the statements used to express such thoughts. It is plausible to suppose that the object referred to by a perceptual demonstrative term is essential to the semantic character of the statement to which that term contributes.[5] By 'essential', I mean that the object referred to is constitutive of what is said thereby: if there were no object, there would be no statement; if some other object were picked out, a different statement would have been made. If this principle did not hold, then perceptual demonstrative statements would still count as such even if there were no object for them to refer to. But, without a referent, the statement could not be assessed as true or false. If there is no pen, the question of whether the putative statement 'this pen is shoddy' is true or false simply could not arise. And there is every good reason to resist the notion that attempts might issue in statements that fail to determine a truth-value. For then we should have to admit a third truth-value to apply to the resulting category of items: those that count as statements but which are nevertheless assessable as neither true nor false. It is clearly preferable to conclude that such uses would not count as statements in the first place.

Object dependency about perceptual demonstrative thoughts may then be seen as simply translating these claims and applying them to thoughts. The object referred to by a perceptual demonstrative term contained within the embedded propositions of a thought is essential to that thought. No object, no thought; different object, different thought. If they were not object-dependent, then perceptual demonstrative thoughts would still count as such even if there were no object for them to be about. And if there were no such item, the thought could not be assessed as true or false – for the same reason that prevents statements being so assessed. Now the defining function of such thoughts is their role in carrying information about the perceptible world; they are determinable as true or false in relation to that world. So we should resist ascribing content to attempts at perceptual demonstrative thought which fail to determine a truth-value. For then we should have to admit a third truth-value and apply it to items which count as perceptual demonstrative thoughts, as conveyors of perceptual information, but which are nevertheless assessable as neither true nor false. Again, it is clearly preferable to conclude that such attempts lack the content of perceptual demonstrative thoughts in the first place. And object dependency justifies this conclusion.

The crucial parts of this argument are those which depend on claims about the defining function of perceptual demonstrative thoughts. These claims are supported by what may be considered intuitively plausible about communicating, and failing to communicate, such thoughts. What would it take for you to grasp what I am thinking if I point to the thin air before us and say 'this computer screen is flickering'? It is not enough that you know what it is like for computer screens in general to flicker, or even what it would be for some particular computer screen to flicker. You need to be in a position to know what it is for *this* computer screen to do so. And, apparently, you cannot. For there is no such computer screen; no object for any pointing use of 'this' – mine or yours – to pick out. In the computer screen's absence, what I said is not determinable as true or false; and, where perceptual demonstrative thoughts are concerned, this seems to undermine any chances you might otherwise have of understanding me. Thus one necessary condition of your grasping my thought appears to be this: that there be an object; and not just *any* object, but 'that one', corresponding to my pointing. In the computer screen's absence, there is just no such thought for you to grasp.

Does this thought nevertheless exist, though incapable of being grasped? It would seem not – and not just because the notion of logically incommunicable thoughts is notoriously problematic. For, in its absence, there is nothing that would count even for me as knowing what it is for this computer screen to be flickering; nothing for me to pick out or point to; nothing by which what I have said might be determined as true or false. Consider your natural reaction on hearing me. It may be one of puzzlement. But not about what it is I am thinking; rather about *why* I have expressed myself this way, *how* I may be deluded, and so on. Thus you do not suppose there is some logically incommunicable thought here you cannot understand. Rather, you simply recognize that there is no thought here you can ascribe to me. There will be other thoughts you can ascribe me, certainly, which will explain my behaviour – for example, 'He thinks there is a computer screen before us that is flickering.' Those thoughts will correspond to what I do and other things I say. But they will not include the thought expressed as 'this computer screen is flickering'. In the absence of the object itself, it would make no sense either to you or to me.

So it may seem that perceptual demonstrative thoughts are object-dependent: they do not exist unless there is an object – and the right object ('*that* object') – for them to be about. This claim should not be so shocking, perhaps. The defining function of perceptual demonstrative thoughts is to convey information about the perceptible world – and, hence, to be assessable as true or false. So we have little reason, if any, to protest that there simply must be such a thought when there is nothing for it to be true about – that is, when the question of its truth or falsity cannot even arise.

Varieties of externalism

The foregoing examination of perceptual demonstrative thinking suggests a tighter way of presenting object dependency.

A thought/proposition is object-dependent if one or more of the referring expressions embedded in the statement expressing it is object-dependent. And a referring expression is object-dependent just in case the contribution it makes to the significance of that statement, in the given context of its being thought or uttered, depends essentially on the existence and identity of the object to which it putatively refers: that is, the object it is about or directed on.

So the existence and identity of object-dependent thoughts/ propositions depend essentially on the existence and identity of the objects they are about or are directed on. It follows that object-dependent thoughts have different and distinct contents if they are about different and distinct objects; and they do not have any content, or any component of content, in the absence of their objects (thoughts without contents are, of course, no thoughts at all). Expressed counterfactually – where the supposition of not-p is contrary to the known fact that p – this is to say that, if its object had not existed, the object-dependent thought itself would not have existed.[6]

This formulation may be converted back into terms that appeal more obviously to the Fregean background with which we started. The significance of a thought/proposition is dependent on the significance of its parts, whose significance in turn is a function of their power to affect the truth-value of the thoughts/propositions in which they occur. In thoughts/propositions expressed by statements containing perceptual demonstrative singular terms (like 'this pen' in 'this pen is shoddy'), that power is determined by the relation of those terms to their extra-linguistic referents in the subject's experience. And there is nothing to determine the truth-value of a thought/proposition expressed by a statement containing an 'empty' perceptual demonstrative singular term (a term purporting to refer to a particular bearer even though that particular bearer does not exist). So such thoughts/propositions are empty, without significance. Hence the subject did not think anything expressed by the statement 'this pen is shoddy'. Perhaps other thoughts were available to him in his hallucinatory state. But in the absence of the object to which 'this pen' putatively referred, none of those thoughts would have been the particular perceptual demonstrative thought the subject took himself to have.

Object dependency clearly entails what has been called 'externalism' for the thoughts/propositions concerned: having them must imply the co-existence of the thinker with specific environmental and extra-cuticular states of affairs. Externalism itself can be, and usually is, held in a much weaker form.[7] We gain a clearer insight into McDowell's version by distinguishing it from such weaker forms.

According to what we might call 'moderate' externalism, thinking about grass entails that one is embedded appropriately in the right sort of socio-physical environment. So you cannot suppose that grass is green, or have any other mental states with grass as an intentional object, unless you are appropriately related to samples of herbage. Zonk, who lives in a grassless world, can no more think about grass than he can graze on it. The same applies to envatted brains that have never roamed free of their vats and to immaterial minds in a world empty but for an omnipotent deceiver. None of these unfortunates has the appropriate sort of intercourse with grass to be able to think about it.

According to the 'strong' externalism expressed by object dependency, having certain kinds of thoughts about grass entails moderate externalism – that one is generally embedded in a grassy world – and more besides: namely, that one is appropriately related to specific samples. Thus I cannot entertain the thought/proposition 'that grass-patch is dying' unless there is a particular patch there available for inspection and unless I am, or could be, linked to it perceptually. Say that I, a citizen of a grassy world, have been deluded and there is no specific patch before me. According to moderate externalism, that demonstrative thought just specified is still available to me – all that matters is that I have lived in this grassy world

for long enough to establish the environmental connections necessary for grass-thoughts. According to strong externalism, whatever
I thought, it was not 'that grass-patch is dying'. For, without the
particular extra-cuticular entity partially constituting that very
demonstrative thought, the thought itself must be unavailable to
me.[8]

Perceptual demonstrative concepts

McDowell's object-dependent views have a significant place in the
present account for three main reasons. The first we have already
seen: his views on this part of thought and experience provide a
reliable guide to his views on the whole. His appeal to (ontological)
openness is meant to be read as claiming not conformity or identity
between thoughts as such and the world, but dependence; and that
dependence exists between the contents of these acts of thinking
(not the acts themselves) and facts conceived as worldly objects (not
mental proxies). So McDowell remains robustly realist. How things
are is independent of one's thinking (except in the very special cases
where how things are just is that one thinks such-and-such); one's
experience is of something objective, independent of the experience
itself.

A significant set of objections to McDowell's conceptualism trig-
gers the second application of his object dependence views: they
help furnish a sufficient defence. Conceptualism of the kind
McDowell espouses, as we have seen, implies that the subject's
experience is constrained by the concepts and conceptual capacities
in his possession. More specifically, it entails that states of affairs
will appear to a subject in experience as if it is the case that p (that
this computer screen is flickering, for example) if and only if that
subject is in possession of the concepts necessary for believing
that p, for judging that p. Thus no subject can be accredited an experience with a given representational content unless he possesses the
concepts of which that content is composed – COMPUTER SCREEN,
for example. And this may seem straightforwardly false. How
things appear to a subject is certainly restricted by his sensitivity to
the world. But it may seem that this sensitivity is not constrained
in this way by whatever concepts the perceiver has. Indeed, it may
be thought quite implausible that a subject has as many experience-
concepts as there are sensibly discriminable features of the world
made accessible to him in perceptual experience. Our ability to

speak about and fully articulate experience is clearly constrained by concepts; but it is not obvious that the same applies merely to the having of experience.[9]

In McDowell's view, this objection ignores our ability to think demonstratively about objects. We have only to appreciate that ability, and its object-dependent basis, for the objection to disappear. McDowell takes our visual experience of coloured objects as an example on which to construct this kind of reply. Consider the subject who sees a canvas daubed with different shades of crimson. We might sort these shades according to the colour-words we know. So amongst the various kinds of red, we might distinguish kinds of crimson, and amongst the kinds of crimson, we might distinguish Harvard crimson. At that point of discrimination, or soon thereafter, we would have no specific names to distinguish between colours that we would nevertheless be able sensibly to discriminate. 'I see that these are two different types of Harvard crimson,' we might say, 'but I don't know what they are called.'

If this means that we do not have the concepts to distinguish between these types either, then we can discriminate more experientially than we can conceptually. If that is so, then conceptualism must be false; our ability to have the world appear to us in experience in various ways cannot be constrained by the concepts we have. But it is not so; we have the words, as well as the concepts they express, to distinguish quite as many colours as we can experientially discriminate. For we can point saying 'that shade of Harvard crimson is different (darker, less reflective, deeper, and so on) from that shade.' In doing so, we have deployed two perceptual demonstrative concepts of the form *That F*; concepts that are on this occasion about or directed on two specific and sensibly discriminable colours. The concepts have what has been called a 'correctness condition' relating them to these specific colours; something else will count as having 'that shade' just in case it has the same shade as the colour pointed at by the subject on this occasion.[10]

Thus it is the object dependency of the concept-form *That Shade* which is crucial to answering the original objection. Sensible experience is remarkably replete with fine-grained detail, but our conceptual capacities are adequate to capture that detail. For we have at our disposal concepts (perceptual demonstrative concepts) which are about or directed on their objects in virtue of the existence and identity of those objects themselves of which we have sensible experience. Indeed, concepts of the form *That F* will usually only have secure application in the presence of the original sample. It is because the subject's thought is thus essentially about and directed on a specific experienced sample that the concept-form *That Shade* is sufficiently fine-grained to capture experience of coloured objects in all its determinate detail.

This may not satisfy the opponent. McDowell (so it may be said) has just shown that, having experienced a richly coloured array, a subject will have demonstrative concepts at his disposal to describe it. But conceptualism claims that the perceiver experiences the array in virtue of the concepts at his disposal. So what McDowell needs to show is that the perceiver has the fine-grained concept prior to attending to the particularity of his experience.

But it is by no means clear that this requirement should follow from the conceptualist premise. Ordinary experience of colour certainly presupposes background conceptual capacities which coordinate the use of particular concepts and permit their application. But McDowell need not claim that the subject has the particular concept corresponding to the form *That Shade* when it is used about the specific sample in question before recognizing which one particular colour falls under it. Particular concepts, as opposed to their background, are exercised precisely in what we sensibly discriminate. Experience need not presuppose a store of concepts awaiting application if the conceptualist is correct that experience is the exercise of concepts. It may seem that, in order to match discriminatory capacities, McDowell has concepts popping up with a suspicious obligingness. But there need be no mystery. The particular concept of the form *That Shade* which is about or directed on a specific sample at some particular time is available in the very way that experience teaches the subject differences – as when he notes 'that is a slightly paler shade of green than that.'

The suggestion that McDowell is gesturing to a distinction between background conceptual capacities and particular concepts assists him in other ways. If experiential content is conceptual, the subject's perceptual capacities for discrimination at the time of an experience must be constrained by the concepts he has at that time. But I may remember seeing a computer screen in my childhood, a time when I did not possess that concept. And there are easily imaginable examples of cases in which distinctive features of a subject's experience on one occasion come to his attention only later when attending closely to what he can recall of how things were.[11]

But such cases need not embarrass the conceptualist. For the opponent has not shown what he needs to show: namely, that memory can be a source of evidence about how things were experienced in the past quite independently of what the subject then believed or conceived to have been the case. The conceptualist can claim that the subject's later more florid recall is entirely constrained by the particular concepts – of size, shape, colour, function, and so on – available to him at the time of the experience. The fact that he is now able to marshal the evidence in new ways is due to background capacities already possessed, in rudimentary form at least, on earlier occasions.

Conceptual structure

There is a third reason to focus attention on perceptual demonstrative concepts and the object dependence they exhibit: they take up a structurally basic position in the conceptual structure which makes two-way rational intentionality possible and in McDowell's account of that structure. That this is the case follows from the main features of his view as we have traced them in this part of the book.

Perceptual demonstrative concepts are peculiarly directly connected with experience in a way that many other thoughts are not. I need not mean *the pen I am now seeing* (or perceptually experiencing in some other way) when I think 'the pen I borrowed from Heloïse is shoddy'. But that is precisely what I must mean in the perceptual demonstrative case, in thoughts containing concepts expressed by the form *This Pen*, for example. This direct dependence on experience gives such concepts the structural aspect of two-way rational directedness exhibited by experience. For the concept bears on the world and the world on the concept in the strong sense that that particular concept would not exist if what it was about did not exist. The subject is thus peculiarly aptly described as receptive to the world in having thoughts which incorporate such concepts. The subject is passive, in the sense that what he thinks is determined by the way the world is; but the subject is also alert, in the sense that he must be (in this case) seeing the way the world is.

Conversely, there are respects in which experience itself depends on perceptual demonstrative concepts. In McDowell's view, experience and concept use are two aspects of the same arrangement, for he regards them as interdependent. This follows from the two-way rational intentionality of experience and what is required to secure it: experience is receptive and spontaneous, equipped with conceptual content that leaves no ontological gap with what is the case. The concepts without which experience would be impossible themselves derive from experience, either directly or indirectly. And it is from precisely those simple experiences expressed by perceptual demonstrative thoughts that concepts derive. These experiences provide identifying reference to the basic items about which we think and talk and whose totality makes up the world. It is the enjoyment of such experiences and the acquisition of such concepts which, in McDowell's view, mark the human infant's initiation into the space of reasons and the achievement of its second nature. If it is in virtue of their object dependence that such concepts articulate our primary intentional relations with the world, then object-dependent concepts may plausibly be regarded as reflecting the fundamental features of those relations. This being so, object-dependent concepts are basic to our conceptual structure.

In brief: perceptual demonstrative concepts and the thoughts they make possible are necessary for and paradigmatic of the openness of human beings to the world; that openness which is expressed in terms of the two-way rational intentionality of experience, thought and talk; the intentionality which requires capacities associated with the autonomous space of reasons; that space which is incorporated into nature once our conception of nature is revised to include second nature.

Part IV

The Exercise of Second Nature

Central Elements

If McDowell is right that revising our view of nature 'gives philosophy peace', and that it does so by discovering a way to secure our Default picture of openness to the world in our experience, thought and talk of it, then revised nature should offer the correct perspective from which to address and resolve questions about how we can know, how we can value, and how we should live. For philosophy is disquieted by these kinds of question also; there are recognizably 'philosophical' problems which arise in each case and which are treated under the headings 'epistemology', 'aesthetics' and 'ethics'.

So far, we have only been concerned with questions of the form 'what is there?' and 'how is it possible that what there is is?' In McDowell's view, as we have seen, there is experience; experience exhibits a two-way rational intentionality between subjects and the world; that relation is only possible if we characterize the contents of experience as conceptual, so that experiencing the world always already engages the subject's ability to deal conceptually with it. Acknowledging this puts an end to philosophy's disquiet, so long as we revise our view of nature and include within it the subject's autonomous rational-conceptual capacities, his 'second nature'.

If this answer to the question 'what is there, and how is it possible?' is the decisive move in philosophy overall, how precisely does it help answer epistemological questions like 'what do we know, and how is knowledge possible?', aesthetic questions like 'what do we value, and how is evaluation possible?' and ethical questions like 'how should we live?' There must be significant features of epistemology and ethics which are clarified and elucidated once our view of nature is revised and our rational-conceptual capacities are thereby incorporated into it. So we should now explore those features and discover what profound interrelations exist between them and our openness to the world in experience that securing this Default view has so decisive an effect on philosophy overall.

It is McDowell's claims about the content of experience which explain why the revision of nature has a profound effect on epistemology and on questions about what (and how) we can know. For his central epistemological claim is an immediate consequence of his views about experience.

> Suppose someone is presented with an appearance that it is raining. It seems unproblematic that if his experience is in a suitable way the upshot of the fact that it is raining, then the fact itself can make it the case that he knows that it is raining. But that seems unproblematic precisely because the content of the appearance is the content of the knowledge. And it is arguable that we find that match in content intelligible only because we do *not* conceive the objects of such experiences as in general falling short of the meteorological facts. That is: such experiences can present us with the appearance that it is raining only because when we have them as the upshot (in a suitable way) of the fact that it is raining, the fact itself is their object; so that its obtaining is not, after all, blankly external.[1]

In this passage, McDowell implicitly appeals to claims that we have already investigated concerning the content of experience, the way the world appears to its subject to be (for example, 'that things are thus and so'). As well as being conceptual,

(a)   The content of a subject's experience can be the content of a judgement.

And

(b)   The content of a subject's experience can be what is the case, a state of the world.

McDowell now claims that the way in which the world appears to be to the subject in experience can be what the subject knows. Thus

(c)   The content of a subject's experience can be the content of a subject's knowledge.

Claim (c) is proposed as being as uncontroversial as (a) and (b), something we do not need to be argued into. It is neatly concurrent with the other claims and can be expressed together with them. The way things appear to a subject to be in experience can be what the subject commits himself to in judgement, what is the case in the world, and what the subject knows.

The deep interrelation between McDowell's earlier claims and his epistemological views is revealed if we examine what, in each case, turns the possibility that experiential content 'can' be such and such into actuality. The way things appear to a subject to be in experience 'is' what he commits himself to in judgement when that is how he takes things to be, and it is what is the case in the world when the subject turns out to be right. The question then arises: what more is required if the way things appear to a subject to be in experience is to count as what the subject knows? 'Nothing', the passage suggests. It may appear to the subject of experience that things are thus and so ('it is raining'), and, on the basis of that experience, he may judge that this is how things are; if this is how things are in fact, then the subject judges knowledgeably.

It might be thought that this response risks making knowledge too easy; in particular, that a subject who merely makes a lucky guess when judging that things are thus and so counts, against our intuitions, as knowing that things are thus and so. But we can block this thought by recalling McDowell's demanding conception of judgement. The subject does not count as judging that things are thus and so unless he has engaged those checking procedures relevant to the evidence which constitute the exercise of control over his cognitive life. This rules out the possibility that a subject who judges something might merely be guessing it.

Nothing more is required for knowledge than judgement and the obtaining of the relevant facts. And, according to McDowell (as we have seen), what is philosophically problematic about judgement and the obtaining of facts is resolved once our view of nature is revised and our rational-conceptual capacities are thereby incorporated into it. So that revision also disposes of whatever might appear philosophically problematic about knowledge.

The best way to appreciate McDowell's overall position on epistemological questions is to examine its application in specific kinds of case; so we shall look at the so-called 'problem of other minds'. McDowell motivates his claims here by appeal to an interpretation of Wittgenstein's writings on criteria, and there are questions to be raised about the success of this manoeuvre.

The question of what values are and how evaluative thought is possible raises different problems. But, in McDowell's view, these are also to be resolved by appeal to our openness to the world in experience and thought, and in particular to the notion of 'second nature'.

> The idea of value experience involves taking admiration, say, to represent its object as having a property that (although there in the object) is essentially subjective in much the same way as the property that an object is represented as having by an experience of redness – that is, understood adequately only in terms of the appropriate modification of human (or similar) sensibility.[2]

There are two basic claims to which this passage refers and on which McDowell's account of value and evaluative thought is based. In his view, there is a close analogy between the role of reason in evaluative thinking, thinking of and about values, and the role of perceptual awareness in colour experience, experience of and about colours. Just as objects are really colourful, objects or actions are really valuable. So, like colours,

(d)   Values are real and objective.

But colours are objective in a qualified sense; they are not objective in the way that certain other properties of objects are objective – such as the size or shape of an object. For an object's having some colour, say red, is its being such as to look red. Contrast this with that same object's having the property of being square; the object could have that property quite independently of however it is, or is to be, experienced. Now an object's being such as to look red is not dependent on actually looking red to anyone on a particular occasion. But it does depend on the possibility of subjects of experience with the relevant concepts, subjects capable of having that object look precisely red to them.

The same applies to values, in McDowell's view. So being such as to recognize value and engage in evaluative thinking is like being such as to recognize red objects and engage in thinking about such colours: it requires acquisition of the relevant concepts through education and sensitivity to the properties in the world that they pick out. This is what McDowell means by 'the appropriate modification of human (or similar) sensibility'. Thus

(e)   Value properties and evaluative thought depend on the exercise of second nature.

So for something to have value – like an action, or a situation, or a person, or an institution – it must be internally related to some exercise of the sensibility that is acquired as second nature. And having sensibility of this sort depends on being educated in various ways, on acquiring habituated tendencies to be attracted towards objects or actions of various kinds.

Insofar as value and evaluative thought are philosophically problematic, therefore, they are just a particular case of a general problem: how we are to make sense of second nature. And McDowell has provided an answer to that general problem, as we have seen, with his naturalism of second nature. So, again, the revision of our view of nature which secures our Default view of openness to the world should also dispose of any residual philosophical disquiet about value.

One kind of evaluative thinking is moral-ethical thinking; one subset of value properties is the set of moral-ethical properties. Given this relationship, it is not surprising to find that the same appeal to revised nature which lies at the heart of McDowell's account of value also grounds his response to the final set of philosophical questions with which we shall deal: namely, moral-ethical questions of the form 'how should we live?'

> In moral upbringing what one learns is not to behave in conformity with rules of conduct, but to see situations in a special light, as constituting reasons for acting; this perceptual capacity, once acquired, can be exercised in complex novel circumstances, not necessarily capable of being foreseen and legislated for by a codifier of the conduct required by virtue, however wise and thoughtful he might be.[3]

To be troubled by philosophical worries about how one should live is to be troubled by questions like the following: what are moral-ethical requirements? How do we know what they are? What justifies their status as such? In McDowell's view, moral-ethical requirements should be thought of as a certain species of reason for acting. When we are trying to explain why an agent acted as he did, for example, we will appeal (among other things) to his reason(s) for acting. And certain background conditions have to be satisfied for us to explain the agent's behaviour by appeal to specifically moral-ethical reasons. Most obviously, the agent would at least have to be sensitive to such reasons in the relevant situations.

(f) The agent's sensitivity to moral-ethical reasons for acting is a perceptual capacity.

This is one reason why, as we have seen, McDowell models moral-ethical properties on colour properties; they are both kinds of thing we experience. That the old lady needs help to get across the road is not the only thing that the suitably sensitive agent perceives; he also 'sees' that he ought to help her. The moral requirement is an objective feature of the situation. The reference to 'moral upbringing' in the quoted passage highlights a further claim which we have to expect anyway about any capacity that counts as experiential:

(g) The perceptual capacity relevant to moral-ethical reasons for acting is the exercise of second nature.

The abilities and opportunities constitutive of the agent's ability to act on specifically moral-ethical reasons presuppose education, learning to recognize and apply specifically moral-ethical concepts in relevant situations, and so on. Moreover,

(h) Moral-ethical reasons for acting are autonomous.

Again, this claim is simply a particular application of a general claim that is central to McDowell's attempt to secure the Default: the autonomy of the space of reasons. In the moral-ethical case, McDowell makes the point with a specific appeal to a Wittgensteinian metaphor. Reasons of this type operate as such within certain forms of life – those in which use of the relevant concepts is taught, for example. And the rationality of such reasons, their counting as the reasons they are, is not intelligible from a standpoint external to such ways of living.[4]

So what holds for knowledge- and value-problems holds also for moral-ethical questions. What is philosophically problematic about all these questions is, at root, what is philosophically problematic about our openness to the world in our experience, thought and talk of it: namely, how we are to make sense of second nature. If McDowell has indeed resolved that problem, then his suggested revision of our view of nature will take care of whatever seemed philosophically problematic about morality/ethics also.

12

Knowledge

McDowell makes various claims about the content of an experience, the way the world appears to its subject to be ('that things are thus and so'). The content of experience is conceptual; it can be the content of a judgement; it can be a state of the world. In each case, we are presented with a claim that captures a different facet of McDowell's attempt to secure the Default, to explain how it is possible for experience to manifest a two-way rational intentionality between subjects and the world. In this chapter, we shall examine a further claim about experiential content: that it can be the content of the subject's knowledge.[1] This will be so in cases where what appears to be the case to the subject in his experience is what he judges to be the case and what is in fact the case.

We have examined McDowell's account of judgement already, so we shall concentrate here on the other crucial aspect of this fourth claim about experience: the implications for epistemology of what we have called openness.[2] Openness has various facets, but there are two that we have focused on and which will be critical to what follows. When one is spontaneously receptive to the world in one's experience of it (sense one), what one experiences or thinks is what is the case (sense two). The former is 'receptive openness', the latter 'ontological openness'. The points to be made do not rest on the distinction, so we shall simply refer in what follows to 'receptive-ontological openness'.

McDowell's notion of receptive-ontological openness is expressed by him in various ways that have clear implications for our ability to know things about the world. 'Experience [is] openness to the layout of reality.'[3] We should 'take seriously the idea of an unmediated openness of the experiencing subject to "external" reality'.[4] 'When we are not misled by experience, we are directly confronted by a worldly state of affairs itself, not waited on by an intermediary that happens to tell the truth.'[5] On this view, it is worldly items – objects, properties, states of affairs, and so on – rather than any substitute which are presented in non-deceptive perceptual experience. This is, as we have seen, just part of what it means to say that the contents of experience do not 'fall short of' the facts.

Intentionality and epistemology

To suppose that the contents of experience only ever *do* fall short of the facts is problematic for various reasons, as we have seen. Throughout the book, we have been distinguishing issues about intentionality from epistemological issues in order to concentrate on the former. And the main problem with alternatives to receptive-ontological openness concerned intentionality. Unless experiences can be conceived of as being open to the world, in the sense of being ontologically dependent on it, so that their existence and identity depend on the existence and identity of the worldly objects they are about or directed on, experiences cannot be conceived of as being 'about' or 'directed on' the world at all. And if this is the case, as we discovered, we cannot retain our Default view that a relation of two-way rational intentionality exists between subjects and the world in their experience thought and talk.

Having examined the intentionality point, we may now look at another kind of problem that arises if we cannot find room for receptive-ontological openness in our conception of the relations that exist between subjects and the world: namely, scepticism about the world and other minds.[6] By scepticism, I mean in particular doubts about our ability to know whether or how the world exists either in whole or in part; doubts about our ability to know whether other minds exist or what they are thinking and experiencing. This clearly epistemological problem was raised briefly in chapter 1 with the crude story about how experience might be conceived of, and we should now return to it.

Scepticism, at least in its traditional forms, depends precisely on maintaining that subjects are not open to the world in their experience of it. Experience 'falls short' of the facts. Far from being ontologically dependent on the world for their existence and identity, experiences and thoughts are conceived of in this picture as being private to the subject, sets of entirely subjective episodes. They could exist just as they are whether or not the world or other minds existed, and however the world or other minds existed. That is why subjects of experience should doubt their ability to know the world or other minds. If experience, so conceived, puts subjects in touch with the world at all (the intentionality problem), it is certainly not such as to give them knowledge of it (the epistemology problem).

According to McDowell and the receptive-ontological openness conception he advocates, experience is not private or exclusively subjective. However, it is important to recognize that there is nothing in his argument which suggests that he denies a subjective *character* to experience. There is, he maintains, 'something it is like' to enjoy experiential access to the world;[7] indeed he maintains that 'nothing could be recognizable as a characterization of this domain of subjectivity if it did not accord a special status to the perspective of the subject.'[8] And he insists that the characterization of inner facts in terms of first-person seemings is 'the most conspicuous phenomenological fact there is'.[9]

If McDowell is right that intentionality requires receptive-ontological openness, then we are free to regard the sceptic's position as simply unintelligible because contradictory. For sceptics have to assume that at least some of their thoughts are intentional: namely, those expressing their doubts 'about' whatever they are doubting. Yet sceptics (at least of the traditional type with which we are concerned) must deny openness to generate the epistemology problem. So, if intentionality requires openness, sceptics would have to assume (even if only implicitly) what they must (explicitly) deny.

The argument could be resolved at this point and in this way, simply by reiterating the claims about intentionality that we have already examined. But since McDowell has specific things to say about the epistemological issues arising, we can set this response to one side for the moment and concentrate on them. The root of his views in this area is his interpretation of certain remarks Wittgenstein makes about criteria in *The Blue Book*. Correctly construed, these remarks are supposedly sufficient to make a case for openness about other minds.[10] Like the argument from intentionality just sketched, this case does not simply assume that scepticism is false or abhorrent; so it is free to draw anti-sceptical conclusions without begging the question. Indeed, if cogent, it would give us the 'intellectual right to shrug our shoulders at sceptical questions'.[11]

Criteria

In McDowell's view, non-deceptive perceptual experience discloses to its subject what is the case – 'facts', conceived as occupants of the world – and not any substitute. Thus, 'If [someone's] experience is in a suitable way the upshot of the fact that [*p*], then the fact itself can make it the case that he knows that [*p*].'[12] When someone believes truly that *p* via the kinds of experience in question, receptive-ontological openness claims that what he believes is what is the case. Thus openness has both ontological and epistemological dimensions. On the one hand, in the cases in question, there can be no ontological gap between the sort of thing someone believes and the sort of thing that is the case;[13] on the other hand, the content of such experiences is the content of the knowledge acquired thereby.[14] 'So since the world is everything that is the case . . . , there is no gap between thought, as such, and the world.'[15]

But what *are* 'the cases in question'? One set, according to McDowell, are those in which we experience behavioural criteria that fix the identity of 'inner processes'. A criterion of something is generally taken to be a way of telling that it is the case. But McDowell uses the term in the more specialized way made possible by Wittgenstein's discussion of criteria.[16] It will be useful to have some cases in mind, so consider the following:

- *A's angina:* This is Wittgenstein's own example. If medical science calls angina an inflammation caused by a particular bacillus and we discovered that bacillus in A's blood, we would have found a criterion of A's suffering from angina.
- *B's arson:* If we found B maliciously setting a house on fire with the intention of gaining financial reward, that would be experiencing a criterion of B's being guilty of arson.

Crispin Wright has argued that we should regard criteria as defeasible evidence in this particular sense: 'A claim made on the basis of satisfaction of its criteria can subsequently be jettisoned consistently with retention of the belief that criteria were indeed satisfied.'[17] Thus experiencing a criterion that *p* might warrant a claim to know that p; it might provide evidence in support of such a claim. But since it would always be compatible with p being false, it must fall short of either knowing that p or experiencing the fact that p. A two-way independence exists between experiencing a criterion that p and either knowing that p or experiencing the fact that p if criteria are regarded in this way: a kind of evidence that yields only defeasible support for the relevant claim.

That this seems to be the wrong way to account for the kind of criteria mentioned above may be brought out by considering Wittgenstein's *Blue Book* distinction between the 'two antithetical terms' criteria and symptoms.[18] Suppose that, in A's case, we had discovered not a particular bacillus but that A was suffering from an inflamed throat; or that, in B's case, we had found he was carrying a box of matches. We would then have found 'criteria', in the usual sense: evidence of how things are; 'ways of telling' that A is suffering from angina and B is guilty of arson. But there is a deep distinction in the nature of the support given by this evidence. For we can reject this conclusion while continuing to believe the evidence: A is not suffering from angina even though his throat really is indeed inflamed; B is not really guilty of arson even though he is carrying matches. They are 'symptoms', therefore, in Wittgenstein's usage.

Contrast this with the ways of telling that the *Blue Book* encourages us to reserve the term 'criteria' for – call them '*Blue Book* criteria': the presence of the bacillus in A; the fire-starting of B under the intention of gaining financial reward. Where *these* ways of telling are concerned, we cannot reject the conclusion while believing the evidence. If A has the bacillus, then A has angina, and that's all there is to it. It is because the presence of the bacillus is not 'defeasible evidence' of angina in the way that an inflamed throat is that it merits the specialized name '*Blue Book* criterion'. If we first advance a claim (e.g. that B is an arsonist) on the basis of satisfaction of its *Blue Book* criteria (e.g. we found B maliciously setting fire to a house in the hopes of financial reward), we cannot subsequently withdraw that claim consistently with continuing to believe that *Blue Book* criteria were satisfied – if such criteria were satisfied, B committed arson, and that is an end of it.

The same goes for other examples. Witnessing the final cessation of C's vital functions is experiencing a very specific 'way of telling' that C is dead; a *Blue Book* criterion. Its truth is not compatible with C's continuing to live. So it strikes a false note to describe the experience of *Blue Book* criteria as one in which we have 'evidence' or 'warrant' for beliefs that C is dead. In C's case, it just is to know that C is dead, to experience that fact.

Wright has objected that 'criteria would not be interestingly different from (public) truth-conditions if defeasibility was waived.'[19] It is not obvious why this would be problematic even if it were true. But it seems false. Criteria remain interestingly different from public truth-conditions in their defining role of being 'ways of telling'. It is logically possible that the truth conditions of an utterance be specifiable in a way that forever transcends our ability to tell whether or not the world is such that the utterance is true of it or not. Truth conditions of this sort are different from criteria because they are not 'ways of telling'.

It might be objected that *Blue Book* criteria are ways of telling whether something satisfies a certain concept where one's grounds are not obviously given by what is available to one in experience at all but by what Wittgenstein would have called the grammar of the relevant concepts. Wittgenstein seems to stress this point: 'To say "A man has angina if this bacillus is found in him" is a tautology or it is a loose way of stating the definition of "angina".'[20] This is true, but I do not think the overall objection is telling. If an experience gives me grounds for thinking that p where p is criterial for thinking that q, then it would seem odd to deny that it is that experience which gives me grounds for thinking that q. For example, I may be justified in believing that B maliciously set fire to the house because I saw him do so. And precisely because of those grammatical phenomena licensing use of the word, it is that same experience which gives me grounds for thinking that he is committing arson.

How do these remarks about *Blue Book* criteria connect with receptive-ontological openness? To return to the spatial metaphor, defeasible evidence like A's symptomatic inflamed throat and B's possession of matches 'falls short' of the facts – the fact that such evidence obtains is consistent with the falsity of the conclusions they are taken to support. Not so with *Blue Book* criteria. There is an indefeasible connection between the actual satisfaction of a *Blue Book* criterion (e.g. the presence of a particular bacillus) and knowledge of the particular state of affairs for which it is a 'way of telling' (e.g. the patient's angina). Experiences are 'ways of telling' that things are thus and so. If *Blue Book* criteria *are* satisfied in experience and we are not misled, what we observe is not evidence that gets us part way to what is the case; what we observe just *is* what is the case. So this particular 'way of telling' does not stop short of the facts. It may be said to 'reach' them in precisely the way that perceptual experiences must if they are to count as 'opening us to', or 'interpenetrating with', reality. What is manifest to the observer is the fact that things are thus and so, not some substitute.

So experiencing a *Blue Book* criterion is a potential support for receptive-ontological openness. When one is not deceived, so the claim goes, what one believes on the basis of criterial experience *is* what is the case. If, for example, it can be shown that experiencing the behaviour of others counts as experiencing such criteria for their 'inner' processes, then openness about other minds is correct. In the relevant cases, what we see in another's behaviour is *that* they are angry (happy, upset, calm, in pain, etc.) and not some substitute, some piece of defeasible evidence that gets us part way to that fact.

The main question to which these considerations direct us, then, is this: *is* experiencing the behaviour of others experiencing *Blue Book* criteria?

Other minds

Consider one such case of observing the behaviour of others: *D's pain*. We see D wince, writhe or grimace and hear him saying 'I am in pain'. In observing these kinds of behaviour, we may be said to be experiencing 'ways of telling' that D is in pain. But do these 'ways' count as *Blue Book* criteria or as symptoms?

It is worth noting certain features of cases involving *Blue Book* criteria. One reason why it seems correct to say that, in seeing B maliciously set fire to the house, I saw him committing arson is that an internal relation obtains, leaving no room for inference. It would be quite false to say that I infer that B is an arsonist when I see him maliciously set fire to a house – though it would be appropriate if my only evidence were B's possession of matches. Similarly, I might infer an eclipse from sudden darkness at noonday but not from seeing the moon pass directly between me and the sun.

Now McDowell is principally interested in cases involving the ascription of psychological predicates to other persons – as in the case of D's pain. And these cases seem quite different from those involving *Blue Book* criteria. Seeing D's writhing does not entail seeing him in pain; it is neither a necessary nor a sufficient condition for seeing him in pain; though one may come to that conclusion, it is not decisive; it may be undermined by further evidence and affected by circumstantial information; no obvious internal relations exist between D's writhing and D's being in pain.

If McDowell wants receptive-ontological openness to hold for the behavioural criteria by which we determine the existence and nature of 'inner processes' in others and thus make psychological ascriptions, he must show that those criteria are not defeasible. One way of doing so seems overly problematic – showing that they are relevantly similar to *Blue Book* criteria. McDowell offers another argument; a negative one this time.[21] If we make behavioural criteria defeasible, then they become inferential – a conclusion that we should avoid on pain of implausibility and a launch into scepticism.

But the conclusion scarcely seems to follow from the evidence. Suppose we agree that the relation between seeing D writhing and believing D is in pain is not internal and that it is not inferential. All that seems to follow is that we require another relation, not that the former be an indefeasible indication of the latter.

So the argument in favour of showing that behavioural criteria are indefeasible certainly needs supplementing. It might be supplemented by arguing that there is no conceivable alternative kind of relation that would be consistent with making behavioural criteria defeasible. But this seems incorrect. It is plausible to suppose that perceptions are instances of non-internal and non-inferential relations – 'I see D writhing around' may be a good answer to the question 'how do you know D is in pain?'; I am not then inferring that D is in pain, but nor am I committed to the position that what I have said is decisive, provides absolute confirmation of my belief, or is unrevisable. So this alternative is, of course, consistent with the claim that behavioural criteria are defeasible. I claim D is in pain on the basis of satisfaction of certain criteria – seeing his writhing; and when I find that my claim is false, that he was pretending, I retain my belief that criteria were satisfied.

McDowell makes one attempt to rule out this possibility, appealing to Wittgenstein's example of ways of telling that it is raining – when the barometer falls; when we have certain sensations of wet and cold, and so on.[22] The problem set by the passage is what to say when we are deceived. According to McDowell, it is tempting but false to interpret Wittgenstein as claiming that, in such cases, criteria for rain are satisfied, although no rain is falling: 'the fact is not that criteria for rain are satisfied but that they *appear* to be satisfied.'[23] But this seems false. Suppose someone were to ask 'why do you say it will rain?' This is precisely a case in which it seems perfectly appropriate to answer 'because the barometer says so.' And when I find that my claim 'It is raining' is false, and the barometer is faulty, I retain my belief that it was precisely *criteria* which were satisfied, and not the *appearance* of criteria. To suppose that the barometer was *appearing* to tell me that it would rain is to be describing a very different case – one in which it might very well have been accurate but I misread it, for example.

For these various reasons, McDowell's positive argument for openness about other minds seems problematic. If the argument is to be made using ways of telling, those ways must not be of a kind that could count as defeasible evidence. Some ways of telling are indeed not defeasible evidence – *Blue Book* criteria. But nothing has been said to rule out the possibility that the ways of telling with which McDowell is concerned are defeasible – those behavioural signs on the basis of which we make psychological predications. (Whether or not we count such ways of telling as evidence seems more a matter of taste.)

Insofar as criteria are to be regarded as defeasible evidence, experiencing them need not 'open the layout of reality' to the subject – so much is agreed. And insofar as criteria are *not* to be regarded as defeasible evidence, for all McDowell shows, they do not concern the kind of facts relevant to openness about others.

Illusion

We may broaden the issue. A familiar way of casting doubt on claims like receptive-ontological openness is to adapt the argument from illusion. There are cases in which, if one were to believe that p (e.g. that a person was in pain) because of experiencing criteria that p (e.g. seeing the person's writhing), one would be misled. What we experience in such cases is indistinguishable from what we experience in non-deceptive cases. So experiencing criteria cannot be having a way of telling that p, but only ever having a way of telling that p appears to be the case.

McDowell ridicules this position as dependent on an unwarranted 'highest common factor' approach to experience.[24] On this approach, one simply assumes that 'experience' is what veridical and non-veridical cases have in common; to account for the difference, one appeals to something extra, an add-on that is not essential to any experience being the experience it is – that in the veridical case, the way things appear is the way they are.

The 'highest common factor' approach is tempting if one is cautious; it enables one to draw in one's horns and remain with what is safe. Experiencing the criterion (e.g. seeing the writhing) gets us to the position of justifiably believing 'the person appears to be in pain' but not all the way to justifiably believing 'that person is in pain'. It is safe because, should the case be deceptive, the belief would still be true. McDowell offers an alternative, 'disjunctive', conception.[25] When things appear to be thus and so to a subject, we should distinguish between cases in which those appearances are just that, 'mere' appearances, and cases in which what the subject perceives is what is the case. McDowell writes:

> suppose we say – not at all unnaturally – that an appearance that such-and-such is the case can be *either* a mere appearance *or* the fact that such-and-such is the case making itself perceptually manifest to someone. As before, the object of experience in the deceptive cases is a mere appearance. But we are not to accept that in the non-deceptive cases too the object of experience is a mere appearance, and hence something that falls short of the fact itself. On the contrary, the appearance that is presented to one in those cases is a matter of the fact itself being disclosed to the experiencer.[26]

Given this possibility, 'what we experience' is *not* indistinguishable in deceptive and non-deceptive cases. We may separate 'conceptually' or 'notionally' those cases where 'the object of experience' is 'a mere appearance' that *p* from cases in which 'the object of experience' is a 'manifestation' of 'the fact' that *p*.[27] In the latter case, the facts themselves are present to the mind; in the former case, mere appearances are present to the mind. In neither case can they be conceived as mediating between subject and world. Appearances must either be manifestations or non-mediating mere appearances; in neither case is there some representative which substitutes for a fact present to the mind.

But it is hard to see why this disjunctive conception should trouble McDowell's opponent. It is of course true that deceptive and non-deceptive cases can be distinguished 'conceptually' or 'notionally' – how else could we have a *use* for the distinction? But much more needs to be shown if the version of the argument from illusion is not to go through: namely, that the cases are distinguishable 'experientially' or 'phenomenologically'. For what we are interested in is precisely what *experiencing criteria* tells us – does it tell us that *p* or merely that *p* appears to be the case? It is of no help to us here that we have a use for the distinction between deception and non-deception. If we cannot tell when we are being deceived, we cannot tell that *p*, only that *p* appears to be the case.

It is important to distinguish this objection from one that McDowell is able easily to shrug off. He discusses the claim that the disjunctive conception fails to show that the subject is able to make a non-question-begging demonstration from a neutrally available standing point that what he takes himself to be experiencing is indeed the fact that p made manifest.[28] But this heads off in entirely the wrong direction. What the disjunctive conception needs to show and does not is that, when a person has a fact made manifest to him in experience, he is able to tell that this is so. It is precisely the point of experiences deemed 'criterial' that they give one the ability to tell.

Furthermore, McDowell's use of the disjunctive conception seems to trade on a crucial ambiguity. 'What we experience' may mean 'how things appear to us to be' or 'what it is given us to experience'. It is true that the subject may be entitled to distinguish deceptive and non-deceptive cases in the latter sense.[29] But McDowell's position requires that the subject's experience entitle him to distinguish cases in the former sense. And, of course, no such entitlement *is* offered from within the perspective of how things appear to the experiencing subject – that is precisely the condition for the possibility of deceptive cases. As McDowell accepts, a 'subject of experience' is such that, in any case, 'what it is like to enjoy access or apparent access' is the same.[30]

McDowell needs to undermine the view that, because we cannot tell deceptive and non-deceptive cases apart, what we experience in either case is an 'appearance'. Otherwise, *pace* receptive-ontological openness, our experiential intake always falls short of the facts. It is precisely acceptance of this claim that, in McDowell's view, makes traditional epistemology vulnerable to the threat of scepticism. For it places what he calls an 'interface' between the experiencing subject and reality – all the subject can experience are certain kinds of appearance, and those appearances may or may not be true to the facts. McDowell writes:

> Am I suggesting that the disjunctive conception of appearances precludes the idea that experience mediates between subject and world? It depends on what you mean by 'mediate'. If experience is conceived in terms of openness to the world, it will not be appropriate to picture it as an interface. (I am sceptical whether such a conception of experience as anything but an interface is available within the dominant contemporary philosophy of mind.)[31]

The disjunctive conception proposes that a subject's best theory of his current perceptual standing (the appearance that such and such is the case) is that it is *either* a mere appearance *or* the fact that such and such is the case making itself perceptually manifest. But no opponent of receptive-ontological openness, and particularly no sceptic, need deny this. Their conclusion is only that, in every case, one must suspend judgement as to *which*. McDowell's argument seems to lack the power to move one either way: experiencing a criterion provides no ground for *insisting* that either option is in fact true.

To summarize. McDowell has a variety of ways available to him in which to respond to the sceptic. The main way is to appeal to the claims about intentionality on which the earlier parts of this book have focused. If two-way rational intentionality depends on a claim that the sceptic is committed to denying – i.e. receptive-ontological openness – then so much the worse for the sceptic. A different kind of response explores the impact of an interpretation of a certain variety of criteria (those Wittgenstein described in *The Blue Book*) on scepticism about other minds. The intention is to provide a self-sufficient case for openness about other minds, one that does not depend on the arguments from intentionality.

McDowell is correct to characterize the kind of criteria Wittgenstein describes as indefeasible. This makes them potentially supportive of his self-sufficient case for openness about other minds. But, for all McDowell shows, *Blue Book* criteria are not of the type invoked on the occasions that are in question. Hence this specific way of motivating openness about other minds is not sufficiently supported by McDowell's Wittgenstein-inspired account of criteria. Moreover, this specific way of motivating openness is not sufficiently protected against versions of the argument from illusion.

13

Value

McDowell is a realist about value, but of a sophisticated or quali-fied sort.[1] And the subtlety of his position depends on its appeal to second nature, to those rational-conceptual capacities that subjects and agents naturally have, but because they naturally acquire them rather than because they are naturally born with them. It will ease exposition of McDowell's claims in this area if we first summarize his overall position.

Values as dispositional properties

To say that McDowell is a realist about value is to say among other things that, in his view, our judgements concerning ethical and aes-thetic matters (these are his central examples) can be true or false. Perceptual experience is the correct model for understanding how this can be so; how values can be as the realist construes them. For the truth or falsity of our value judgements is partly dependent, as in the experiential case, on the identity and existence of the ethical and aesthetic properties they are about or directed on. And these ethical and aesthetic properties are objective: they really exist in the world and are not projected there by the person judging.

There are important differences in the class of properties that count as objective. Moral and aesthetic properties are of the sort that are not fully describable or intelligible without reference to the effect they have on subjects of experience and agents. In that sense, they are more like the colour- or taste-properties that an object might have than like those shape- or size-properties it has. All these properties are objective; but whereas shape- and size-properties are fully describable and intelligible independently of our sensitivity to them, colours, tastes and values are not.

This is because colours, tastes and values are a particular kind of objective property: they are dispositions of objects to appear a certain way to suitably sensitive observers in suitable conditions. An object's having the colour-property 'red', for example, just is its being such as to look red given these circumstances. Given the same circumstances, an object's having the aesthetic value 'beautiful' just is its being such as to appear beautiful, and a person's having the ethical value 'kind' just is his being such as to appear kind. So the existence of such properties depends partly on the existence of beings with the capacity to observe them and pick them out. Being a suitably sensitive observer of aesthetic or ethical properties depends on the acquisition and exercise of those rational-conceptual capacities that count as the second nature of certain – i.e. human – beings. So the existence of ethical and aesthetic proper-ties depends partly on the existence and exercise of second nature.

Perceptual awareness of colour- and taste-properties models the role of reason in evaluative thinking. But this is only an analogy and should not be pressed too far. If an object is red, and a subject of experience judges it to be so, we would not claim that the judge-ment is merited by the object's having that property; at best, the judgement is something which is drawn out of the subject by the object's having that property. Value-properties are quite different in this respect: the judgement that an object is beautiful or that a person is kind is merited by the properties these items have.

Again, if an object is red, we would not expect controversy about whether it is indeed red, or about whether, if it is red, the object counts as having a genuine colour-property. If an object is beauti-ful or a person just, on the other hand, it is possible and likely that debate will arise over whether this is indeed the case, or over whether, even if it is the case, the object or the person counts thereby as having a genuine aesthetic or ethical property.

Varieties of property

On one view of objectivity, what is objectively there in the world is the kind of thing that physics tells us is there. And it is tempting to suppose that this is to think of the world as fully describable in terms of objects, properties, events, and so on, that are intelligible quite independently of their effects on sensitive or sapient beings. This is clearly a view of objectivity that McDowell must reject, for it has no place for the objectivity of (ethical or aesthetic) values. If they can be counted as existing at all in this picture, they cannot be regarded as doing so objectively. So debate on the issue turns on the status of properties that are not intelligible independently of sentient and sapient responses to them. Are there such properties? Are they in the world? Are they *objectively* in the world?

Elucidation of the precise claims to which McDowell is committed and of the debate to which they give rise will be greatly helped if we have certain defined terms at our disposal. So, first, consider a distinction between properties that we may call 'intrinsic' and 'relational'. Let us say that relational properties, like being married or being one mile from Berlin, imply the actual co-existence of the item with that property with the existence of another item. If you were the only human being in the world, you could not be married; if Berlin did not exist, nothing could have the property of being one mile from it. Intrinsic properties do not imply such co-existence. A triangle has the property that its angles add up to 180 degrees; nothing and no one else need exist for that to be the case.

'Dispositional' properties differ from their non-dispositional counterparts in their conditional aspect: they imply what relations *would* exist if something else *were* to exist. If we think colours are dispositions, for example, that is presumably because we think coloured objects have the property of being disposed to give rise to experiences of redness in suitably sensitive observers in suitable circumstances. Because dispositional properties are conditional in this way, they need not be relational: they do not imply the actual existence of any other thing. This pen does not stop being red when the light is turned off or when no one is actually looking at it.

'Sensory' properties are properties that imply both actual co-existence with certain sensitive beings, and the existence of a certain relation with those beings on the condition that they are suitably situated – namely, that they would cause a particular kind of sensory state in those beings if they were so situated. Thus sensory properties are both relational and dispositional. Non-sensory properties may be defined by contrast as all those that are not sensory – that is, all properties that are either non-relational or non-dispositional, and all properties that are relational and dispositional but either do not imply actual co-existence with certain sensitive beings, or do not imply that a particular kind of sensory state would be caused in those beings if suitably situated. We should not confuse the sensory/non-sensory distinction with a distinction between sensible or observable properties and those that are not sensible or observable. A sensitive being may be sensible of, or observe, a property even though the existence of that property implies the existence of neither that being nor that state.

Given these definitions, many coarse or fine ways of assembling properties are made available. There are three assemblies crucial to what follows; they do not, of course, exhaust those available.

First, there are properties that are non-sensory, intrinsic and non-dispositional. These are properties like the extensive magnitude, shape and size of physical objects. They are located in the object and need have nothing to do with anything else.

Second, there are properties that are sensory, relational and dispositional. These are properties like colours, in McDowell's view of what colours are. They are powers to affect the sensory experience of suitably sensitive subjects and they are located in the object.

Third, there are properties that are non-sensory, relational and dispositional. These are properties like magnetism and solubility. They are powers to affect other objects but need have nothing to do with the sensory experience of suitably sensitive subjects.

These three assemblies map onto one way of conceiving the distinction between so-called 'primary', 'secondary' and 'tertiary qualities'. The main point is that values, in McDowell's view, are to be located by analogy with the secondary level; they are quasi-sensory, being 'powers' that have essentially to do with suitably sensitive (i.e. rational-conceptual) creatures.[2]

Objectivity and realism

Values are objective. But they are objective in a qualified sense in McDowell's view. The point rests on a crucial distinction between, on the one hand, what it takes to think of anything as being objective, and, on the other hand, what it takes for something to be objective.

In McDowell's view, the possibility of objective thought is dependent on the existence of the primary properties of space-occupying matter and on our ability to distinguish between properties that are mind-dependent and mind-independent.[3] For being able to think objectively requires that one have a use for the distinction between oneself and one's states, on the one hand, and something not oneself, or a state of oneself, of which one is thinking or having experiences, on the other.[4] And having a use for this distinction depends on being able to think of objects as existing unperceived, as distinct from any particular experience of them, and as capable of existing independently of any experience of them. Being able to think of objects in this way requires that objects exist with primary qualities and that we be suitably equipped to experience them.

This view qualifies the objectivity of values in the following way. If the world were constructed entirely out of the kind of properties which values are, secondary qualities, we would be incapable of thinking objectively about it. And since the objectivity of such qualities is a dispositional matter, one that precisely depends on our being able to think objectively about them, those properties would not even be objective in such a world. Given the distinction between what is objective and what is necessary to think objectively, together with the existence of primary properties, however, McDowell can claim the following: that objective thought is possible, and that the kind of property which a value is, a secondary quality, is objective.

The objectivity of ethical and aesthetic values enables McDowell to take up a realist construal of ethical and aesthetic judgement. Ethical and aesthetic beliefs and judgements can be true or false. Ethical and aesthetic properties really exist in the world. These values are things to which moral agents and aesthetic judges can be sensitive or insensitive. These values are really there to be discovered; they are not projected onto the world, willed into existence or constituted by emotional reactions. They are distinct from discrete affective experiences that individuals may or may not have when confronted with them. They make a real difference to the situations or individuals that possess or lack them. Values are not objective in the sense in which primary qualities are objective. For they are not fully describable without essential reference to the effect they have on suitably sensitive beings; we cannot adequately understand what it is for an object or person or action to have a value without appeal to its dispositions to give rise to certain experiences, thoughts or judgements in suitably sensitive subjects. Values remain objective, however. For they are fully describable without essential reference to any effect they may have on a particular occasion to a particular sentient being; we can adequately understand what it is for an object or person or action to have a value without appeal to any particular exercise of a subject's sensitivity to that value, to any particular experience, thought or judgement concerning it or to which it gives rise.

Colours

We can obtain a better grasp on these matters and specifically on McDowell's account of value by thinking about distinctions between various views about colour. Here, we can ask 'are (physical) objects coloured?'; and, if so, 'what is the nature of colour properties?' We can distinguish, fairly crudely, between four relevant positions on these issues.

Dispositionalists (like McDowell) claim that objects are coloured, and that the nature of this property is a disposition to produce certain perceptual states (if the object is red, it has the property of being disposed to look red in suitable circumstances). So colour is a relational and sensory property – i.e. secondary. Value properties are of this sort.

Physicalists claim that objects are coloured, and that the nature of this property is physical, relational, but non-sensory (if the object is red, it has the property of selectively reflecting incident light at certain wavelengths, etc.). So colour is a relational but non-sensory property – i.e. tertiary.

McDowell rejects this claim on the grounds that it misdescribes the phenomenology of colour vision, what it is like to experience coloured objects.[5] In his view, what a colour *is* is deeply responsive to a description of how it *looks*. And colours do not look the way they should look if the physicalist were right; it is not as something differentially responsive to certain wavelengths of light that we see red objects, for example.

Strong objectivists claim that objects are coloured, and that the nature of this property is intrinsic. If the object is red, that property grounds its disposition to look red; just as if an object is fragile, its molecular structure is the ground of its disposition to shatter when struck (though strong objectivists are free to affirm or deny that colours are microphysical; they may or may not be 'transparent' under conditions of normal observation). So, on this view, colour is an intrinsic, non-relational, non-sensory property – i.e. primary.

Again, McDowell takes the vital place of phenomenology to count against this claim. Colours, in his view, do not look the way they would have to look were they to be as the strong objectivist describes them: the grounds of dispositions.

Finally, *error theorists* like J. L. Mackie claim that objects are not coloured; for that would be to say that colours are 'in' objects, and colour is no more in the object which causes one's colour-experiences than pain is in the pin which causes one's pain sensations. Thus phenomenology is charged with error. Objects do have the power to produce experiences in us of colour; but these powers in the object are not colours; and since 'what it is like' to have such experiences is to experience those powers as colours, 'what it is like' is erroneous.[6]

In Mackie's view, the same holds for ethical value. We gain a clearer sense of McDowell's position on ethics and ethical evaluation by comparing and contrasting it with that of Mackie, so that is what we shall examine in a moment.

McDowell's treatment of colour plays an important role in his account of value, but it should not be exaggerated. The extent to which McDowell's position is dependent on the case of colour is appreciable if we distinguish his argument into two steps. First, we should give a dispositional account of colour. Colour is a secondary quality. That is to say: colour is an objective property with a subjective character, something that really exists in the world but whose existence is not intelligible independently of its effect on suitably sensitive observers.[7] Second, we should understand ethical and aesthetic value by analogy with colour. So, if it should turn out that colour is not a secondary quality, or cannot be given a dispositional account, we might still understand value in the way McDowell desires: that is, by analogy with some other quality that *does* count as a dispositional and secondary quality.

The point can be put in another way. We can understand McDowell as saying the following: 'Why shouldn't we understand value as we understand colour – in the world, though internally related to the exercise of sensibility?' If we respond: 'because that is not how colour works', that does not undermine McDowell's overall claim about value. Even if colour does not work that way, other things might, and they would provide an effective model for value. On the other hand, if we respond 'because values and value-sensitivity are not like colours and colour-sensitivity, thus conceived', that would be an effective response.

Consequently, if our goal is to understand McDowell on value, we need not worry overmuch whether his account of colour is correct. What matters is whether he is right to think of values as secondary qualities, properties that are objective in a qualified sense. It is to that question we now turn, building on the groundwork laid by distinguishing types and assemblies of objective properties.

Moral realism

To focus on the specifically ethical applications of McDowell's views on value and evaluative thinking, it will help to consider some conceptual geography; we gain a fix on McDowell's own position by relating it to some well-known alternatives.[8] Consider four claims that, as we have seen, McDowell holds:

  (i)   Ethical beliefs and judgements can be true or false.
 (ii)   Ethical properties (values) exist.
(iii)   Ethical properties are things to which moral agents can be sensitive or insensitive.
(iv)   Ethical properties are objective.

Emotivists deny (i) and (iv). In their view, moral judgements are merely expressions of emotion, so they cannot be either right or wrong, true or false. We falsely assume that we can take sentences like 'stealing is wrong' and ask 'is it true that *p*?' But we cannot. For what that sentence actually means, all that its expressive content amounts to when phrased perspicuously, is something like 'boo to stealing'.

Prescriptivists also deny (i) and (iv). But, contrary to the emotivists, they do not hold that moral judgements are merely expressions of emotion. In their view, all ethics amounts to, or should amount to, is conceptual analysis, a set of accounts of the meaning of statements. It is not, for instance, factual analysis. Moral beliefs are not really assessable as being true or false; they are only to be investigated as being meaningful or meaningless. They are meaningful just in case they have applications to and within given forms of life.

J. L. Mackie denied (i), (ii) and (iv).[9] Contrary to the prescriptivists, he claimed that ethics is beholden to factual analysis. For example, he argued that if ethics claims there are values and we can know what they are, our ontology and epistemology had better find a place for them. In his view, however, our ontology and epistemology cannot find such a place. Hence (ii) and (iv) are false. There is nothing for our moral judgements to be about, no value, for example, that makes this action or person or event or institution or form of life either right or wrong, good or bad. If this is so, it follows that (i) is false. For if there is nothing for our moral judgements to be about, there is nothing in virtue of which they can be said to be true or false or known.

One way to gain entry to McDowell's specifically ethical views is to examine his response to these arguments. In his view, as we shall see, (i)–(iv) can be recaptured once we conceive adequately of the objective and of the rational-conceptual capacities exercised in second nature. For it is in engaging with the world in the way that second nature makes possible that we recognize ethical values for the objective, secondary properties that they are.

Phenomenology

In McDowell's view, values occur in our evaluative thought as features of reality. Ordinary evaluative thought 'presents itself as a matter of sensitivity to aspects of the world'.[10] This is a phenomenological claim; it is about what it is like for us to apprehend values, whether as ethical or aesthetic properties, whether as properties of objects, actions, people or situations. Ethical or aesthetic experience 'typically presents itself, at least in part, as a confrontation with value; an awareness of value as something residing in an object and available to be encountered'.[11] This is not a point of disagreement with Mackie; indeed, it is precisely because Mackie thinks that our evaluative thought does unquestionably present values as being aspects of the world that he charges phenomenology with error. The way in which we seem not to be able to help experiencing the world is, in Mackie's view, a way that cannot help but represent the world falsely.

McDowell argues that a perceptual model helpfully represents our evaluative thought, and that this follows from the phenomenological claim.[12] 'Given that Mackie is right about the phenomenology of value, an attempt to accept the appearances makes it virtually irresistible to appeal to a perceptual model.'[13] But perceptual experience is only ever meant to be a model for evaluative thinking, and not an exact one at that. Since the apprehension of value is an intellectual rather than a sensory capacity, the perceptual awareness of qualities can only mirror the role of reason in evaluative thinking.[14] Mackie has no objection on this score.

In Mackie's view, our evaluative thinking presents our awareness of value like experience presents our awareness of primary qualities. And this is the heart of the problem. McDowell agrees with Mackie on the definition of primary qualities. They are perceptible qualities of objects that are causally efficacious and intelligible independent of human sensibility, and they include properties like solidity, number, mobility, shape and extension. And he agrees that, if the phenomenology of evaluative thought really does present our awareness of value as an awareness of properties like these, then so much the worse for that phenomenology and for the evaluative thinking it describes. The reasons they give for this conclusion differ, however, and in ways that indicate McDowell's positive views.

Mackie argues that, if what it is like for us to be presented with value is what it is like for us to be presented with primary properties, then the phenomenology can be assessed by a simple empirical test. Are there, in fact, items in the world which both count as values and have the properties of primary qualities – perceptibility; causal efficacy; intelligibility independent of human sensibility? There are not. Moreover, our ontology and epistemology could not permit such items. There are no such features of the world, and no forms of awareness that could provide us with experience of them. Hence our evaluative thinking is empirically false; our phenomenology is in error.

McDowell offers different grounds for the claim that our phenomenology would be at fault if it presented our evaluative thinking as awareness of primary qualities. He need not hold the controversial view that an empirical test could reveal our phenomenology to be false, for he argues instead that there would simply be a contradiction in a phenomenology of this type. Primary qualities are properties that are intelligible independently of human sensibility. It is an essential feature of values, on the other hand, that they elicit (and merit) various cognitive and conative states from those who are aware of them. So they could not be intelligible independently of the sensibility required for such states. This claim will become clearer in a moment, once we have examined the positive aspect of McDowell's proposals.

Secondary qualities

Rather than presenting us with properties that are characteristic of primary qualities, in McDowell's view, the phenomenology of evaluative thinking presents us with values as if they were secondary qualities. McDowell and Mackie agree on the kinds of thing that count as secondary qualities – colours and tastes, for example. But they disagree on what defines them as such.

In Mackie's view, they are qualities the perception of which is by definition erroneous. The mind cannot help perceiving colours and tastes as if they were primary qualities. This is an error which the empirical test reveals: there is no feature of the world that both is a colour and has the property of being intelligible independently of certain kinds of subjective sensibility (e.g. human kinds); there is no form of awareness that could give us experience of such features of the world if they did exist. The error is projective at its root; the mind seemingly cannot helping projecting primary attributes onto secondary qualities.

By contrast, McDowell regards secondary qualities as non-erroneous dispositions of objects to appear a certain way perceptually. Colours are secondary qualities, for example, on the following grounds. The property of being some colour is to be identified with the disposition to cause in (normal) perceivers in (standard) circumstances visual experiences of a certain kind. So an object's having the property of being red, for example, 'is understood as something that obtains in virtue of the object's being such as (in certain circumstances) to look, precisely, red'.[15] More precisely, 'A secondary quality is a property the ascription of which to an object is not adequately understood except as true, if it is true, in virtue of the object's disposition to present a certain sort of perceptual appearance; specifically, an appearance characterizable by using a word for the property itself to say how the object perceptually appears.'[16] If this is correct, of course, then 'what it is to be, say, red is not adequately conceived independently of the idea of looking red.'[17] Hence it is not intelligible independently of certain kinds of (e.g. human) sensibility: 'A subjective property, in the relevant sense, is one such that no adequate conception of what it is for a thing to possess it is available except in terms of how the thing would, in suitable circumstances, affect a subject – a sentient being.'[18]

Mackie could not accept that our evaluative thinking presents our awareness of value like our awareness of secondary qualities, for, given his definition of such qualities, the phenomenology would be false by virtue of definition. Whereas, in his view, the phenomenology is empirically false. McDowell, on the other hand, is free to assert that this is indeed how we are aware of value. And this pays dividends by providing support for claims (i)–(iv) above.

For we may assert that, like colours, values exist in a real and objective way; like colours, they are properties to which suitably educated concept-users can be sensitive or insensitive; and like colour judgements, value judgements can be true or false. This can be maintained without falling into the trap of supposing values are like primary qualities. Like colours, again, they are not intelligible from a standpoint independent of certain (e.g. human) kinds of sensitivity. What it is for something to have a value cannot be adequately understood 'otherwise than in terms of dispositions to give rise to subjective states'.[19]

So the debate centres on whether or not the phenomenology of our evaluative thought is vindicated. Mackie thinks it is not: it presents values as like primary qualities, and they are not. McDowell thinks it is: it presents values as like secondary qualities, and they are.

This puts matters a little too simply, of course, for both agree that there are crucial disanalogies between values and secondary qualities. For Mackie, the kinds of experience associated with secondary qualities are misleading or erroneous by definition, whereas it is by empirical investigation that evaluative thought is shown to be so. McDowell places the distinction elsewhere, as we have seen. He emphasizes the fact that value judgements (like 'that is beautiful', 'he is just') are contentious in a way that secondary quality judgements (like judging 'that is red') are not, and that values merit the appropriate attitudes in suitably sensitive observers whereas secondary qualities merely elicit them, draw them out.[20]

Value judgements

It follows from the debate we have rehearsed that McDowell and Mackie would provide different answers to the question 'What is it for something to have value?' Mackie famously called 'queer' the kind of properties something would have to have to count as a value.[21] For those properties must ground the 'because' in sentences like 'That is wrong *because* it is deliberately cruel.' And, given his understanding of the phenomenology of evaluative thinking and the results of the empirical test he applies as a consequence, it is not surprising that he asks, rhetorically, 'just what *in the world* is signified by this because?'[22] In McDowell's account, for something (e.g. actions, situations, persons, institutions) to have value, it must be internally related to some exercise of (e.g. human) sensibility. And there need be nothing queer about this sensibility. If it is the outcome of a human being's education into rational-conceptual capacities, for example, it is to be found occurring quite naturally in the natural world.[23]

Mackie and McDowell agree that our ordinary moral judgements aim at objective values. There is an implicit claim to objectivity in the meaning of moral terms and in moral discourse. They contain, for example, an objectively prescriptive element – reasons for acting regardless of one's wants. They disagree, of course, on whether there are in fact such values for our moral judgements to aim at. In Mackie's opinion, there is only a misleading phenomenology. If there *were* such values, they would be utterly different, and our ways of knowing about them would be utterly different, from anything else in the universe. And since our ordinary moral judgements aim at objective values, they involve an error. In McDowell's view, such values do exist for our judgements to aim at. They are objective in the qualified sense that colours are.

> Secondary-quality experience presents itself as perceptual awareness of properties genuinely possessed by the objects that confront one. And there is no general obstacle to taking that appearance at face value. An object's being such as to look red is independent of its actually looking red to anyone on any particular occasion; so, notwithstanding the conceptual connection between being red and being experienced as red, an experience of something as red can count as a case of being presented with a property that is there anyway – there independently of the experience itself.[24]

Just as an object's having the colour red is its being such as to look red to a suitably sentient observer, so a person's being just is their being such as to appear just to a suitably sapient observer. And just as an object continues to be red (if it is) even though it may not look red to some particular person on some occasion (the lighting may be bad; the observer may be colour-blind), so a person continues to be just (if he is) even though he may not seem so to some particular person on some occasion (the context may make his action difficult to interpret; the observer may lack the ability to discriminate character sufficiently subtly). Values are not *strongly* objective as strong objectivists think colours are. If values were strongly objective, then a person's being just would be his having properties that ground the fact that they are such as to appear just to suitably sapient observers. For on this view, values turn out to be primary qualities; their identity and existence would not depend on the experiences or judgements to which they gave rise. And, in McDowell's view, Mackie was quite correct to deny that this could be the case. Nothing 'in the world' corresponds to values conceived in this way.

The question then arises for McDowell of how we know what objective values there are, and how they relate to our judgements. (For Mackie, of course, the question does not arise; there are no such things to know about or relate to.) His answer, not surprisingly, is a specific application of the general case that we have examined in relation to naturalism. We develop our abilities to engage in rational-conceptual ways with the world and with others, and in so doing acquire the concepts necessary to offering case-by-case explanations of human behaviour. In this way, we establish that some human behaviour is a response to things that are really valuable; show what makes these things valuable; explain these responses as rationally grounded in awareness of value; and thus gain knowledge of value.[25] McDowell uses the example of fear to make the point about value: 'we make sense of fear by seeing it as a response to objects that *merit* such a response. . . . For an object to merit fear just is for it to be fearful.'[26] McDowell takes his views to point towards what he calls 'uncodifiability'.[27] 'We need a conception of rationality in evaluation that will cohere with the possibility that particular cases may stubbornly resist capture in any general net.'[28]

Conclusion

If we could achieve a firm hold on a naturalism of second nature, a hold that could not be shaken by any temptation to lapse back into ordinary philosophical worries about how to place minds in the world, that would not be to have produced a bit of constructive philosophy . . . . In Wittgenstein's poignant phrase, it would be to have achieved 'the discovery that gives philosophy peace'.

McDowell, Mind and World[1]

In this passage, McDowell clearly signals what he takes to be the goal of his inquiries. To judge whether he has achieved it requires knowing what is meant by 'giving philosophy peace'. Wittgenstein's phrase, which McDowell has conflated here, occurs in a context that makes it ambiguous on the crucial point: 'The real discovery is the one that makes me capable of stopping doing philosophy when I want to. – The one that gives philosophy peace, so that it is no longer tormented by questions which bring *itself* into question.'[2] Depending on whether we stress the first sentence or the second, we obtain significantly different senses of what is to be achieved; what it means for philosophy to be at peace. On the first interpretation, it is for us to stop philosophizing altogether; on the second, it is to stop philosophizing about philosophy.[3] So 'the real discovery' might be one of two things: something that makes philosophy illegitimate and rules out all ways of practising it; or something that legitimizes philosophy, ruling out misguided ways of engaging in it in favour of correct ways. Wittgenstein himself probably took the second view.[4] But it is not always clear which interpretation best captures the goal McDowell sets himself. He argues that we are caught in a web of our own making and that we have to escape from it. But is it philosophy itself that we will have shaken off when successful, or just particular ways of doing philosophy? Certainly McDowell offers reasons to reject specific ways of engaging in philosophy: those he calls 'substantive' and 'constructive', for example.[5] These kinds of philosophy are particularly problematic because they ensnare their advocates in fruitless self-questioning. But this does not imply that McDowell regards other ways as above suspicion.[6] Indeed, he implies on occasion that the goal is to be rid of philosophy *simpliciter*.[7] We should attain 'a frame of mind in which we no longer seem to be faced with problems that call on philosophy'.[8] The goal, in other words, is not to set philosophy straight and on the right tracks, but to take the tracks away and show that it has nowhere to go.

We have examined the steps by which McDowell hopes to achieve his aims; it may help to recall the main steps. We should be naturalists. Naturalism forces us to regard our second nature as part of nature, and that includes our capacity to recognize and live within the autonomous space of reasons. This incorporating move forces us to revise our current view of nature. Once this view is revised, it is shown to express the Default. We can appreciate the fact that our relationship to the world in experience, thought and talk is one of openness. Or in another phrase that McDowell uses, 'the world is where a human being lives, where she is at home.'[9] So the proposed revision of our conception of nature puts us 'at home' in the world and puts philosophy 'at peace'. These are the goals McDowell seeks to achieve.

It can seem that these effects – putting us at home and putting philosophy at peace – are similar or even the same. For being 'at home' often suggests being comfortable, at ease, relaxed, calm, free from anxiety; in other words, 'at peace'. But if these states often accompany being at home, they are not identical with that condition. Someone who is heavily sedated, for example, will be comfortable, at ease, and so on, but not at home. If one is at home, one is secure, composed, confident, sure. Moreover, the person who is at home has acquired certain powers which he may exercise in his situation, given the opportunity. The aspect of acquisition is plain: when we say of someone that he is at home, we mean he is accustomed or used to things, familiar with them; he is experienced in certain ways. And the role of powers or capacities is clear when we note that describing someone as 'at home' is to say that he is in control, skilled, knowledgeable, proficient.

So if revised nature shows us to be at home in the world, it does not imply that we are at peace with it. It implies that we are related to the world in ways that reveal a preparedness to act in it and on it, and to respond differentially to what it is likely to throw up. Being at peace is a quite different matter. Indeed, there are frequent occasions in which the two contrast with each other. One's way of being at home in any situation of threat, for example, requires renouncing ease, relaxation and comfort while retaining confidence, skill and a sure manner. So it is just as well that, having shown that we are at home with the world, McDowell's account does not imply that we are at peace with it (and not just because being dead is the paradigm of that condition). Conversely, if revised nature puts philosophy at peace, it does not imply that we are at home with it. At most it implies that the revision takes away those kinds of anxiety which sustain 'constructive' or 'substantive' philosophy. Again, it is just as well that McDowell's account does not imply that we are at home with philosophy, at least if he takes the stronger view. For being at home in a setting is to be related to it, as we have seen. And if the decisive move gets rid of philosophy, there is nothing here for us to be related to, no setting within which we can continue to exercise acquired skills and capacities.

As McDowell's goals become clearer, it is easier to distinguish between the deep questions with which his account leaves us and more superficial queries and difficulties, such as those we have noted on the way. In drawing to a close, we may note examples of the former sort and thus indicate lines for further inquiry.

The first set of questions has to do with the roots of McDowell's attempt to give philosophy peace. The crucial move here is the revision of our conception of nature. To be at peace is at least to be comfortable and free from anxiety, as we have seen. Yet McDowell himself seems not to envisage a future free from the 'philosophical impulse' and the tensions it generates.[10] He does not claim, for example, that swapping a science-determined conception of nature for one that makes proper sense of our rational-conceptual capacities could give more than temporary and occasional respite. There is no tension here with the claim that, by this same move, we have been shown to be at home in the world, to be open to it. For openness will be the case, no matter how pessimistic we may be about our chances of appreciating it in a constant manner. Indeed, it may be that being at home in the world partly involves coping skilfully with the temptation to lose sight of revised nature and the openness it confers. But there are pessimistic aspects to this picture of our relationship with the world. If blindness to openness is not simply a possible threat but somehow endemic, it is difficult to see how philosophy is ever to be considered truly at peace. Always prey to the philosophical impulse and anxious about its next irruption, the best we can hope for is a state of cold war.

This condition makes itself felt in various ways. There is an excellent example of one variety in a passage from Saul Bellow's novel *The Dean's December*. It is very plausible to suppose that no revision of our conception of nature could entirely inoculate one against experiences like this: 'A dog barked, whined as if a beater had given him a whack, then barked again. The barking of a dog, a protest against the limits of dog experience (for God's sake, open the universe a little more!) – so Corde felt, being shut in.'[11] Bellow tricks us for a moment, pretending that the dog has a perspective on its own aching poverty. But it is Bellow's human character, Corde, who has interpreted the bark as the dog's protest against its own lack of openness to the world. And he has done so in sympathetic extension from his own position and situation. The limits and the receding horizon of the world are there for him, not for the animal. It is Corde who captures the lie of the land at this point, who feels unable to penetrate the limitations it presents. In fact, the world is open to him and he is at home in it; but this is not how it seems to him. So he experiences that anxiety which heralds the return of what McDowell regards as typical of the philosophical impulse: namely, the urge to satisfy what is already satisfied. We may treat the logical mistakes in philosophy which prevent us appreciating what is the case, that we are at home in the world; then urges of this sort will abate, perhaps. But if they do not entirely vanish, we can never quite be at peace. And this constant tension may just be part of what it is to be at home. Complicated.

The second set of concerns with McDowell's project relates to the roots of his attempt to make us at home in the world. Again, as we have seen, the crucial move is the revision of our conception of nature. Such a revision is a major undertaking; a prudent conservatism would suggest we resist it unless it is forced on us. We are obliged to revise, in McDowell's view, because our current conception of the natural order has no place for the rational-conceptual capacities of human beings. There are various questions the reluctant conservative might ask first, and we have addressed them. Is our science-determined conception of the natural order really unable to make proper sense of these capacities? Are these capacities really essential to human beings? But suppose the conservative accepts McDowell's answers to these questions and digs down to a deeper one. Rational-conceptual capacities form a small part of all the features relating to human beings; human beings form an infinitesimally small part of the natural order. Why revise our whole conception of nature in order to accommodate this subset of a subset?

It is not sufficient to reply that rational-conceptual capacities are a part of nature, no matter how small, and hence nature must be made to accommodate them. For science is developing and with it our conception of the natural order. The reluctant conservative, who identifies the latter with what the former determines, will note what prudence demands in these circumstances: no revision of the natural order should be made to incorporate such minor details until it is clear that no major development of science is going to result in their being incorporated anyway. So it is crucial to persuade the conservative that rational-conceptual capacities are a major feature of the natural order; that accommodating them is a pressing matter.

This would be the case, of course, if the human beings to whom such capacities belonged were treated as centrally significant. Call such a position 'humanism'. It comes in two different sorts, as we have had occasion to note before; which sort is at issue depends on whether human beings are made the point of focus or the point of view.[12] The first kind gives human beings central place amongst the objects to be investigated but does not oblige one to adopt any particular perspective on them; the second gives precedence to what is particular about the human perspective on things but does not oblige one to adopt any particular ordering of the objects to be investigated. If the conservative could be persuaded of either form of humanism, human capacities would be of sufficient significance to make revision of the natural order pressing. But he may, in his reluctance, insist that humanism is merely a prejudice; we are not rationally obliged to make human beings our point of focus or of view.

It will not be sufficient to reply that taking any other point of focus or view is incoherent because it would be trying to make sense of the things under investigation 'sideways-on', that is, from a position outside, or from a perspective beyond, that in which it is possible to make sense of those things.[13] For the conservative, clinging to his conception of science-determined nature, will deny that he does step outside what is necessary in answering these questions: the set of natural things, or the natural perspective. What is a natural object or a natural perspective is determined by science; human beings and their perspective are a part of the natural order; so we do not take a position outside what is human or a perspective beyond it by trying to make sense of humanity in terms of science. To reply that we cannot help trying to make sense of that order 'sideways-on' while human rational-conceptual capacities are excluded from the natural order begs the question at issue. Without a strong dose of humanism, the conservative will continue to endorse a science-determined view of the natural order which regards these capacities as of minor significance and so prudently delays consideration of how to incorporate them. In short, humanism of either sort may be credible, appealing or even compelling. But if it is still a prejudice, then the conservative is not unreasonable in resisting revision of our current conception of nature. Without such a revision, McDowell will not have succeeded in making us at home in the world. But if Adorno is right that today 'it is part of morality not to be at home in one's home', it may be appropriate to resist a thoroughgoing humanism and suffer the ensuing unease.[14]

Notes

Preface

1 'the world is where a human being lives, where she is at home' (McDowell 1994a, p. 118).
2 Novalis 1997, pp. 135, 131.
3 By adhering to this policy, I hope to overcome some particularly sharp tensions between accessibility and scholarliness. In practice, it has meant quoting mainly from McDowell 1982a, 1985b, 1994a, and giving full supporting references to the breadth of McDowell's writing in the notes.

Chapter 1   Challenge

1 West 1971.
2 1978, p. 22.
3 The key articles include 1977, 1978a, 1979, 1982a, 1985b, 1986b.
4 McDowell's style is consciously unsettling and presents many different kinds of challenge to readers. Since his mode of communicating is intimately related to his views about what philosophy is and what tasks philosophers should be about, we shall often return to it in what follows.
5 It is possible that full appreciation of the integrated picture took time to dawn on McDowell also. These two sentences from a paper published in 1987 capture what is essential, as we shall see; but note how prospective they sound: 'I can think of no better project for philosophy than to try to understand the place of content – of conceptual consciousness – in the world. This is a task that is both more pressing

and more difficult in an age in which Enlightenment views of man and
his relation to nature are in the ascendant' (1987a, pp. 106–7).

6 Dibdin 2002, p. 1.

7 He summarizes his view as one that 'take[s] seriously the idea of an
unmediated openness of the experiencing subject to "external" reality'
(1982a, p. 392); it 'puts us in a position to speak of experience as openness to the layout of reality' (1994a, p. 26).

8 McDowell expressly allows that a reason can be a cause, 'though it is
not by virtue of its rational relationships that it stands in causal relations' (1994a, p. 75, n. 6). See also his 1995b and 1999.

9 Wallace Stevens' phrase for a certain conception of reality ('Man Carrying Thing', 1997, p. 306).

10 One aspect of the crudity of this picture is that I ignore, for the
moment, the fact that experience can sometimes (wholly) mislead us
about the world. McDowell also often avoids complicating the slogan
of openness with the necessary caveat – as he puts it on one occasion,
we should 'see experience *at its best* as openness to how things are'
(2002a, p. 291).

11 The crude pattern of thought I shall follow is not meant accurately to
portray any particular thinker's view. But it is not meant to be a straw
man either. So it is designed intentionally to recall certain key elements
of John Locke's discussion in his 1975. References to particular passages follow in further notes.

12 Our ideas of 'solidity, extension, figure, motion or rest, and number',
the so-called primary qualities of bodies, 'are all of them the images,
or representations of what does exist' (Locke 1975, II.xxx.2); they are
'*resemblances* of them, and their patterns do really exist in the bodies
themselves (1975, II.viii.15); speaking of material objects that are circular or square, Locke claims 'A circle or square are the same, whether
in *idea* or existence, in the mind or in the [material object]' (1975,
II.viii.18). (Locke explicitly rejects the claim that all our ideas are
images; those of secondary qualities, for example, are not; 1975,
II.viii.15; xxx.2.)

13 'For, methinks, the *understanding* is not much unlike a closet wholly
shut from light, with only some little openings left, to let in external
visible resemblances, or *ideas* of things without; would the pictures
coming into such a dark room but stay there, and lie so orderly as to
be found upon occasion, it would very much resemble the understanding of a man, in reference to all objects of sight and the *ideas* of
them' (Locke 1975, II.xi.17).

14 Locke describes what occurs when we look at a round globe of any
uniform colour:

> 'tis certain, that the idea thereby imprinted in our mind, is of a flat circle
> variously shadow'd, with several degrees of light and brightness
> coming to our eyes. But we having by use been accustomed to perceive,

what kind of appearance convex bodies are wont to make in us; what alterations are made in the reflections of Light, by the difference of the sensible figures of bodies, the judgement presently, by an habitual custom, alters the appearances into their causes. (Locke 1975, II.ix.8)

15 'Consciousness is the perception of what passes in a man's own mind' (Locke 1975, II.i.19).

16 'we are no more able to discover, wherein the *ideas* belonging to body consist, than those belonging to spirit. From whence it seems probable to me, that the simple *ideas* we receive from sensation and reflection, are the boundaries of our thoughts; beyond which, the mind, whatever efforts it would make, is not able to advance one jot; nor can it make any discoveries, when it would prie into the nature and hidden causes of those *ideas*' (Locke 1975, II.xxiii.29).

17 'words, in their primary or immediate signification, stand for nothing, but the *ideas* in the mind of him that uses them, how imperfectly soever, or carelessly those *ideas* are collected from the things, which they are supposed to represent' (Locke 1975, III.ii.2).

18 As we shall see, it is difficult (but not impossible) to interpret McDowell as invariably true to this non-constructive commitment. There are passages, for example, where he seems straightforwardly to be advancing a theory (a modest form of empiricism; for an explicit mention, see McDowell 2002a, p. 287).

19 Plato, *Theaetetus* 148e–151d; 1973, pp. 11–15, 116–17.

20 McDowell 1999, p. 89.

21 McDowell 1993b, p. 278.

22 See 1994a, pp. 93–5, 175–80.

23 I am assuming that there is much less danger of misleading anyone into thinking that McDowell draws directly from 'deconstruction' as that phrase is associated with Jacques Derrida and others (though I am sure there are instructive parallels; in any case, I am not equipped to draw them accurately).

24 With reference to Nietzsche 1994. On this connection and its context, see Geuss 1999.

25 See 1994a, p. 85.

26 For example, he appeals to the hold that Protestant individualism exercised over Kant to explain why Kant was peculiarly blind to the values of tradition and, hence, to an Aristotelian conception of our nature as primarily *second* nature (1994a, p. 98).

27 However unaware he himself may be of this. Anthony Kenny's impressive confidence that the *Tractatus Logico-Philosophicus* of Wittgenstein *can* be read in a single afternoon (Kenny 1973, p. 4) pales considerably beside McDowell's proposition that the six lectures of *Mind and World* were *meant* to be read 'at a single sitting' (1994a, p. vii).

28 Compare: 'we must uncover the source of the error: otherwise hearing what is true won't help us. It cannot penetrate when something is taking its place. To convince someone of what is true, it is not enough to state it; we must find the *road* from error to truth' (Wittgenstein, 1979, p. 1).

29 For the therapy image, see Wittgenstein, 1958, §255, p. 91: 'The philosopher's treatment of a question is like the treatment of an illness'; also see McGuinness 1967, p. 186. For the knot image, see Baker and Hacker 1980, p. 288.

30 McDowell certainly appeals to the model (even extending the metaphor on occasion to describing philosophy as a disease – certain manoeuvres lead to 'an outbreak of philosophy' and are to be rejected for that reason; 1994a, p. 183), though less often and less centrally than some commentators obviously suppose.

31 I am referring here to all of McDowell's writing, not just to those parts published in their original lecture form.

Chapter 2 Response

1 He defines transcendental *knowledge* thus:

> In transcendental knowledge, so long as we are concerned only with concepts of the understanding, our guide is the possibility of experience. Such proof does not show that the given concept (for instance, of that which happens) leads *directly* to another concept (that of a cause). The proof proceeds by showing that experience itself, and therefore the object of experience, would be impossible without a connection of this kind. (Kant 1933, A 783, B 811)

The interpretation is austere because Kant himself used the term in a wider sense, on occasion, to mean the conditions of possibility of items other than experience: for example, the preconditions of logic, the unity of apperception, illusion and the faculties.

2 Kant 1933, A 295, B 352.

3 For recent work on this subject, see Stern 1999b.

4 McDowell himself retains the label for intentional use, calling an argument of Wilfrid Sellars 'transcendental' precisely because it is directed towards McDowell's own goal: 'showing our entitlement to conceive subjective occurrences as possessing objective purport' (1998f, p. 445).

5 See Gareth Evans, 'Semantic theory and tacit knowledge', in his 1985, pp. 322–42, esp. § III.

6 See Sellars 1997, p. 76.

7 1998f, p. 433.

8 Thus McDowell distinguishes and holds a third way. On the one hand, he resists those who make the referential aspect basic, such as those

whose views are characterized by the 'Augustinian' picture which is the target of the opening sections of Wittgenstein 1958. On the other hand, he resists those who make the logico-deductive aspect basic, for example the 'inferentialism' which is defended by Robert Brandom in his 1994. As Brandom puts it, the 'major explanatory challenge' for theorists who support inferentialism is 'to explain the representational dimension of semantic content – to construe *referential* relations in terms of *inferential* ones' (1997, p. 156). McDowell indicates his holistic view – that neither can be construed in terms of the other; the possibility of construing either is a package deal, something that comes with the construal of both – most clearly in his contribution to a discussion of Brandom's work (McDowell 1997c). In keeping with the Default-imposed strategy, the force of McDowell's argument here is directed not towards motivating the holistic view, but towards showing that Brandom's position is unmotivated. In McDowell's view, inferentialism (i.e. making the logico-deductive dimension basic) is only motivated if it provides the only alternative to representationalism (i.e. making the referential dimension basic). With the possibility of the holistic view (neither is basic in relation to the other), inferentialism is not the only alternative and is thus not motivated. 'Given that [Brandom's] inferentialism is not necessitated by the unacceptability of representationalism, why should we regard it as anything but wildly implausible?' (1997c, p. 160).

9   This is an obvious point that nevertheless needs constant repetition; as we shall see, many opponents of McDowell assume that being a conceptualist about experience is to regard an experience as, or reducible to, some type of propositional attitudes, perhaps even a belief. But to say that concepts are essential constituents of both beliefs and experiences does not entail that the two are identical, or that their contents are identical (any more than saying that water is an essential constituent of mammals and beer makes the two identical, or their contents identical).

10   E.g. Crane 1992, p. 152.

11   See in particular 1998f, pp. 464ff. 'Concepts, which make thought what it is, can intelligibly be what they are – thought can intelligibly be of the objective at all – only because we can see how there can be conceptual occurrences in which objects are manifestly there for thinkers, immediately present to their conceptually shaped sensory consciousness' (1998f, p. 465).

12   Indeed, given the transcendental form of McDowell's approach and his emphasis on experience, it may be tempting to describe him as a 'transcendental empiricist' (McDowell himself seems to do so: 'I think a minimal empiricism, transcendentally slanted, is compelling'; 'In transcendental empiricism as I have described it'; in McDowell 2002a, p. 287). I think we should resist the temptations such easy labelling pushes us towards – forgetting the nature of the challenge McDowell

faces, and confusing his approach with the advancement of (yet another) rival position.

13 Following Davidson:

> Empiricism, like other isms, we can define pretty much as we please [but, note, as Davidson continues, it is clear that the bounds are still set by epistemology], but I take it to involve not only the pallid claim that all knowledge of the world comes through the agency of the senses, but also the conviction that this fact is of prime epistemological significance. (1990, p. 68)

14 Brandom characterizes this view as 'semantic empiricism' (2002, pp. 92–3).

15 This is perfectly consistent with allowing that what underlies or motivates forms of empiricism also underlies McDowell's philosophical interventions: namely, 'the idea that thought can be intelligibly nonempty only by virtue of answerability to experience' (McDowell 1999, p. 98).

16 He is explicit about this: 'saying how we should conceive experience [is] the main thing I try to do here' (1994a, p. viii).

17 So, although there are occasions on which McDowell seems prepared to accept the 'transcendental empiricist' label (see note 12 above), this would be out of keeping with his own conception of what his work is basically about. Another way to express the third worry is that the very notion of 'transcendental empiricism', to which McDowell himself appeals, is at best tautologous – certainly if it means what a straightforward interpretation suggests: a philosophical position taken by any who stress the primary importance of experience for experience.

18 Where 'closed off from the world' is taken to mean isolated or withdrawn from the world, confined outside it. See above (p. 5) for the appropriate antonyms of 'openness'.

19 This is not to deny that mental images might be 'involved' in some broad sense (they might pass through the mind while having the experience; they often do). It is to deny that such images could be essential or intrinsic to the experience. What is essential to an experience, given the Default, are the myriad possibilities opened to it for engaging in rational relations with other items. And these possibilities are provided for by the concepts of which they are constituted; no appeal to mental images is necessary.

20 See Descartes 1984, II; *Meditations* I–II.

21 If this position seems too strong – that there is a deep sense in which openness characterizes all our experience, even hallucinations and other false-seemings – a weaker one suffices for McDowell's point. *Some* of our experience is characterized by openness; finding room for

the possibility of experience of that sort is sufficient to generate his interdependence claims.

22 What follows is a version of the notorious 'argument from illusion'. I have phrased it in terms of hallucination, as most do, since the hard problem is not generated out of the possibility that we misperceive an object that exists (i.e. we are 'illuded' about what properties an object manifests), but that we take ourselves to perceive an object that does not in fact exist (i.e. we are 'deluded' about whether an object exists).

Chapter 3   Implications

1   Kant 1933, A 51, B 75.
2   See McDowell 1993a.
3   See 1994a, pp. 99–124; 1998c.
4   Specifically Gareth Evans; see 'Things without the mind' in his 1985, pp. 249–90.
5   See McDowell 1979, 1980c, 1996a, 1998e.
6   See McDowell 1983, 1985b, 1994a, 1997b, 1998c, 1998f, 2000a, 2000b.
7   See McDowell 1977, 1982b, 1984a, 1991b.
8   See McDowell 1978c, 1981a, 1981b, 1982a, 1984b, 1989b, 1989c, 1991a, 1993b, 1994a, 1998c.
9   'achieving what Kant wanted to achieve' (1994a, p. viii). See also McDowell 1995a, 1998f, 1999, 2000a, 2000b.
10 On Davidson, see McDowell 1976a, 1976b, 1978b, 1980b, 1985a, 1999, 2002b. On Dummett, see McDowell 1978c, 1981a, 1987a, 1989a, 1997a.
11 One consequence of rethinking mind–world relations in the way McDowell advocates is that Evans' externalism, often dismissed as counter-intuitive, stands revealed as 'deeply right, at least in general outline' (1994e, p. 107). On externalism, see McDowell 1982b, 1984a, 1986b, 1990, 1991b, 1992, 1998d.
12 Particularly clear examples are his rejections of behaviourism and psychologism in his account of language (1987a, 1997a); the Myth of the Given and coherentism in his account of experience (1994a); and strong referentialism and strong inferentialism in his account of conceptual content (1997c). All three are also examples of cases in which McDowell tries to free us from an unfortunate oscillation. In the first case, for example, the argument goes as follows. We need to secure the 'openness to view' of language; we are tempted to think that behaviourism is the only way to do so; but we accept that behaviourism is bad and recoil from it into the opposed position – a psychologism about language (it is a code of a certain sort); this position loses us openness about language; so we recoil from it into behaviourism; and so on. The exit from oscillation in this case is only possible if we give up thinking that we can (should) give a 'sideways-on' account of lan-

guage and the conceptual; i.e. one that takes its perspective from outside language and the conceptual.

13 See McDowell 1986b, 1987a, pp. 90–1; 1997a, pp. 130–1.
14 See in particular McDowell 1982a and 1986b. Note the role of privilege in the argument from illusion described above; it is from this perspective that deceptive and non-deceptive cases are indistinguishable, giving support to the claim that, as regards the content of *experience* at least, they are identical.
15 For the perceptual model in ethics, see McDowell 1979; in evaluative thought more generally, see McDowell 1983, pp. 117ff.
16 See McDowell 1982a. The argument is investigated at length in chapter 12 below.
17 See McDowell 1986a, 1997b, 1998c.
18 Strawson 1959, pp. 9–12. I have broadened Strawson's distinction in the spirit in which it was made, from metaphysics to philosophy.
19 This is not contrary to Strawson's design; as he notes, 'Perhaps no [philosopher] has ever been, both in intention and effect, wholly the one thing or the other' (1959, p. 9).

Part II   Central Elements

1 Book III, § 109; Nietzsche 2001, p. 110.
2 McDowell 1994a, p. 86. The Wittgenstein quotation is from his 1958, § 133, p. 51.
3 1994a, p. 70.
4 1994a, p. 85.

Chapter 4   Naturalism

1 1996, pp. 2, 6.
2 See Aristotle 2000, book I, ch. 1, p. 3.
3 For McDowell's views on naturalism, see in particular 1994a, pp. 66–86; 1996b.
4 The label 'reductionist naturalism' is sometimes used for what I shall call 'scientism'. I distinguish the two labels since it is crucial to McDowell's point that science ('law') is not the only mode to which a naturalistic explanation might reduce. (To distinguish at the level of labels, of course, leaves it completely open whether McDowell is right about this: 'non-scientistic reductive naturalism' might denote the empty set.)
5 Jerry Fodor, for example, is happy to adopt the label, though it is not very clear whether he adopts what it denotes. Implicitly, he seems to on many occasions (see his 1998, pp. 3–8, 189–202); explicitly, he means something much milder. 'Scientism claims, on the one hand, that the

goals of scientific inquiry include the discovery of objective empirical truths; and, on the other hand, that science comes pretty close to achieving this goal at least from time to time' (1998, p. 189). The first claim is not deniable on any plausible definition of scientific inquiry, and there is nothing reductive (or even necessarily deferential) about the second claim.

6   This way of putting the point owes to Bernard Williams (2002, p. 22).

7   McDowell himself uses the lower case to distinguish the view often called 'Platonist' in the philosophy of mathematics (that logical or mathematical entities subsist independently of the natural and empirical world and of human thought) from what he regards as Plato's own views.

8   These alternatives are close to what McDowell calls 'rampant platonism' and 'bald naturalism', respectively.

9   For McDowell on second nature, see in particular 1994a, pp. 66–87; 1996b, pp. 188ff.

10   1994a, p. 84.

11   1994a, p. 84.

12   1994a, p. 77. This phrase is intended accurately to capture McDowell's true position, even though he employs it when putting words into the mouth of an opponent who misrepresents him in other ways (mistaking his position for rampant platonism).

13   For McDowell on the relevant aspects of Aristotle, see in particular 1979, 1980c, 1996a, 1998e.

14   Aristotle 2000, book II, ch. 1, p. 23.

15   This is Aristotle's example, not McDowell's. Since Aristotle goes on to speak of hearing and seeing, it is likely that by 'senses' he means perceptual abilities rather than our capacity for experiencing (bodily) sensations. But, as we shall see, McDowell would reject the example whichever is meant: both count as the exercise of second nature abilities.

16   Aristotle 2000, book II, ch. 1, p. 23.

17   Aristotle 1984a, § 13, p. 36.

18   A point emphasized and explored for the case of vision by John Hyman (1994).

19   Aristotle 2000, book II, ch. 1, p. 24.

20   For the role of language in his account, see in particular McDowell 1976b, 1980a, 1987a, 1992, 1997a, 1981a, 1994a, pp. 108–26.

21   1994a, p. 126.

22   1994a, p. 125.

23   See Sellars 1997, p. 76.

24   1994a, p. 82.

Chapter 5   Reasons

1 Williams 2002, p. 23.
2 Williams 2002, pp. 26–7.
3 This phrase, which McDowell borrows from Sellars, was introduced in chapter 3 above. In McDowell's usage, the essential idea is as follows: 'The space of reasons is the space within which thought moves, and its topography is that of the rational interconnections between conceptual contents; we might equally speak of the space of concepts' (1995a, p. 408).
4 In Davidson 1980, p. 222. McDowell notes the connection, carefully distinguishing those parts of Davidson's argumentation he agrees with from those he does not, at 1994a, pp. 72–6; esp. p. 74. I have been helped in finding a way to explicate Davidson's claims by Evnine 1991, pp. 17–20, to which book, together with the Davidson essay, I refer the reader. For McDowell's relationship to the work of Davidson, see his 1976a, 1976b, 1978b, 1980b, 1985a, 1999, 2002b.
5 Davidson 1980, p. 222.
6 G. E. M. Anscombe's example of the man who goes shopping with a list and the detective who makes a list of what he buys – any discrepancy between what is bought and what is on the list is a problem with what is bought in the former case, and what is on the list in the latter – has been helpful in formulating these points. See her 1957, § 32, pp. 56–7.
7 Davidson 1980, p. 223.
8 I take the notion of such a verb from Wittgenstein's extended reflection on Moore's paradox, 1958, pp. 190–2.
9 1994a, p. 74.
10 For the relevant discussions of meaning and its place in language in McDowell's writing, see in particular 1976a, 1980a, 1981a, 1987a, 1992, 1997a.
11 I shall present eliminativism about meaning using Quine because he is the figure most clearly associated with the position, not because he always clearly held it in its strong form. On occasion, he seems to have held the weaker position that there are no (or only a few) 'determinate' facts about translation (and hence meaning). If this is a viable position, of course, its advocates must be prepared to say what non-determinate facts could be.
12 So-called because it turns on the indeterminacy of sub-sentential expressions (i.e. putatively referring terms). See Quine 1960, pp. 51–4, 68–79; and Quine 1969, pp. 1–6, 30–5.
13 See Schiffer 1987, pp. 1–2.
14 The essential point can be captured if we employ the use/mention distinction. Two rather different functions are signified by the term 'meaning' (or, rather, at least two). In constructing translation manuals, the term 'meaning' is a function mapping one *mentioned*

expression onto another (*translation manual*: 'Das Pferd ist hübsch' means 'The horse is pretty'). In constructing theories of meaning, or semantic theories, however, the term 'meaning' is a function mapping one *mentioned* expression onto a *used* expression, a semantic entity denoting those items satisfying it (*semantic theory*: 'The horse is pretty' means the horse is pretty). Thus we can say that translation manuals tell us when two words have the same meaning (first sense), but only semantic theories tell us what either mean (second sense). They do so, for each well-formed declarative sentence of the language under consideration, by offering a theorem stating the meaning of that sentence in terms of truth conditions (*semantic theorem*: 'The horse is pretty' is true if and only if the horse is pretty). Thus, unlike translation manuals, theories of meaning state semantic truths, require the use of expressions as well as their mention, and employ the concepts truth, denotation and satisfaction. The meaning of a sentence is given by its *truth* conditions; the extension of a term is that thing which it *denotes*; the extension of a predicate is the set of things *satisfying* it; and so on. See Evans, 'Identity and predication', in his 1985, pp. 25–48; esp. pp. 25–7.

15 See Quine, 'Epistemology naturalized', in his 1969, pp. 69–90; esp. p. 75.

16 See note 15.

Chapter 6   Nature Revised

1 See 1994a, pp. 66–126; 1996b.

2 See McDowell 1994a, pp. 66–86; 1995a.

3 'On the notion of cause', in Russell 1953, pp. 171–96; esp. pp. 179–86. See also Russell's 'On scientific method in philosophy' in the same volume, pp. 95–119.

4 There is a benefit to describing the debate in terms of a reason/law divide rather than a reason/cause divide; it does not rule out by definition the possibility that reasons might be causes.

5 Aristotle 1984b, book 1, § 1, p. 315.

6 See Annas 1981, p. 7.

7 As Nietzsche points out, there may be (perhaps ironically) no less anthropomorphism about the post-revolution conception of nature than about the conception it replaces.

> Let us beware even of believing that the universe is a machine; it is certainly not constructed to one end, and the word 'machine' pays it too high an honour . . . . The total character of the world is for all eternity chaos, not in the sense of a lack of necessity but of a lack of order, organization, form, beauty, wisdom, and whatever else our aesthetic anthropomorphisms are called . . . . It has no drive to self-preservation or any other drives; nor does it observe any laws. Let us

beware of saying that there are laws in nature. There are only necessi-
ties: there is no one who commands, no one who obeys, no one
who transgresses. Once you know that there are no purposes, you also
know that there is no accident; for only against a world of purposes does
the word 'accident' have a meaning. (Nietzsche 2001, book III, § 109,
pp. 109–10)

8   So there is a nice concurrence between McDowell's account of the con-
    fusion inherent in our post-Scientific Revolution conception of nature,
    science and reason, and Laurence Sterne's satire on that world, and
    particularly on the reception of Locke's philosophy, in his *The Life and
    Opinions of Tristram Shandy, Gentleman*. Conceived in circumstances
    which confusingly identify the natural with the mechanical (his
    parents' lovemaking is interrupted by his mother, who asks her
    husband 'Pray my dear, did you remember to wind up the clock?'),
    Shandy's character and opinions are thereby informed with the same
    identity confusion. Taking the mechanical world for the whole of
    nature, he tries to interpret and account for his mental life as merely
    the instantiation of physical laws. A great deal of the comic value of
    the book lies in Shandy's highly inventive attempts to incorporate all
    that he experiences and thinks within the realm that physical laws
    alone make intelligible, attempts which Sterne ably portrays as futile
    and absurd. Shandy's opinions also reflect the influence of what
    McDowell calls 'the rise of Protestant individualism', which brings
    with it 'a loss or devaluation of the idea that immersion in a tradition
    might be a respectable mode of access to the real. Instead it comes to
    seem incumbent on each individual thinker to check everything for
    herself' (1994a, p. 98). Shandy aims to be wholly self-reliant in this
    way, comically exaggerating the range of introspection and the value
    of private reasoning at the expense of public knowledge and shared
    tradition, with predictably bizarre results.
9   We might ask, in addition, about the notion of 'freedom' in play here.
    Is it the kind of freedom an agent has which may aptly be described
    as autonomy? McDowell's dependence on Aristotle's ethical views
    might suggest this. On the other hand, his appeal to Kant suggests
    another kind of freedom: the independence from natural law and
    merely causal processes characteristic of someone at home in the space
    of reasons. Are these indeed two different kinds of freedom or aspects
    of the same phenomenon? If they are different kinds, is McDowell con-
    flating them?
10 The necessary constraints appear to be internal to the individual for
    McDowell; they are what make and keep one the individual one is. So
    McDowell cannot appeal to St Augustine's comforting distinction,
    which accommodates the need for discipline while keeping it at bay:
    'Let constraint be found outside; it is inside that the will is born'
    (Sermon 112.8; quoted in Brown 2000, p. 232).

Part III Central Elements

1 1958, p. 177.
2 McDowell 1994a, p. 26.
3 See 1994a, p. 28.
4 See 1994a, pp. 23, 25.
5 1994a, p. 162.
6 See 1994a, p. 27.
7 1994a, p. 27.

Chapter 7 Experience

1 For McDowell on experience, see in particular 1986b, 1994a, 1994b, 1998f, 1999, 2000a, 2000b.
2 We may stop short of the functionalist conclusion; an answer to the question 'what is its function?' directs us towards an answer to the question 'what is it?' without actually providing that answer.
3 McDowell probably holds the stronger view, that without experience we would have no reason for what we think and say. It is difficult otherwise to see what passages like this come to: 'The thinkable contents that are ultimate in the order of justification are contents of experiences' (1994a, p. 29). But this view is not essential to the current argument; the weaker claim is sufficient.
4 See 1994a, p. 28.
5 See 1994a, pp. 23, 25. Elsewhere, McDowell describes spontaneity as 'simply a label for the involvement of conceptual capacities' (1994a, p. 9). This cannot be quite right, as we shall see when examining the Kantian context from which this usage derives. Spontaneity is more like the *precondition* for the involvement of conceptual capacities – i.e. the power or faculty in virtue of which a concept-user exercises those capacities.
6 1994a, pp. 11–12.
7 1994a, p. 23.
8 1994a, p. 162.
9 1994a, p. 71.
10 1994a, p. 41.
11 1994a, p. 23.
12 Kant 1933, A 51, p. 93.
13 It is true that reasons necessitate; but for Kant, rational necessitation is not just compatible with, but constitutive of, freedom.
14 1933, A 51, p. 93.
15 1933, A 68, B 93, p. 105.
16 1933, A 29–30, B 45, p. 73.
17 McDowell commends Wilfrid Sellars for remaining 'firm in his conviction' that Kant should be interpreted in such a way that 'intuitions

are representations of individuals that already involve the under-standing, the faculty associated with concepts'. Developing this view somewhat, McDowell describes intuitions as 'shapings of sensory con-sciousness by the understanding' (1998f, p. 452). For McDowell's rela-tionship to the work of Sellars, see his 1995a, 1998f, 1999, 2000a, 2000b.

18 See McDowell 1994a, p. 8.

19 See McDowell 1994a, p. 5.

20 Sydney Shoemaker notoriously denies that 'self-awareness involves any sort of perception of oneself'; see his 1994a, p. 89. Whether the kinds of bodily awareness listed here count as 'of oneself' need not come into question at this point; what is important is that they satisfy the conditions on ordinary kinds of sense perception listed by Shoe-maker himself (see 'Self-knowledge and inner sense' in his 1996, pp. 204–6). Three features are most important in these cases. First, the capacity to perceive something is to some extent under the subject's voluntary control (he can move his fingers if he wants to feel them bent; not eat or sleep if he wants to affect his metabolism sufficiently to feel hungry and tired, and so on; though, as with visual percep-tion, for example, it is of course not up to him what he perceives once he is so positioned – experience is passive). Second, the way things then appear perceptually is distinct from the object perceived and from any belief the subject may form (its appearing to him that his arm is bent is not the same thing as his bent arm, nor as his believing his arm is bent – he may not form this belief at all if he is suffering from cramp and knows about the kinds of attendant illusion). Third, the outcome of these perceptions in the ordinary (non-illusionary) case is aware-ness of facts (awareness *that* his arm is bent, and so on).

21 See Armstrong 1968, ch. 10; Pitcher, 1971; Peacocke, 1983, ch. 1.

22 Note that this is not the extreme view that giving an accurate descrip-tion of the contents of one's experience will involve listing *propositions* – even if aposiopetically.

23 I have focused on the inferential features of concepts in this chapter to make McDowell's path to conceptualism clear. It should not be for-gotten that, in his view, the referential or representational features of concepts are equally fundamental (e.g. 1997c). This aspect of his claims was discussed at length in chapter 2 and in the notes to that chapter.

Chapter 8　Conceptualism

1 See McDowell 1986b, 1994a, pp. 3–65, 1994b, 1998f, 1999, 2000a, 2000b.

2 See in particular Burge 1977; Evans 1982, pp. 123–4; McGinn 1989, pp. 58–62; Cussins 1990, pp. 380–401; Davies 1991; Crane 1992; Martin 1992; Peacocke 1992. For a recent defence of conceptualism that is akin to but distinct at many points from McDowell's, see Brewer 1999, esp. ch. 5.

3   Evans 1982, p. 227.
4   See Sellars 1997, § 28, p. 62.
5   Lewis 1956, p. 38.
6   Lewis 1956, p. 39.
7   For Kantian and neo-Kantian elements in McDowell's approach on
    these matters, see his 1983, 1985b, 1994a, 1997b, 1998c, 1998f, 2000a,
    2000b.
8   Bradley 1897, p. 198.
9   Richard Rorty expresses the connection neatly in his definition of the
    Myth (which he calls 'the doctrine of the Naturally Given'): 'knowl-
    edge is either of the sort of entity naturally suited to be immediately
    present to consciousness, or of entities whose existence and properties
    are entailed by entities of the first sort (and which are thus "reducible"
    to those of the first sort)' (1980, p. 105).
10 Although Sellars concentrates his attack on views which make foun-
    dationalist claims, he acknowledges that such views are '*one* of the
    forms taken by the Myth of the Given' (1997, § 32, p. 68, my empha-
    sis). See McDowell 1995a, 1998f, 1999, 2000a, 2000b.
11 See 1994a, pp. 17–18.
12 To put matters another way. Pointing is supposed to offer the pos-
    sibility of warrant; but before we can ask whether a *judgement* is war-
    ranted, and hence knowledge, we need to ask about the concepts of
    which the judgement is formed. For the possibility of warrant is con-
    stitutive of a concept's being what it is, and hence constitutive of its
    contribution to any thinkable content in which it figures. Unless point-
    ing can offer *that* kind of warrant, we do not even have a judgement
    which might or might not be knowledge.
13 See McDowell 1994a, p. 20. McDowell connects the point with his
    interpretation of Wittgenstein's private language argument. The Myth
    claims that

>   a concept is constituted by a justificatory linkage to a bare presence,
>   which is what its being a private concept would amount to. . . . Making
>   the abstraction that would be necessary to form such a concept would
>   be giving oneself a private ostensive definition. In effect the idea that
>   concepts can be formed by abstraction from the Given just is the idea of
>   private ostensive definition. So the Private Language Argument just is
>   the rejection of the Given, in so far as it bears on the possibilities for lan-
>   guage; it is not an application of a general rejection of the Given to a
>   particular area. (1994a, p. 20)

14 Russell 1912, pp. 3–5.
15 As Sellars notes, 'For we now recognize that instead of coming to have
    a concept of something because we have noticed that sort of thing,
    to have the ability to notice a sort of thing is already to have the
    concept of that sort of thing, and cannot account for it' (1997, § 45,
    p. 87).
16 1994a, p. 8.

17   See BonJour 1985 and Davidson 2001, pp. 137–57.
18   1994a, p. 11.

Chapter 9   Judgement

1   See McDowell 1986b, 1994a, pp. 3–65, esp. p. 26 (quoted at the begin-
     ning of part III); 1998f, 1999, 2000a, 2000b.
2   1994a, p. 27.
3   In order to retain continuity with earlier usage in explicating
     McDowell's views, I am replacing his own preferred term to cover
     occasions where conceptual capacities are not exercised by the subject
     but are passively drawn on; 'engage' for 'actualize'. For McDowell's
     usage, see his 1998f, throughout.
4   See McDowell 1998f, p. 434.
5   1998f, p. 463. McDowell takes this explicitly for 'an implication of the
     position I am finding in Kant'.
6   1998f, p. 439; see also pp. 438–40.
7   I am not suggesting that this is the only way to distinguish experien-
     cing from judging, or that someone who wants to do so while holding
     McDowell's conceptualist views is forced to renounce the relaxed view.
8   1998f, p. 458. See also pp. 440–1. McDowell is here drawing on and
     partially explicating Wilfrid Sellars' notion of visual experience as
     cases of ostensible seeing which contain claims about a visible region
     of objective reality; see Sellars 1997, §16, pp. 40–1. This is to treat the
     assertion that experiences contain claims as synonymous with the
     assertion that they are actualizations of conceptual capacities; see
     McDowell 1998f, p. 471.
9   Evans 1982, p. 227. Evan's non-conceptualism is of a comparatively
     sophisticated variety, as McDowell recognizes when discussing it
     (1994a, Lecture III); only subjects capable of judgement are to be attrib-
     uted those kinds of non-conceptual information state which can be
     accounted 'experiences'.
10   Evans 1982, p. 227.
11   Reid 1941, pp. 151–2.
12   Reid 1941, p. 155.
13   See Evans 1982, pp. 123–4; McGinn 1989, pp. 58–62; Crane 1992,
     pp. 136–57.
14   McDowell 1998f, p. 463.
15   For the anti-conceptualist use of the repleteness of experience and its
     specificity, see Burge 1977, pp. 338–62; Evans 1982, p. 229; McGinn
     1989, p. 62.

Chapter 10   Openness

1   See the passage quoted at the beginning of the introduction to this part
     of this book, from McDowell 1994a, p. 26.

2　1994a, p. 27.

3　1994a, p. 27.

4　1994a, p. 27. See Wittgenstein 1961, § 1, p. 1.

5　1994a, p. 27.

6　Wittgenstein 1958, § 95, p. 44. McDowell's writing is particularly indebted to close readings of the later Wittgenstein; see his 1978c, 1981a, 1981b, 1982a, 1984b, 1989b, 1989c, 1991a, 1993b, 1998c.

7　1994a, p. 26.

8　Wittgenstein 1958, § 428, p. 127 and 1974, pp. 154–8.

9　Nietzsche 2001, p. 204.

10　1986b, p. 237.

11　As Wittgenstein himself does on occasion, though cautiously: e.g. 'An "inner process" stands in need of outward criteria' (1958, § 580, p. 153). Note that only one term of this spatial relation is hedged, giving one some reason to suppose that Wittgenstein was content with the spatial metaphor itself and had separate reasons to be wary of the 'inner'.

12　'Mere appearance'; McDowell 1982a, p. 386. 'Interface'; 1982a, p. 393, fn. 45. 'Interpenetrating', 'separated'; 1986b, p. 250. 'Gulf', 'bridge'; 1986b, p. 237. 'Tract of the environment', 'present to consciousness', 'not an image'; 1994a, p. 191.

13　See 1994a, p. 28.

14　1994a, p. 10.

15　1994a, p. 26.

16　1994a, p. 40.

17　For McDowell's dependence on and discussions of this Fregean background, see his 1977, 1982b, 1984a, 1991b.

18　Frege 1967, pp. 34–5.

19　Frege, of course, also regards thoughts as 'the sense of a whole sentence'. I shall specify what I mean by 'sense' wherever confusion threatens.

20　See Frege 1980, p. 59 and 1918, p. 29.

21　See Frege 1980, p. 57.

22　See Frege 1967, throughout.

23　The claim that the object dependency of propositions containing singular terms is supported by parallel arguments in Frege has been disputed. Michael Dummett, for example, claims that it was the 'early' Frege (that is, prior to the distinction between sense and reference) who argued that propositions containing empty singular terms fail to be significant. The later Frege appears to have been, at the very least, more tolerant of empty singular terms, even in non-fictional usage (see Frege 1980, p. 62), and for the following reason. A proposition containing an empty singular term would lack a referent and hence be without semantic value; but it might still have a sense (a cognitive value) and thus lay claim to expressing a communicable and evaluable thought. See Dummett 1993, chs 5 and 7.

24　1994a, pp. 179–80.

25 For discussion of these issues, see Dodd 1995. Dodd regards McDowell as caught in an impasse; he does not recognize the exit afforded by his object-dependent views.
26 1994a, p. 28.
27 See in particular 1977, 1982b, 1984a, 1986b, 1990, 1991b, 1992, 1998d. Perhaps surprisingly, McDowell's advocacy is not explicit in his 1994a, merely hinted at (cf. pp. 104–7).

Chapter 11 World Dependency

1 See in particular McDowell 1977, 1982b, 1984a, 1986b, 1990, 1991b, 1992, 1998d.
2 Referring terms were the subject of McDowell's first published paper in philosophy (1970); for details of his developing approach, see his 1977, 1982b, 1984a, 1986b, 1998c.
3 Of particular relevance to what follows are McDowell's editorial contributions to Evans 1982 and his 1990.
4 It is natural to suppose that different kinds of referring expression have different ways of generating an object dependence in the thoughts/propositions in which they figure – depending, largely, on the kinds of information necessarily invoked by the particular term used, the possible diversity of ways its referent has of being thought about as the same, and so on. Some singular terms may not generate object dependency at all. If 'descriptive names' may be considered as a distinct group within the class of referring expressions, then there appear to be *some* singular terms which compose contents available to be thought in the absence of their referents (see Evans 1982, p. 328). The cases of ordinary proper names and definite descriptions are more controversial.
5 See Strawson, 'On referring', reprinted in his 1971, pp. 1–27; and his 1952, pp. 173–9 and pp. 184–90.
6 The identity and existence of an object, and its appropriate (causal) relations to the thinker, are necessary conditions for the availability of object-dependent thoughts about it but, obviously, not sufficient: such thoughts might be rendered unavailable through any number of causes – the absence of an entity capable of thought, for example; the lack of an attempt on a thinker's part to think such a thought; or the absence of an appropriate relation between the thinker and the thought.
7 The kind with which the following, for example, are associated: Putnam 1975; Burge 1994; Shoemaker 1994b.
8 The anti-Cartesian aspects of this position are supported by a whole structure of arguments in McDowell's writings; see in particular his 1982a, 1984a, 1986a, 1986b, 1991b, 1994b, 1997b, 1998f. For the implications of such views on the inner–outer and on subjectivity more generally, see in addition 1982b, 1989b, 1989c, 1991a, 1998d.

9   For anti-conceptualist strategy here, see Evans 1982, p. 229; Burge 1977, pp. 338–62; McGinn 1989, p. 62.
10   McDowell 1994a, p. 170.
11   The resolution of Vladimir Nabokov's novel *Despair* (1981) is based on this conceit. For the anti-conceptualist use of temporal priority and memory arguments, see Campbell 1986, p. 280; and Martin 1992, especially p. 759.

Part IV   Central Elements

1   1982a, pp. 388–9.
2   1985b, p. 143.
3   1978a, p. 85.
4   See 1979, p. 63.

Chapter 12   Knowledge

1   For McDowell's approach to knowledge, see in particular his 1980a, 1981a, 1982a, 1986b, 1993a, 1995a.
2   For the implications on subjectivity generally, see McDowell 1982a, 1982b, 1984a, 1986a, 1986b, 1989b, 1989c, 1991a, 1991b, 1994a, pp. 18–23, 99–104, 114–23, 1994b, 1997b, 1998d, 1998f.
3   1994a, p. 26.
4   1982a, p. 392.
5   1994a, p. 143.
6   For scepticism about the world, see in particular McDowell 1986b; for the other minds problem, see in particular McDowell 1982a; for the way in which that problem relates to questions about the testimony of others, see in particular McDowell 1993a.
7   1986b, p. 240.
8   1986b, p. 251.
9   1986b, p. 243.
10   This argument is developed in its greatest length and detail in McDowell 1982a.
11   McDowell 1994a, p. 143.
12   1982a, p. 388. If someone has a fact made manifest to him in experience, he forms the belief caused by that fact and is not prey to an illusion, then that is sufficient epistemic justification for his belief. This is apparently an externalist position (even if the ontological dimension of McDowell's position blocks its characterization in terms of that which is within or without the thinker's 'cognitive perspective'). For it seems that one may be justified in believing that p given only that this belief is caused by the relevant fact; there is no requirement that one be able to recognize or point out that fact as precisely relevant to the belief.
13   'No ontological gap' (McDowell, 1994a, p. 27).

14   See McDowell 1982a, p. 388. It should be noted that, although complementary to each other, the metaphysical and epistemological components of receptive-ontological openness are apparently logically independent. Say that, between what I think and what is the case, there is no ontological gap (however that troubling phrase is to be interpreted); it may nevertheless be denied that experiencing the fact that *p* can be sufficient for knowing that *p*. For experiencing the fact that *p* may not be sufficient for believing *justifiably* that *p*. Conversely, experiencing the fact that *p* may constitute my epistemic standing when believing that *p*, even though the contents of my thoughts and of my experiences should be placed in strictly distinct ontological categories.

15   McDowell 1994a, p. 27.

16   See Wittgenstein 1969a, pp. 24–5.

17   1980, p. 97. Wright footnotes this: 'This aspect of the notion of a criterion . . . may have escaped McDowell.'

18   1969a, p. 24.

19   1984, p. 384.

20   1969a, p. 25.

21   See 1982a, § 3, esp. pp. 387–9.

22   Wittgenstein 1958, § 354, pp. 112–13; McDowell 1982a, pp. 380–1.

23   1982a, p. 381.

24   1982a, p. 386.

25   For earlier accounts detailing the possibility of taking a position of this sort, see Hinton 1973 and Snowdon 1981.

26   1982a, pp. 386–7. The final sentence originally read: 'On the contrary, we are to *insist* that . . . .'

27   To put the case in McDowell's own terms: 1982a, pp. 386–7.

28   1982a, pp. 389–90.

29   As William Child formulates the disjunctive conception, we may claim that 'there is no single type of state of affairs common to' both (1994, p. 144).

30   1986b, p. 240.

31   1982a, p. 393, fn. 45.

Chapter 13   Value

1   For McDowell's views on value, see in particular his 1983, 1985b.

2   See 1985b, pp. 133ff.

3   He appeals to the discussion of these matters by Gareth Evans in 'Things without the mind' in the latter's 1985, pp. 249–90.

4   See Strawson 1959, p. 69.

5   On the phenomenological point, see in particular McDowell 1985b, pp. 131ff.

6   See Mackie 1977.

7   Note that McDowell seems committed to the claim that dispositions

can be perceived. For he argues that colours are both visible properties of objects and dispositions to produce colour experiences.

8 For the relevant papers, see in particular McDowell 1978a, 1979, 1980c,
1987b, 1995b, 1996a, 1996b, 1998c.

9 Mackie 1977.

10 McDowell 1985b, p. 131.

11 McDowell 1983, p. 112.

12 For the perceptual model in evaluative thought generally, see
McDowell 1983, pp. 117ff. For its role in ethics specifically, see 1979, p.
51, where McDowell states specifically that what he has in mind is 'a
sort of perceptual capacity' (one should not be put off by the slight
vagueness; he does not say 'sort of a perceptual capacity').

13 McDowell 1985b, p. 132.

14 See McDowell 1983, p. 117 and 1985b, p. 132.

15 McDowell 1985b, p. 133.

16 McDowell 1985b, p. 133.

17 McDowell 1983, p. 113.

18 McDowell 1983, p. 113.

19 McDowell 1985b, p. 136.

20 McDowell 1985b, pp. 141–6.

21 McDowell adopts the same terminology, though he sometimes modi-
fies the description to 'weird'; see McDowell 1983, pp. 115ff.

22 Mackie 1977, p. 41.

23 McDowell raises and discusses the question of whether the particular
sensibility required for value-experience should be accounted a form
of intuition; see his 1985b, pp. 133 and 149.

24 McDowell 1985b, p. 134.

25 See McDowell 1985b, pp. 143–4.

26 1985b, p. 144.

27 See 1979, pp. 57 and 65ff; 1985b, p. 149.

28 See 1979, throughout; and 1985b, pp. 146–50, esp. p. 149.

Conclusion

1 1994a, p. 86. McDowell is quoting from Wittgenstein 1958, § 133, p. 51.

2 1958, p. 51.

3 Other passages of Wittgenstein are similarly ambiguous on this point.
For example: 'The philosopher strives to find the liberating word, that
is, the word that finally permits us to grasp what up until now has
intangibly weighed down our consciousness' (Wittgenstein 1993, § 87,
p. 165). It is unclear whether or not Wittgenstein thought that, when
the weight has been grasped, the philosopher still has a profession.

4 Context suggests this; the passage occurs in the last of a run of sections in *Philosophical Investigations* which are dedicated to repudiating
as incoherent not philosophy as a whole but a particular conception

of the philosopher's task – constructing an ideal, complete and determinate language (1958, §§ 89–133). And the incoherence of this conception is manifest precisely in the self-questioning torments induced in its advocates. Since it is on these specific torments that Wittgenstein focuses, rather than those induced by just any conception of philosophy, and since he does not attack any other conception, the peace-giving discovery is more likely to be one that puts false ways of doing philosophy to rest rather than one that puts philosophy itself to rest. Anecdotal evidence also supports this interpretation: Wittgenstein is reported to have repudiated the first sentence in conversation with Rush Rhees; see Baker and Hacker 1980, p. 246.

5 See 1993b and 1994a, pp. 93–5, 175–8.
6 Elsewhere, McDowell sometimes qualifies 'philosophy' with 'ordinary'. This raises the slim possibility that, when he speaks of the philosophy to be quieted, he might *simply* mean those particular conceptions of the philosophical task he calls 'substantive' or 'constructive'. But I suspect this is too cautious: there is no obvious difference between these adornments in McDowell's use of them in the passages relevant to this question; no mention of 'extra-ordinary' philosophy or what it would be; no sense of what legitimate philosophizing might be like, or what tasks face it, after the rest-giving discovery (other than to offer regular reminders of that discovery, for McDowell regards a definitive cure as out of the question; we are habitual recidivists and backsliders; cf. 1994a, p. 177).
7 It is remarkable, for example, that when discussing different possible interpretations of the Wittgenstein passage (1994a, p. 177), McDowell only ever considers versions of the first alternative. He accepts that Wittgenstein probably did not look to a future in which 'the real discovery' would absolve him from doing philosophy altogether. But, in McDowell's interpretation, that is not because Wittgenstein thought he could renounce bad ways of philosophizing for the sake of better ways; it is because he knew he could only temporarily stop doing philosophy of any kind – he knew he would never be entirely rid of the impulse to philosophize.
8 1994a, p. 86. See also his discussion of 'the philosophical impulse'; 1994a, p. 177.
9 1994a, p. 118.
10 See the poignant discussion of these issues in relation to Wittgenstein; McDowell 1994a, pp. 177–8.
11 1982, p. 16.
12 The disjunction is not exclusive, of course; one might adopt both forms of humanism.
13 McDowell himself often makes this charge, particularly of incoherent attempts to account for language and experience; see his 1987a, pp. 90–1; 1997a, pp. 130–1; 1986b.
14 Adorno 1974, § 18, p. 39.

Select Further Reading

By John McDowell

Most of McDowell's published papers to date are collected in two volumes: McDowell 1998a and 1998b. The following are particularly useful for offering insights into his overall position: McDowell 1982a, 1985b, 1986a, 1986b, 1994a (the paperback edition adds a useful 'Introduction'), 1999, 2000b. Helpful essays on McDowell 1994a are McDowell 1998g and 1998h and those contained in Smith 2002, which includes replies by McDowell himself. See the notes for suggested further reading on specific subjects.

By other authors

Part I: Overview

In general For an account of various forms of challenge to the Default, particularly Cartesianism and traditional empiricism, see McCulloch 1995. Robinson 1994 offers an introduction to the general debate over perceptual experience and a defence of one particular challenge to the Default (sense datum theory). For a reflective initiation into Wittgensteinian views of philosophy and philosophical method, see Pears 1971 and 1987, particularly part one. Brandom 1994 sets out in considerable detail the kind of inferentialism from which McDowell ultimately distances himself, but with which he has much in common.

On McDowell For overviews of McDowell's work from different perspectives, see the following in particular. From a historical perspective which foregrounds post-Kantian and post-Hegelian philosophical traditions, see Friedman 1996. From the perspective of various available forms of empiricism, see Brandom 2002. From the perspective of various available forms of naturalism see Wright 1996. McDowell takes the opportunity to respond to each of these papers and to correct misinterpretations in his 'Responses' in Smith 2002: pp. 270–4 (Friedman); pp. 279–81 (Brandom); pp. 286–91 (Wright).

Part II: A Naturalism of Second Nature

In general For an historically grounded introduction to ideas of nature and the natural, before and after the Scientific Revolution, see Taylor 1975, ch. 1. Rorty 1980, part three, discusses the implications of philosophical history for naturalism. For a reflection on current and viable views of naturalism, see Williams 2002, chs 1–3. Bertrand Russell's provocative essays 'On scientific method in philosophy' and 'On the notion of cause' in his 1953 provide context for McDowell's conception of science and scientific method. For background on his conception of the space of reasons and its autonomy, see Sellars 1956 and Davidson 1980.

On McDowell On naturalism, see Wright 1996 and Bübner 2002. On the connection between naturalism and the space of reasons, see Blackburn 2001 and Papineau 1999. On the space of reasons, see Brandom 1995.

Part III: An Intentionality of Second Nature

In general For the neo-Kantian background to McDowell's views on experience, see Strawson 1959 and 1966, and Sellars 1956. For the Fregean background, see Frege 1967 and 1980. For the coherentism McDowell distances himself from, see Davidson 2001. For a sophisticated version of the non-conceptualism to which McDowell's conceptualism is a response, see Evans 1982. This work, which McDowell himself edited, also contains vivid argumentation for the view with which McDowell aligns himself: that thoughts expressed using a variety of singular terms are object-dependent. For a recent defence of conceptualism that is akin to McDowell's, but distinct at many points, see Brewer 1999, especially ch. 5.

On McDowell   On the rational bearing of experience on perceptual judgements, see Hinton 1996 and Brandom 1998. On 'the Given', see Schantz 2001. On the relation between McDowell's views of experience with the Kantian and post-Kantian tradition, see Stern 1999a. On non-conceptual content, see Peacocke 1998 and Heck 2000. On the identity theory of truth, see Hornsby 1997.

Part IV: The Exercise of Second Nature

In general   Wittgenstein 1958, 1969a and 1969b are of particular importance for an understanding of McDowell's approach to epistemology. For the interpretation of Wittgenstein against which McDowell establishes his own, see in particular Wright's essays 'Realism, truth-value links, other minds and the past' and 'Second thoughts about criteria' in his 1993. Aristotle's *Nichomachean Ethics* (Aristotle 2000) establishes the background for McDowell's work on value and ethics. McDowell develops his own views most vividly in contrast with Mackie 1977 and Foot 1978.

On McDowell   For discussion of the epistemological implications of McDowell's views on the object dependency of singular thoughts, see Brueckner 1993. On McDowell's interpretations of Aristotle, see Wiggins 1995. In relation to McDowell's views of evaluative thought, see Blackburn 1994.

References

Cited works by John McDowell

Given here are details of original publication and of reprinting in the collections McDowell 1998a and 1998b. Page references in the notes are to these collections when a paper is reprinted there.

1970   'Identity-mistakes: Plato and the Logical Atomists', *Proceedings of the Aristotelian Society*, 70, pp. 181–95. Reprinted in McDowell 1998a, pp. 157–70.

1973   *Plato: Theaetetus;* Translation with Notes (Oxford: Clarendon Press).

1976a   'Introduction' with Gareth Evans, *Truth and Meaning: Essays in Semantics*, ed. Gareth Evans and John McDowell (Oxford: Clarendon Press), pp. vii–xxiii.

1976b   'Truth-conditions, bivalence and verificationism', *Truth and Meaning: Essays in Semantics*, ed. Gareth Evans and John McDowell (Oxford: Clarendon Press), pp. 42–66. Reprinted in McDowell 1998a, pp. 3–28.

1977   'On the sense and reference of a proper name', *Mind*, 86, pp. 159–85. Reprinted in McDowell 1998a, pp. 171–98.

1978a   'Are moral requirements hypothetical imperatives?', *Proceedings of the Aristotelian Society*, Supplementary Volume 52, pp. 13–29. Reprinted in McDowell 1998b, pp. 77–94.

1978b   'Physicalism and primitive denotation: Field on Tarski', *Erkenntnis*, 13, pp. 131–52. Reprinted in McDowell 1998a, pp. 132–54.

1978c   'On "The Reality of the Past"', *Action and Interpretation: Studies in the Philosophy of the Social Sciences*, ed. Christopher Hookway and Philip Pettit (Cambridge: Cambridge University Press), pp. 127–44. Reprinted in McDowell 1998a, pp. 295–313.

1979   'Virtue and reason', *The Monist*, 62, pp. 331–50. Reprinted in McDowell 1998b, pp. 50–73.

1980a   'Meaning, communication and knowledge', *Philosophical Subjects: Essays presented to P. F. Strawson*, ed. Zak van Straaten (Oxford: Clarendon Press), pp. 117–39. Reprinted in McDowell 1998a, pp. 29–50.

1980b   'Quotation and saying that', *Reference, Truth, and Reality*, ed. Mark Platts (London: Routledge and Kegan Paul), pp. 206–37. Reprinted in McDowell 1998a, pp. 51–86.

1980c   'The role of *eudaimonia* in Aristotle's Ethics', *Proceedings of the African Classical Associations*, 15, pp. 1–14. Reprinted in McDowell 1998b, pp. 3–22.

1981a   'Anti-realism and the epistemology of understanding', *Meaning and Understanding*, ed. Herman Parret and Jacques Bouveresse (Berlin: Walter de Gruyter), pp. 225–48. Reprinted in McDowell 1998a, pp. 314–43.

1981b   'Non-cognitivism and rule-following', *Wittgenstein: To Follow a Rule*, ed. Steven Holtzman and Christopher Leich (London: Routledge and Kegan Paul), pp. 141–62. Reprinted in McDowell, 1998b, pp. 198–218.

1982a   'Criteria, defeasibility and knowledge', *Proceedings of the British Academy*, 68, pp. 455–79. Reprinted in McDowell 1998a, pp. 369–94.

1982b   'Truth-value gaps', *Logic, Methodology, and Philosophy of Science VI: Proceedings of the Sixth International Congress of Logic, Methodology and Philosophy of Science, Hanover, 1979*, ed. L. Jonathan Cohen (New York: North-Holland Publishing Co.), pp. 299–313. Reprinted in McDowell 1998a, pp. 199–213.

1983   'Aesthetic value, objectivity, and the fabric of the world', *Pleasure, Preference and Value*, ed. Eva Schaper (Cambridge: Cambridge University Press), pp. 1–16. Reprinted in McDowell 1998b, pp. 112–30.

1984a   '*De re* senses', *Philosophical Quarterly*, 34, pp. 283–94. Reprinted in McDowell 1998a, pp. 214–27.

1984b   'Wittgenstein on following a rule', *Synthese*, 58, pp. 325–63. Reprinted in McDowell 1998b, pp. 221–62.

1985a 'Functionalism and anomalous monism', *Actions and Events: Perspectives on the Philosophy of Donald Davidson*, ed. Ernest LePore and Brian McLaughlin (Oxford: Blackwell), pp. 387–98. Reprinted in McDowell 1988b, pp. 325–40.

1985b 'Values and secondary qualities', *Morality and Objectivity*, ed. Ted Honderich (London: Routledge and Kegan Paul), pp. 110–29. Reprinted in McDowell 1998b, pp. 131–50.

1986a 'Introduction', with Philip Pettit, *Subject, Thought and Context*, ed. Philip Pettit and John McDowell (Oxford: Clarendon Press), pp. 1–15.

1986b 'Singular thought and the extent of inner space', *Subject, Thought and Context*, ed. Philip Pettit and John McDowell (Oxford: Clarendon Press), pp. 137–68. Reprinted in McDowell 1998a, pp. 228–59.

1987a 'In defence of modesty', *Michael Dummett: Contributions to Philosophy*, ed. Barry Taylor (Dordrecht: Martinus Nijhoff), pp. 59–80. Reprinted in McDowell 1998a, pp. 87–107.

1987b 'Projection and truth in ethics', Lindley Lecture 1987, University of Kansas, in McDowell 1998b, pp. 151–66.

1989a 'Mathematical Platonism and Dummetian anti-realism', *Dialectica*, 43, pp. 173–92. Reprinted in McDowell 1998a, pp. 344–65.

1989b 'One strand in the private language argument', *Grazer Philosophische Studien*, 33/34, pp. 285–303. Reprinted in McDowell 1998b, pp. 279–96.

1989c 'Wittgenstein and the inner world', *The Journal of Philosophy*, 86, pp. 643–4.

1990 'Peacocke and Evans on demonstrative content', *Mind*, 99, pp. 255–66.

1991a 'Intentionality and interiority in Wittgenstein', *Meaning Scepticism*, ed. Klaus Puhl (Berlin: De Gruyter), pp. 148–69. Reprinted in McDowell 1998b, pp. 297–321.

1991b 'Intentionality *de re*', *John Searle and his Critics*, ed. Ernest LePore and Robert van Gulick (Oxford: Blackwell), pp. 215–25. Reprinted in McDowell 1998a, pp. 260–74.

1992 'Putnam on mind and meaning', *Philosophical Topics*, 20, pp. 35–48. Reprinted in McDowell 1998a, pp. 275–91.

1993a 'Knowledge by hearsay', *Knowing from Words: Western and Indian Philosophical Analysis of Understanding and Testimony*, ed. B. K. Matilal and A. Chakrabarti (Dordrecht: Kluwer), pp. 195–224. Reprinted in McDowell 1998a, pp. 414–43.

1993b 'Meaning and intentionality in Wittgenstein's later philosophy', *Midwest Studies in Philosophy, vol. 17: The Wittgen-*

stein Legacy, ed. Peter A. French, Theodore E. Uehling, Jr and Howard K. Wettstein (Notre Dame, Ind.: University of Notre Dame Press), pp. 40–52. Reprinted in McDowell 1998b, pp. 263–78.

1994a *Mind and World* (Cambridge, Mass.: Harvard University Press).

1994b 'The content of perceptual experience', *The Philosophical Quarterly*, 44, pp. 190–205. Reprinted in McDowell 1998b, pp. 341–58.

1995a 'Knowledge and the internal', *Philosophy and Phenomenological Research*, 55, pp. 877–93. Reprinted in McDowell 1998a, pp. 395–413.

1995b 'Might there be external reasons?', *World, Mind, and Ethics: Essays on the Ethical Philosophy of Bernard Williams*, ed. J. E. J. Altham and Ross Harrison (Cambridge: Cambridge University Press), pp. 387–98. Reprinted in McDowell 1998b, pp. 95–111.

1996a 'Incontinence and practical wisdom in Aristotle', *Identity, Truth and Value: Essays for David Wiggins* (Oxford: Blackwell), pp. 95–112.

1996b 'Two sorts of naturalism', *Virtues and Reasons: Philippa Foot and Moral Theory*, ed. Rosalind Hursthouse, Gavin Lawrence and Warren Quinn (Oxford: Clarendon Press), pp. 149–79. Reprinted in McDowell 1998b, pp. 167–97.

1997a 'Another plea for modesty', *Language, Thought and Logic: Essays in Honour of Michael Dummett*, ed. Richard G. Heck, Jr (Oxford: Oxford University Press), pp. 105–29. Reprinted in McDowell 1998a, pp. 108–31.

1997b 'Reductionism and the first person', *Reading Parfit*, ed. Jonathan Dancy (Oxford: Blackwell), pp. 230–50. Reprinted in McDowell 1998b, pp. 359–82.

1997c 'Brandom on representation and inference', *Philosophy and Phenomenological Research*, 57, pp. 157–62.

1998a *Meaning, Knowledge, and Reality* (Cambridge, Mass.: Harvard University Press).

1998b *Mind, Value and Reality* (Cambridge, Mass.: Harvard University Press).

1998c 'Referring to oneself', *The Philosophy of P. F. Strawson*, ed. L. E. Hahn (Chicago: Open Court), pp. 129–45.

1998d 'Response to Crispin Wright', *Knowing Our Own Minds*, ed. Crispin Wright, Barry C. Smith and Cynthia Macdonald (Oxford: Clarendon Press), pp. 47–62.

1998e 'Some issues in Aristotle's moral psychology', *Ethics*, ed. Stephen Everson (Cambridge: Cambridge University Press), pp. 107–28. Reprinted in McDowell 1998b, pp. 23–49.

1998f 'Having the world in view: Sellars, Kant, and intentionality', *The Journal of Philosophy*, 95, pp. 431–91.

1998g 'Précis of *Mind and World*', *Philosophy and Phenomenological Research*, 58, pp. 365–8.

1998h 'Reply to commentators', *Philosophy and Phenomenological Research*, 58, pp. 403–31.

1999 'Scheme–content dualism and empiricism', *The Philosophy of Donald Davidson*, ed. L. E. Hahn (Chicago: Open Court), pp. 87–104.

2000a 'Transcendental Empiricism', Pittsburgh, ms.

2000b 'Experiencing the world', *Reason and Nature*, ed. Marcus Willaschek (Münster: Lit Verlag), pp. 3–17.

2002a 'Responses', *Reading McDowell*, ed. Nicholas H. Smith (London: Routledge), pp. 269–305.

2002b 'Gadamer and Davidson on Understanding and Relativism', *Gadamer's Century: Essays in Honor of Hans-Georg Gadamer*, ed. J. Malpas, U. Arnswald and J. Kertscher (Cambridge, Mass.: MIT Press), pp. 173–93.

Cited works by other authors

Adorno, Theodor (1974) *Maxima Moralia*, tr. E. F. N. Jephcott (London: New Left Books).

Annas, J. (1981) *An Introduction to Plato's Republic* (Oxford: Oxford University Press).

Anscombe, G. E. M. (1957) *Intention* (Oxford: Blackwell).

Aristotle (1984a) *De Interpretatione*, tr. J. L. Ackrill, *The Complete Works of Aristotle*, I, ed. J. Barnes (Princeton: Princeton University Press), pp. 25–38.

Aristotle (1984b) *Physics*, tr. R. P. Hardie and R. K. Gaye, *The Complete Works of Aristotle*, I, ed. J. Barnes (Princeton: Princeton University Press), pp. 315–446.

Aristotle (2000) *Nicomachean Ethics*, tr. Roger Crisp (Cambridge: Cambridge University Press).

Armstrong, David (1968) *A Materialist Theory of the Mind* (London: Routledge and Kegan Paul).

Baker, G. P. and Hacker, P. M. S. (1980) *An Analytical Commentary on Wittgenstein's Philosophical Investigations* (Oxford: Blackwell).

Bellow, Saul (1982) *The Dean's December* (Harmondsworth: Penguin).

Berlin, Isaiah (1978) 'The hedgehog and the fox', in his *Russian Thinkers* (London: Penguin), pp. 22–81.

Blackburn, Simon (1994) 'Errors and the phenomenology of value', in his *Essays in Quasi-Realism* (Oxford: Oxford University Press, 1994), pp. 149–65.

Blackburn, Simon (2001) 'Normativity à la mode', *Journal of Ethics*, 5, pp. 139–53.

BonJour, Laurence (1985) *The Structure of Empirical Knowledge* (Cambridge, Mass.: Harvard University Press).

Bradley, F. H. (1897) *Appearance and Reality*, 2nd edition (Oxford: Oxford University Press).

Brandom, Robert (1994) *Making it Explicit* (London: Harvard University Press).

Brandom, Robert (1995) 'Knowledge and the social articulation of the space of reasons', *Philosophy and Phenomenological Research*, 55, pp. 895–908.

Brandom, Robert (1997) 'Précis of *Making it Explicit*', *Philosophical and Phenomenological Research*, 57, pp. 153–6.

Brandom, Robert (1998) 'Perception and rational constraint', *Philosophy and Phenomenological Research*, 58, pp. 369–74.

Brandom, Robert (2002) 'Non-inferential knowledge, perceptual experience, and secondary qualities: placing McDowell's empiricism', in Smith 2002, pp. 92–105.

Brewer, M. W. (1999) *Perception and Reason* (Oxford: Oxford University Press).

Brown, Peter (2000) *Augustine of Hippo*, 2nd edition (London: Faber and Faber).

Brueckner, Anthony (1993) 'Singular thought and Cartesian philosophy', *Analysis*, 53, pp. 110–15.

Bübner, Rudiger (2002) '*Bildung* and second nature', in Smith 2002, pp. 209–16.

Burge, Tyler (1977) 'Belief *de re*', *Journal of Philosophy*, 74, pp. 338–62.

Burge, Tyler (1994) 'Individualism and self-knowledge', *Self-Knowledge*, ed. Q. Cassam (Oxford: Oxford University Press), pp. 65–79.

Campbell, John (1986) 'Critical notice of Christopher Peacocke's *Sense and Content*', *The Philosophical Quarterly*, 36, pp. 278–91.

Child, William (1994) *Causality, Interpretation, and the Mind* (Oxford: Oxford University Press).

Crane, Tim (1992) 'The nonconceptual content of experience', *The Contents of Experience*, ed. T. Crane (Cambridge: Cambridge University Press), pp. 136–57.

Cussins, Robert (1990) 'The connectionist construction of concepts', *The Philosophy of Artificial Intelligence*, ed. M. Boden (Oxford: Oxford University Press), pp. 368–440.

Davidson, Donald (1980) 'Mental events', in his *Essays on Actions and Events* (Oxford: Oxford University Press), pp. 207–25.

Davidson, Donald (1990) 'Meaning, truth and evidence', *Perspectives on Quine*, ed. R. B. Barrett and R. F. Gibson (Oxford: Blackwell), pp. 68–79.

Davidson, Donald (2001) 'A coherence theory of truth and knowledge' in his *Subjective, Intersubjective, Objective* (Oxford: Oxford University Press), pp. 137–53.

Davies, Martin (1991) 'Individualism and perceptual content', *Mind*, 100, pp. 461–84.

Descartes, René (1984) *The Philosophical Writings of Descartes II*, tr. J. Cottingham, R. Stoothoff and D. Murdoch (Cambridge: Cambridge University Press).

Dibdin, Michael (2002) *And Then You Die* (London: Faber and Faber).

Dodd, Julian (1995) 'McDowell and identity theories of truth', *Analysis*, 55, pp. 160–5.

Dummett, Michael (1993) *Origins of Analytical Philosophy* (London: Duckworth).

Evans, Gareth (1982) *The Varieties of Reference*, ed. John McDowell (Oxford: Oxford University Press).

Evans, Gareth (1985) *Collected Papers* (Oxford: Oxford University Press).

Evnine, Simon (1991) *Donald Davidson* (Oxford: Blackwell, 1991).

Fodor, Jerry (1998) *In Critical Condition* (Cambridge, Mass.: MIT Press).

Foot, Philippa (1978) 'Morality as a system of hypothetical imperatives', *Proceedings of the Aristotelian Society*, Supplementary volume 52.

Frege, Gottlob (1967) 'The thought: a logical inquiry', tr. A. and M. Quinton, *Philosophical Logic*, ed. P. F. Strawson (Oxford: Oxford University Press), pp. 17–38.

Frege, Gottlob (1980) 'On sense and meaning', tr. Max Black, *Translations from the Philosophical Writings of Gottlob Frege*, 3rd edition, ed. P. Geach and M. Black (Oxford: Blackwell), pp. 56–78.

Friedman, Michael (1996) 'Exorcising the philosophical tradition', *Philosophical Review*, 105, pp. 427–67. Reprinted in Smith 2002, pp. 25–57.

Geuss, Raymond (1999) *Morality, Culture, and History* (Cambridge: Cambridge University Press).

Heck, Richard, Jr (2000) 'Non-conceptual content and the "space of reasons"', *Philosophical Review*, 109, pp. 483–523.

Hinton, J. M. (1973) *Experiences* (Oxford: Oxford University Press).

Hinton, J. M. (1996) 'Sense-experience revisited', *Philosophical Investigations*, 19, pp. 211–36.

Hornsby, Jennifer (1997) 'Truth: the identity theory', *Proceedings of the Aristotelian Society*, 97, pp. 1–24.

Hyman, John (1994) 'Vision and power', *Journal of Philosophy*, 91, pp. 236–52.

Kant, Immanuel (1933) *Critique of Pure Reason*, tr. Norman Kemp Smith, 2nd edition (London: Macmillan).

Kant, Immanuel (1966) *Education*, tr. A. Churton (Ann Arbor, Mich. University of Michigan Press).

Kenny, Anthony (1973) *Wittgenstein* (London: Penguin).

Lewis, C. I. (1956) *Mind and the World Order* (New York).

Locke, John (1975) *An Essay Concerning Human Understanding*, ed. Peter H. Nidditch (Oxford: Oxford University Press, 1975).

McCulloch, Gregory (1995) *The Mind and its World* (London: Routledge).

McGinn, Colin (1989) *Mental Content* (Oxford: Blackwell).

McGuinness, B. F. (ed.) (1967) *Ludwig Wittgenstein und der Wiener Kreis* (Oxford: Blackwell).

Mackie, J. L. (1977) *Ethics: Inventing Right and Wrong* (London: Penguin).

Martin, Michael (1992) 'Perception, concepts, and memory', *The Philosophical Review*, 101, pp. 745–63.

Nabokov, Vladimir (1981) *Despair* (Harmondsworth: Penguin).

Nietzsche, Friedrich (1994) *On the Genealogy of Morality*, tr. Carol Diethe (Cambridge: Cambridge University Press).

Nietzsche, Friedrich (2001) *The Gay Science*, tr. J. Nauckhoff, ed. Bernard Williams (Cambridge: Cambridge University Press).

Novalis (1997) *Philosophical Writings*, tr. and ed. Margaret Mahony Stoljar (Albany: State University of New York Press).

Papineau, David (1999) 'Normativity and judgement', *Proceedings of the Aristotelian Society*, Supplementary volume 73, pp. 17–43.

Peacocke, Christopher (1983) *Sense and Content* (Oxford: Oxford University Press).

Peacocke, Christopher (1992) *A Study of Concepts* (Cambridge, Mass.: MIT Press).

Peacocke, Christopher (1998) 'Non-conceptual content defended', *Philosophy and Phenomenological Research*, 58, pp. 381–8.

Pears, David (1971) *Wittgenstein* (London: Fontana Press).

Pears, David (1987) *The False Prison: A Study of the Development of Wittgenstein's Philosophy* (Oxford: Oxford University Press).

Pitcher, George (1971) *A Theory of Perception* (Princeton: Princeton University Press).

Plato (1973) *Theaetetus*, tr. with notes by John McDowell (Oxford: Oxford University Press).

Putnam, Hilary (1975) 'The meaning of "meaning"', in his *Mind, Language and Reality* (Cambridge: Cambridge University Press), pp. 215–71.

Quine, W. V. O. (1960) *Word and Object* (Cambridge, Mass.: MIT Press).

Quine, W. V. O. (1969) *Ontological Relativity and Other Essays* (London: Columbia University Press).

Reid, Thomas (1941) *Essays on the Intellectual Powers of Man*, ed. A. D. Woozley (London: Macmillan).

Robinson, Howard (1994) *Perception* (London: Routledge).

Rorty, Richard (1980) *Philosophy and the Mirror of Nature* (Oxford: Blackwell).

Russell, Bertrand (1912) *The Problems of Philosophy* (Oxford: Oxford University Press).

Russell, Bertrand (1953) *Mysticism and Logic* (London: Pelican Books).

Schantz, Richard (2001) 'The Given regained: reflections on the sensuous content of experience', *Philosophy and Phenomenological Research*, 62, pp. 167–80.

Schiffer, Stephen (1987) *Remnants of Meaning* (Cambridge, Mass.: MIT Press).

Sellars, Wilfrid (1997) *Empiricism and the Philosophy of Mind*, reprinted (London: Harvard University Press).

Shoemaker, Sydney (1994a) 'Self-reference and self-awareness', reprinted *Self-Knowledge*, ed. Q. Cassam (Oxford: Oxford University Press), pp. 80–93.

Shoemaker, Sydney (1994b) 'Self-knowledge and "inner sense"', *Philosophy and Phenomenological Research*, 54, pp. 249–314.

Shoemaker, Sydney (1996) *The First Person Perspective and Other Essays* (Cambridge: Cambridge University Press).

Smith, Nicholas H. (ed.) (2002) *Reading McDowell: On Mind and World* (London: Routledge).

Snowdon, Paul (1981) 'Perception, vision and causation', *Proceedings of the Aristotelian Society*, 81, pp. 175–92.

Stern, Robert (1999a) 'Going beyond the Kantian philosophy: on McDowell's Hegelian critique of Kant', *European Journal of Philosophy*, 7, pp. 247–69.

Stern, Robert (ed.) (1999b) *Transcendental Arguments* (Oxford: Oxford University Press).

Stevens, Wallace (1997) *Collected Poetry and Prose* (New York: Penguin Putnam).

Strawson, Peter (1952) *Introduction to Logical Theory* (London: Methuen).

Strawson, Peter (1959) *Individuals: An Essay in Descriptive Metaphysics* (London: Methuen).

Strawson, Peter (1966) *The Bounds of Sense* (London: Methuen).

Strawson, Peter (1971) *Logico-Linguistic Papers* (London: Methuen).

Taylor, Charles (1975) *Hegel* (Cambridge: Cambridge University Press).

West, M. L. (ed.) (1971) *Iambi et Elegi Graeci*, I (Oxford: Oxford University Press).

Wiggins, David (1995) 'Eudaimonism and realism in Aristotle's Ethics: A reply to John McDowell', *Aristotle and Moral Realism*, ed. R. Heinaman (Boulder, Colo.: Westview Press).

Williams, Bernard (2002) *Truth and Truthfulness* (Oxford: Princeton University Press).

Wittgenstein, Ludwig (1958) *Philosophical Investigations*, 2nd edition, tr. G. E. M. Anscombe (Oxford: Blackwell).

Wittgenstein, Ludwig (1961) *Tractatus Logico-Philosophicus*, tr. D. F. Pears and B. F. McGuinness (London: Routledge and Kegan Paul).

Wittgenstein, Ludwig (1969a) *The Blue Book*, 2nd edition (Oxford: Blackwell).

Wittgenstein, Ludwig (1969b) *On Certainty*, tr. D. Paul and G. E. M. Anscombe (Oxford: Blackwell).

Wittgenstein, Ludwig (1974) *Philosophical Grammar*, tr. A. Kenny, ed. R. Rhees (Oxford: Blackwell).

Wittgenstein, Ludwig (1979) *Remarks on Frazer's Golden Bough*, tr. A. C. Miles, ed. Rush Rhees (Denton: The Brynmill Press Ltd).

Wittgenstein, Ludwig (1993) *Philosophical Occasions, 1912–1951*, ed. J. C. Klagge and A. Nordmann (Indianapolis: Hackett).

Wright, Crispin (1980) 'Realism, truth-value links, other minds and the past', *Ratio*, 22, pp. 112–32. Republished in Wright 1993, pp. 85–106.

Wright, Crispin (1984) 'Second thoughts about criteria', *Synthese*, 58, pp. 383–405. Republished in Wright 1993, pp. 383–402.

Wright, Crispin (1993) *Realism, Meaning and Truth* (Oxford: Blackwell).

Wright, Crispin (1996) 'Human nature?', *European Journal of Philosophy*, 4, 1996, pp. 235–54. Reprinted with Postscript in Smith 2002, pp. 140–73.

Index